THE FRANCE OF THE LITTLE-MIDDLES

ANTHROPOLOGY OF EUROPE

General Editors:
Monica Heintz, University of Paris Ouest Nanterre La Défense
Patrick Heady, Max Planck Institute for Social Anthropology

Europe is the latest region to attract anthropological research and a region whose variety and speed of change constitutes the strongest challenge to classical anthropology. Situated at the frontier with other social sciences and humanities, the anthropology of Europe has been bred by ethnology, anthropology, folklore, cultural studies before engaging in innovative interdisciplinary approaches. "Anthropology of Europe" publishes fieldwork monographs by young or established scholars, as well as collective or edited volumes on particular regions or aspects of European society. The series pays special attention to studies with a strong comparative component—addressing theoretical questions of interest both to anthropologists and to other scholars working in the general field of social science and the humanities.

Volume 1
The France of the Little-Middles
A Suburban Housing Development in Greater Paris
Marie Cartier, Isabelle Coutant, Olivier Masclet, and Yasmine Siblot

THE FRANCE OF
THE LITTLE-MIDDLES

A Suburban Housing Development in Greater Paris

Marie Cartier, Isabelle Coutant,
Olivier Masclet, and Yasmine Siblot

Translated by Juliette Radcliffe Rogers

berghahn
NEW YORK • OXFORD
www.berghahnbooks.com

Published by

Berghahn Books

www.berghahnbooks.com

English-language edition
© 2016, 2019 Marie Cartier, Isabelle Coutant, Olivier Masclet, and Yasmine Siblot
First paperback edition published in 2019

French-language edition
© 2008
Editions La Découverte
La France des "petits-moyens." Enquête sur la banlieue pavillonnaire

Library of Congress Cataloging-in-Publication Data

Names: Cartier, Marie, author.
Title: The France of the little-middles : a suburban housing development in greater
    Paris / Marie Cartier, Isabelle Coutant, Olivier Masclet, and Yasmine Siblot ;
    translated by Juliette Radcliffe Rogers.
Other titles: France des "petits-moyens". English.
Description: New York : Berghahn Books, [2016] | Series: Anthropology of Europe ;
    volume 1 | Originally published in French as: La France des "petits-moyens" :
    enquête sur la banlieue pavillonnaire [by] Marie Cartier ... [et al.]. | Includes
    bibliographical references and index.
Identifiers: LCCN 2016022448 (print) | LCCN 2016032079 (ebook) | ISBN
    9781785332289 (hardback : alk. paper) | ISBN 9781785332296 (ebook)
Subjects: LCSH: Suburbs—France—Gonesse. | Suburban life—France—Gonesse. |
    Middle class—France—Gonesse—Social conditions. | Gonesse (France)—Social
    conditions.
Classification: LCC HT352.F82 G86413 2016 (print) | LCC HT352.F82 (ebook) |
    DDC 307.740944/361—dc23
LC record available at hbps://lccn.loc.gov/2016022448

British Library Cataloguing in Publication Data

A catalogue record for this book is available from the British Library

ISBN 978-1-78533-228-9 hardback
ISBN 978-1-78920-520-6 paperback
ISBN 978-1-78533-229-6 ebook

CONTENTS

MAPS, ILLUSTRATIONS, AND TABLES

MAPS

ILLUSTRATIONS

TABLES

ACKNOWLEDGEMENTS

This book was greatly influenced by Olivier Schwartz's work on the transformations of the working class, and benefited from his constant encouragement throughout the fieldwork and writing. We extend him our most sincere gratitude.

We also thank Florence Weber, who had an important role in the early stages of this study, as well as Jean-Pierre Hassoun, Nicolas Renahy, and Anne-Catherine Wagner, who also actively contributed to it.

We are very grateful to all the students from the Ecole Normale Supérieur (ENS), the joint ENS-EHESS (École des hautes études en sciences sociales) master's program *Enquêtes, Terrains, Théories,* and the University of Paris 1's economics-sociology master's program and tutors (social science PhD students at ENS-EHESS) who participated in the study at one time or another, and with various degrees of investment, since 2003:

Pascal Marichalar, a master's student, was especially invested in this study from the outset, and additionally took charge of the research group's website; Claire Bader, Aude Béliard, Marianne Blanchard, Thomas Blanchard, Émilie Bonnet, Mathieu Bonzom, Judith Bovensiepen, Vincent Braconnay, Grégoire Brugère, Fabien Brugière, Vincent Chabault, Angèle Christin, Francesco Colonna, Emmanuel Comte, Jean-Robert Dantou, Clément Dherbecourt, Dagmara Drazewska, Jean-Sébastien Eideliman, Eleonora Elguezabal, Virginie Fauchille, Sara-Lou Gerber, Alexandre Hobeika, Christina Kolerus, Laure Lacan, Laure Le Coat, Faty Mbodj, Samuel Neuberg, Alexandra Oeser, Aurélie Ouss, Clémence Patureau, Alice Richard, Delphine Roy, Camille Soutarson, Laeticia Strauch, Marion Tanniou, Solène Thomas, Olivier Vanbelle, and Maud Vu Van Kha.

Appendix 1 contains a list of the interviews used in this book, specifying the date each took place as well as the researchers conducting them.

We also thank Nicole Ruster for the study's administrative and financial organization; Baya Sekraoui, who worked with Jean-Pierre Hassoun to build and exploit the DIA database; Alexandre Kish of the Centre Maurice Halbwachs for access to census data; Cécile Détang-Dessendre of the CESAER Research Center, for the exploitation of census data on mobility, and everyone who transcribed interviews—especially Morgan Cochenec.

This study was mainly financed by the Ethnology Mission of the French Ministry of Culture and the City of Gonesse. It was conducted in association with the *Enquêtes, Terrains, Théories,* master's program at ENS-EHESS, under the auspices of which there was a regular seminar. We submitted a report to the ethnology mission of the Ministry of Culture in 2006, entitled *Pavillonnaires de la banlieue Nord. Une ethnographie des petites mobilités sociales.* This report was written with the collaboration of Jean-Pierre Hassoun, Pascal Marichalar, and Nicolas Renahy. Thanks to A-C Wagner for reading the manuscript and her feedback.

The mayor of Gonesse, Jean-Pierre Blazy, spoke with us and helped us over the course of the study, as did many elected officials and city employees, and we extend our most heartfelt thanks to them. Pascale Didine played an especially crucial role the first two years. We would also like to acknowledge the institutions that contributed to the funding of the translation of this text: the Institut Universitaire de France, the Nantes Sociology Center, Université de Paris 8, CRESPPA-CSU, the TEPSIS Research Center of Excellence supported by the Pres heSam (ANR-11-LABX-0067), and the French National Research Agency (ANR) under the auspices of the "Investissements d'Avenir Paris Nouveaux Mondes" program (ANR-11-IDEX-0006-02).

Lastly, we wish to thank Juliette Rogers, not only for all the care she put into the translation of this book, but for her precious support at every step of our endeavor to publish it in English.

Last, we are especially grateful to all the residents of the Poplars neighborhood who welcomed us and delivered themselves in interviews, often at great length. We hope that we have fully represented the complexity of their relationship to this residential neighborhood, as well as their social trajectories.

FROM PETIT-BOURGEOIS TO LITTLE-MIDDLE

Studying Small Social Mobility

Interest in social class and inequality has experienced a resurgence in French social sciences since the late 1990s.[1] Sociologists and economists have highlighted persistent inequalities in income, net worth, and cultural attainments, suggesting that they may even be on the rise.[2] Alongside these broad, statistically based approaches, other sociologists analyze contemporary French class structure by exploring changing social conditions through ethnographic study of social and occupational categories. Their work has pointed to the disintegration of industrial labor as a social group: today's industrial laborers no longer identify as members of a laboring class as they did in the 1960s.[3] In addition, young people from immigrant backgrounds living in public housing seem to be caught in a particular situation, with a conflictual relationship to institutions manifest in difficulties in school, job insecurity, discrimination, and urban relegation.[4]

Our longitudinal study of changes in a housing development adjacent to public housing in Paris's northern periphery was intended to contribute to this analysis of contemporary French class structure. In this neighborhood, we found neither the working classes nor the middle classes as they are typically described in the literature. It is instead populated by households of diverse geographical backgrounds experiencing small upward social mobility associating both inter- and intra-generational residential and professional ascension. We chose to call them the *little-middles* (*petits-moyens*), picking up on an expression an interviewee used to describe her social position. This designation conveys the fact that a considerable number of the neighborhood's single-family homeowners cannot readily be classified as working class or middle class without oversimplifying the distinctive aspects of their lifestyle, which is typified both by efforts to get ahead and succeed, and fear of backsliding.

By comparing residents' social characteristics and lifestyles at two very different periods in the neighborhood's history (the 1960s–70s and the 1990s–2000s), the book illustrates various kinds of collective social ascension and their consequences on social relations. Whereas the collective social ascension process typical of the 1960s–1970s seemed to break down class boundaries and forge what to all appearances was a comfortable relationship to the social world, the individual social ascension of today, with increasing employment instability, creates uncertainty about the future that feeds conflict and misunderstanding with other social groups. The social structure's intermediate categories are subject to considerable political and media commentary in contemporary France that often only defines them in vague terms, while identification with the middle class has generally expanded to higher and lower categories of the social hierarchy.

But is there not a vast range of inequality within these intermediate categories? The localized ethnographic approach makes it easier to break with homogenizing representations and discourses about the middle class to analyze phenomena of stratification from the perspective of specific local configurations, in this case a neighborhood in a residential city in the northern Parisian suburbs whose population has been significantly renewed since the 1980s by the arrival of immigrants from Asia and sub-Saharan Africa and the children of North African immigrants from adjacent neighborhoods. Crossing urban ethnography with the sociology of social stratification enriches both approaches, especially concerning the spatial aspects of social issues.[5] By combining temporalities (past and present), by encompassing diverse spheres of neighborhood residents' social lives, and by considering residents in terms of their backgrounds and geographical movement as well as their socioeconomic positions and trajectories, this book explores the full complexity of the concrete living conditions of a particular strata of society that hovers between the working and middle classes, and the variety of ways in which its members live together, have a sense of group belonging, and participate in community life. Entering the field through the domestic rather than the occupational scene helps observers to conceive of these mid-range categories of the social structure through their internal relationships as well as their relationships with other social groups living nearby, and to assess whether they have broken away from or maintained their early social circles or lifestyles. It also permits taking couples and households as the unit of analysis, rather than individuals (as statistical studies usually do), which seems all the more necessary given the rise in women's employment. Finally, it offers the possibility of studying forms of public participation and relationships to politics in a finite localized setting over the long term, instead of taking a decontextualized snapshot as is too often the case in postelection studies evoking "the housing development vote" or "Front National voters" that, in so doing, create artificial groups.

STUDYING NEIGHBORHOODS OF SINGLE-FAMILY HOMES

In the United States, there is a long tradition of research in inner-city neighborhoods inhabited by the poor and the underclass, with particular attention to African-American families.[6] This research tradition emerged in the 1960s and has continued ever since, highlighting the persistence of racial segregation and social exclusion alongside the rising weight of the service sector in urban economies and challenges to national-level social policies.[7] In contrast, American suburban residents' lifestyles have more often been condemned and depicted critically than they have benefited from dispassionate scientific study,[8] although Nicholas Townsend reminds, as did Herbert Gans in the 1960s, that suburban homeowners also deserve attentive, empathetic study, free of prejudice.[9] Mary Pattillo-McCoy further observes that researchers have given little attention to the residential experience of the black middle classes compared with African-Americans living in urban ghettos.[10]

Although the urban structure and spatial distribution of social classes are different in France and the United States, we note the same bias in French social science work on urban peripheries. It also has a penchant for the poorest neighborhoods, the 1960s housing projects of towers and fences found in the urban periphery (known as the *banlieue*), and not cities themselves.[11] Since the 1970s, French sociologists have continuously analyzed population flows, forms of sociability, and lifestyles in these neighborhoods on the urban edge that have gradually concentrated immigrants and the poorest members of society.[12] In the 1980s, they were joined by anthropologists wanting to develop an "ethnology of the present" who also took a particular interest in marginal spaces and housing projects.[13] These social scientists were reacting to the stereotypes and stigma haunting these spaces that became fixtures in the media as violence has increased in these settings since the late 1970s. Predictably, the riots in the autumn of 2005 prompted innumerable commentaries in the media and academia alike[14] that immediately led to new studies and publications questioning the limits of the French republican model for integration and addressing the discrimination suffered by young people from immigrant backgrounds in France.[15] Consequently, such neighborhoods (or *cités,* a term designating high-rise public housing developments where the young, insecure, and immigrant are overrepresented, which we translate as "housing projects") are at the heart of academic and everyday representations of the French *banlieue*. This is just as true for the work of American anthropologists of urban France, whose interest in immigration and immigrant integration in France led them to choose public housing neighborhoods as field sites as well.[16]

In contrast, the social sciences have been less attentive to studying neighborhoods of first-time homeownership, despite the fact that they have been proliferating since the 1960s, first on the outskirts of cities and more recently on the edges of rural villages. Nicole Haumont's study of homeowners in the mid 1960s was marginal and quickly forgotten.[17] From the 1950s through the 1970s, French sociologists were suspicious and disdainful of homeowners from working-class backgrounds. In the language of the Marxist-influenced political and intellectual climate of the time, they were seen as embourgeoised workers whose interests as homeowners were thought to distract them from engagement in the labor movement's collective struggle. Socially and politically stigmatized, they were criticized for being "individualists" and "closed in on themselves." The new single-family home seemed like a fairy tale to sociologists who were devoted to denouncing the illusion of social mobility. It also seemed to run counter to residential modernity at a time when high-ranking authorities and urbanists were vaunting communal housing, as Susanna Magri has shown.[18] And yet historians have demonstrated that property ownership does not automatically engender a conservative disposition or individualism at odds with the values of equality and social justice, as Annie Fourcaut proves by connecting the emergence of communist suburbs ("*banlieue rouge*") and laborers' and basic employees' access to homeownership in Bobigny, on the northeast edge of Paris.[19] Along with other historians, she reconstructed the intense social life in neighborhoods of new single-family homes built in the interwar period, where individualism was far from being the way of life.[20] Little inclined to look at these neighborhoods' lifestyles and sociabilities with an open mind, French sociologists contented themselves with studying them from afar by exposing the Statist and economic rationales behind policies for the development of individual housing.[21]

Starting in the 1990s, the expansion of subdivisions in the outer suburbs renewed attention to housing developments, which geographers henceforth saw as symbols of the phenomenon of "peri-urbanization," or suburbanization.[22] There were a few studies devoted to domestic and semi-domestic practices of various social strata of people living in these environments,[23] relations between family, housing, and residential practices,[24] and the social and symbolic consequences of new homeownership in families of working-class or more diverse backgrounds,[25] but they were rarely conducted at the neighborhood level, in contrast to this study's localized ethnographic approach. The world of housing developments, another facet of the French urban periphery, has been understudied, despite the fact that it is a fruitful starting point for renewed study of class difference in light of the transformations that French society has undergone since the 1960s.

STUDYING SMALL SOCIAL MOBILITY

The single-family homeowners we met in the northern outskirts of Paris have similar social trajectories. Whether they are from immigrant families or not, whether they hold a given occupational position or not, they are quite frequently dual-income couples from working-class backgrounds experiencing upward social mobility. The difficulty in putting a name to this population is in part related to the state of research on social mobility in France. Although there is no lack of research, it favors two main models: the most frequently occurring (social reproduction) and the most rare (the great leaps across the social spectrum of class transfuges). They are not especially interested in mobility of small magnitude, which Bernard Lahire calls "small social mobilities."[26] There have also been recent developments on social downclassing.[27] While this is in no way contesting the fact that the wage-earning middle classes are being destabilized, it is important to draw attention to the ordinary trajectories of social ascension that exist in contemporary French society, despite mass unemployment and deindustrialization.

Furthermore, research on social mobility is dominated by statistical studies. Although they do reveal structural and cyclical factors influencing movement across the social space and are the only way to measure society's overall "flexibility," they are not useful to analysis of modest social displacements, because the statistical categories are often too broad for them to be perceptible. The statistical approach usually overlooks the actors' own interpretations of these shifts in social position and the altered practices and lifestyles that simultaneously precondition the social shift and signal its arrival.

We consequently chose an ethnographic approach to analyze trajectories associating modest inter- and intra-generational mobilities between the working and middle classes, from the informants' perspective.[28] The residential neighborhood selected as a field site was a location for observing such small social mobilities. Many informants expressed their satisfaction with "living like everyone else" and their conviction they were "average," "like the others—no better, no worse." We took these formulations from the field quite seriously so we could better understand how to classify these small homeowners, in sociological terms. What social conditions make slight social ascension possible, in an era of mass unemployment and prolonged education? What does it mean to become a homeowner in a suburban city with a striking presence of high-rise housing projects? Would the inhabited space

not be even more important to little-middles because their social and occupational resources, though on the rise, are still fragile? What consequences
do these small social ascensions have on lifestyles, social relations, and forms
of socializing, or on civic participation and what they think of politics?

FROM PETIT-BOURGEOIS TO LITTLE-MIDDLE

Are these upwardly mobile new homeowners part of the "respectable" working classes,[29] or should they be classified with the lower middle classes? Can
their practices and worldview be included in the category of "petit-bourgeois"?[30] Classifying these households is even more challenging because a
fair number of them are heterogamous. More often than not, sociologists
and anthropologists on both sides of the Atlantic use the categories working
class, middle class, or petite bourgeoisie automatically without really specifying how groups or individuals were categorized. Our work breaks with this
habit to challenge these classifications by opting for an indigenous category,
little-middle, that an informant used to socially situate herself. By adopt-
ing and defining the term little-middles, we are rejecting the idea that social
classes are disappearing in the purported "middling" of French society.

In this regard, our thinking is in continuity with Pierre Bourdieu's work,
especially his well-known book *Distinction*. It made considerable strides in
renewing approaches to social class in France (and elsewhere) by offering a
conception of a multipolar social space that distinguishes between classes
based on their relationship to domination and further identifies fractions
within each class, each with different practices and dispositions depending
on the nature of peoples' resources and trajectories. From this perspective,
social position is derived from the volume and structure of an individual's
economic, cultural, social, and symbolic capitals, and it is defined relation-
ally. Insofar as this approach suggests observing social classes in a variety of
social scenes (including workplaces and people's positions relative to production, but also on the residential scene and everyday family and public life), it
calls for ethnographic methods and a local monograph, a recipe we followed
for this study as others have done for other recent studies in Europe.[31] But
despite *Distinction*'s in-depth study of the French upper and middle classes
(including the petite bourgeoisie) of the 1970s, it gives superficial treatment
to the working classes (which at the time included the census categories "laborers" and "farmers" but not "basic employees"), neglecting differences in
position, taste, and lifestyle within them and thus leading to a homogenizing
and often grim image of the working classes as primarily defined by privation
and "the choice of the necessary."[32] Although our work is clearly in line with
this Bourdieusian approach to social classes (which is experiencing some-

thing of a revival in Europe), we also make a considerable effort to study the lifestyles of modest social categories in all their complexity and detail, and represent how they think and act without resorting to clichés.

While identifying with a so-called Bourdieusian approach, we believe that there is a point in studying social change empirically and that the transformations of the working and middle classes, their cultural borders, and their relations merit documentation. The work of sociologist Olivier Schwartz inspires our work in this regard.[33] Affirming his conviction that the notion of class is relevant, he calls for an update of social class analysis and its terminology: "For the time being, we have no analysis of the class structure of contemporary France, no satisfying interpretation of contemporary France in terms of class that takes account of the developments and transformations that have affected this society since the late 1970s and that could consequently be applied to what this society is today."[34]

Because socially in-between situations force questioning of the homogeneity of each broad class category and its fractions, studying them is a useful strategy for thinking about the issue of social mobility and the boundaries between social groups. So in speaking of little-middles, we hope to counter the tendency to reduce all middle classes to "cultural goodwill"[35] and to break the habit of forever and always coming back to the same working-class culture passed on since its heyday in the 1930s through 1950s. The goal is to try to think about lifestyles that have emerged since the 1960s that have thus far only been described in passing in social science research on the working or middle classes. The working classes' move toward the middle classes has often been described as involving a violent and often painful break, whether through the political or moral judgment of "class treason" underlying Marxist use of the notion of petit-bourgeois[36] or through the "split habitus" analysis developed by Bourdieu. What subjective experiences and feelings are associated with these modest social ascensions, which just happen to be the most common kind? This book approaches the question through the empirical study of the hybrid lifestyles emerging from these small ascensions, the fruit of complex adjustments and arrangements, guided by the following questions: How are little-middles similar to petits-bourgeois? How are they different? How do they imagine society and their position in it? How have the conditions for small social mobilities changed from the 1960s to the 1990s?

A NEIGHBORHOOD BRIDGING
INSECURITY AND SUBURBAN COMFORT

This study is based in a neighborhood of the city of Gonesse, whose population of 25,000 has been governed by Socialist politicians since 1995, after over thirty years of a right-leaning city hall. At first sight, Gonesse looks like so many other disadvantaged cities in Paris's northern suburbs: it has more poor households with low educational levels than the regional average and distinctly fewer people in the highest categories. The significant presence of immigrants, primarily from Turkey, North Africa (the Maghreb), and sub-Saharan Africa, also encourages observers to associate it with the French administrative department of Seine-Saint-Denis, often referred to by its nickname, "the 93" (the department's code) or variations on it (the "9-3" or "9.3"), which for many French symbolizes ghettos, delinquency, and poverty.

But on closer examination, Gonesse has two distinctive qualities making it a transitional space in greater Paris. Located at the limits of the metropolitan area, just where the dense part of the city ends, it marks the beginning of the periurban countryside that attracts the middle and upper classes. It is also on the edge of the poor sector of northeastern Ile-de-France (the administrative region consisting of Paris and its immediate periphery).

But two statistical studies on the socioeconomic transformations of the Ile-de-France dramatically highlight what makes Gonesse so distinctive. The city is still identified as a working class space, where laborers and basic employees are overrepresented and *cadres*[37] distinctly underrepresented in relation to the regional average.[38] But today it has a rising presence of midlevel occupations with a high concentration of public employees. Its transitional situation is confirmed by a study based on household income distribution rather than socioeconomic categories,[39] in which Gonesse appears to have a low presence of wealthy households (although they are numerous in metropolitan Paris overall) and a concentration of households in the middle-income and poor deciles. The types of housing found there reflect this socioeconomic composition: there are vast public housing projects, but also housing developments of single-family homes that help keep home-owning households in the area.

According to both of these studies, the regional trend is toward the disappearance of gradual transition zones between spaces of poverty and those of greater privilege. The gap between these spaces is becoming more dramatic, as seen in Gonesse: several neighboring cities have become poorer since the 1990s (for example, Garges-lès-Gonesse, Aulnay-sous-Bois, and Bondy; see Map 0.1), while other nearby cities concentrate increasingly well-off households (such as Ecouen and Deuil-La Barre, in Map 0.1).

In this part of Ile-de-France, where contrasts are particularly high, Gonesse is a site of transition from poor to better-off towns. Analysis of census data makes this evident: Between the 1990 and 1999 censuses, only six out of ten Gonesse households stayed put, while the other four moved elsewhere. The amplitude of this migration seems to be the key to defining the city's social function since the 1960s. As a space for taking in new populations,

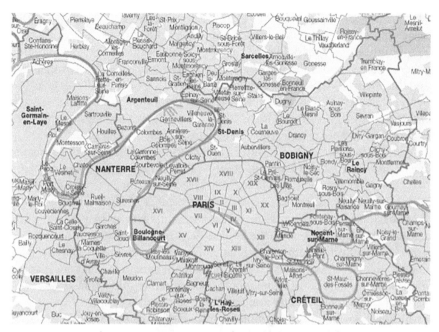

MAP 0.1. Map of greater Paris; Gonesse is found in the upper left. The dark lines indicate the outlines of administrative departments. (Source: Institut d'aménagement et d'urbanisme d'Ile de France)

Gonesse primarily attracts young couples with children and some retirees. New arrivals are predominantly from the working classes: basic employees and laborers represent over half of the newcomers. Inversely, the social categories leaving Gonesse were mainly tradesmen, shop-owners, business-owners, mid-level employees, *cadres,* and high-level intellectual occupations. The higher their position on the social scale, the greater their likelihood of leaving. Census data also reveals that Gonesse is a place for becoming a first-time homeowner or upgrading property ownership for households already settled in greater Paris.

In Gonesse, the study focused on a neighborhood, "the Poplars," that embodies all these processes. Mobility is higher there than in the rest of the city, and the percentage of homeowners is the highest of all Gonesse's neighborhoods (70 percent). The Poplars, at the epicenter of the opposing sociospatial dynamics typical of the Ile-de-France, is indeed marked by increasing internal differentiation. Since 1990, the census divides it into two zones: the Poplars, designating the oldest part of the neighborhood, and the New Poplars, which corresponds to the more recently built areas.

In the New Poplars, there was a decline in the number of laborers and basic employees, a strong increase in mid-level occupations, and a slight rise in the proportion of *cadres* (12 percent) between 1990 and 1999. But basic employees are still the main group present (42 percent), with a very significant presence of public-sector employees. A third of residents in this part of the neighborhood have degrees at the *baccalauréat* level or higher,[40] and the unemployment rate (10 percent) was below the overall city level (15 percent) in 1999. The New Poplars brings together households of relatively comfortable means: the annual median income per consumption unit was 17,544 euros, as compared with 13,882 euros for all of Gonesse.

We find the reverse in the older Poplars zone—a decline in the percentage of mid-level occupations and employees, a strong rise in the percentage of laborers (24.5 percent, and of unskilled laborers among them), while public-sector employees are less present. The percentage of residents without educational qualifications has risen, as has the unemployment rate (17 percent). The median annual income in the Poplars (11,910 euros) is below the city median, which reflects the impoverishment of part of its population. But the economic situation of its households remains overall better than that of residents of Gonesse's public housing neighborhoods, and the proportion of *cadres* (9 percent) is still above the city average. These trends thus indicate that this part of the Poplars is far from being indistinguishable from public housing projects, but that it clearly diverges from the better-off part of the neighborhood.

Census data reaches its limits, however, when it comes to understanding the processes that led to such differences. Each zone (Poplars and New Poplars) has a relatively homogeneous population, and the differentiation is actually found between microneighborhoods on a smaller scale. To comprehend the dynamics in play, then, we must revisit how the neighborhood was urbanized, in a patchwork of construction projects from a wide range of real estate development activities. Local urbanization policy as well as real estate market actors, developers, and builders thus all had their hand in influencing the composition of the neighborhood's population today.

A PATCHWORK OF SINGLE-FAMILY HOMES

The neighborhood is located near Gonesse's downtown and is well served by the metropolitan Paris public transportation system; its residents' social characteristics are wide-ranging, as are the architectural styles and property values of their homes. The Poplars has 1,400 single-family houses, in a broad array of architectural styles resulting from a succession of real estate development initiatives.

Urbanization began in the 1920s with the creation of two garden-city-style developments near a train station, followed by the gradual construction of about 300 houses in a farming zone through the 1950s. The neighborhood only really took off in the 1960s with a boom in the city's population, which quadrupled between 1954 and 1960 largely due to the construction of high-rise housing projects.[41]

From 1958 to 1966, a large-scale development project led to the construction of 644 row houses (also known as grouped houses or townhouses)—three-story attached homes with adjoining side walls (see Illustration 0.1). This project was similar to initiatives in other neighborhoods of Gonesse, greater Paris, and across France. The sales brochure of the time suggests that the appeal of these homes lay in their technical attributes that made them so modern (reinforced concrete, bathrooms with tubs and showers, water closets, central heating, ceramic tiles, parquet floors), and by a certain symbolic prestige conferred by reference to the homes as a "residence" as well as names for various house styles evoking luxurious places in and around Paris such as "Vendôme," "Monceau," and "Chantilly." The rows of houses are of variable lengths, along a street or in a horseshoe around small squares. Their footage is from 85 to 95 square meters, with four to five rooms and a garage, and they have yards of about 150 square meters (see Illustration 0.2). Homeowners' associations manage upkeep of the small squares' shared infrastructure. This makes it a rather specific kind of housing: single-family, but with points in common with collective housing. Businesses and new schools ap-

ILLUSTRATION 0.1. Row houses. (Photo taken by author)

ILLUSTRATION 0.2. Adjoining yards. (Photo taken by author)

peared in the neighborhood in the 1970s. The microneighborhood of row houses is populated by families with young children, fostering an intense social life, and it goes on to become the heart of the Poplars.

The third phase of building, from the mid 1970s to the mid 1980s, was organized in subdivisions. Its 250 two-story houses had footage ranging from 90 to 110 square meters. These houses were either in duplex or free-standing, most of them arranged in a so-called village-style: private cul-de-sacs circled by about twenty so-called grouped (duplex) houses, built by the developer, based on a choice of more or less spacious models in the same style and construction methods, interconnected by footpaths. These houses are slightly larger than the row houses and have rather large backyards (350–600 square meters) that initially bordered farmland (see Illustration 0.3).

But a few years later, these fields became the fourth and final housing zone, following the construction of a golf course there in 1991. Several developer-builders offered the 200 or so properties, locally referred to as the "golf-course" houses, and some houses from this phase of construction (such as those built by the developers Kaufman and Broad, abutting the golf course) are distinctly larger and of higher standing than other houses in the neighborhood (see Illustration 0.4). These developments were aimed at a more affluent clientele than the preceding initiatives.

ILLUSTRATION 0.3. Mid-range single-family homes. (Photo taken by author)

Because of its gradual urbanization, this assemblage of single-family homes thus brings together houses of very different sizes: the surface area can double from one to the next, and plot surface area varies to a factor of five. The row houses (by far the most numerous) are the smallest homes, with the narrowest yards. At the opposite end of the spectrum, the most recent houses are the biggest, with sprawling properties by French standards. The oldest houses and those from the 1970s to 1980s are medium-sized with rather large yards.

The real estate and social values of this housing have changed with time, each wave of construction influencing the standing of the others. This is captured to a certain extent by using selling price as an indicator of houses' relative values. Using a database of property sales tracked by the Gonesse planning office from 1988 to 2005 (DIA—see box "Building and Using the DIA Database") allowed us to quantify the cost differences between sections of the neighborhood (old houses from the 1920s to 1950s; row houses; 1980s subdivisions; recent houses). Thus, in 2005, the most recent houses were worth 50 percent more than the row houses, and the oldest houses and those from the 1980s were worth 30 percent more. This hierarchy seems to have become even more marked over the last decade. Indeed recent developments linked to changes in the national and regional real estate market (a

ILLUSTRATION 0.4. More recent "golf course" houses. (Photo taken by author)

brutal drop in values between 1991 and 1997, then a rapid rise) have uneven consequences on different parts of the neighborhood. The houses from the 1920s to 1950s and the 1970s to 1980s thus experienced a strong upswing in value, while the row houses' value was less affected.

BUILDING AND USING THE DIA DATABASE

This database was built and treated by Jean-Pierre Hassoun and Baya Sekraoui, based on the "Declarations of the Intent to Alienate" (DIA) filed with the city of Gonesse.

The DIA is a statement that notaries handling property contracts must send city hall prior to the closing of a sale. This became mandatory in 1987. The following information appears on each declaration: the property's address, name and address of seller, name of buyer (since 1990), buyer's address at the time of the transaction, the plot's surface area, inhabitable surface area (since 1996), price, and date of signing of the sales agreement.

The database contains this information for 634 transactions between April 1998 and May 2005.

Houses' sales prices make it possible to pin down an internal ranking within the neighborhood that is inseparable from the houses' material characteristics and the social value attributed to them. The main division opposes the row houses at the heart of the neighborhood with all other house types, which then break out into the most highly valued new and recent "golf course" houses, followed by the oldest houses accruing considerable value, and last the 1970s and 1980s subdivision houses whose value also nearly doubled.

This quick tour of the history of the neighborhood's urban development demonstrates that these microneighborhoods are the most relevant scale for studying the Poplars's internal dynamics. But the processes influencing their relative values are naturally also related to changes in the populations living in them. Neighborhood residents hold a range of social positions, from laborers to *cadres,* but beyond that, the group of households we have called little-middles appears to remain central, renewing itself over the generations.

THE ROW HOUSES: FROM "PIONEERS" TO "FOREIGNERS"

It is necessary to study the neighborhood's settlement and its population's social construction process to understand how this stratified patchwork of housing has served as a neighborhood of social ascension as well as (inevitable) downclassing.[42] Of all the levels of housing present, the row-house zone is the core that gives structure to the whole.

Depending on the era, we can characterize the flow of arrivals in the neighborhood and how it developed by combining a variety of complementary archival sources and interviews with some long-time residents still living in the Poplars or elsewhere in Gonesse.

ARCHIVAL DATA ON THE PEOPLING OF THE ROW HOUSES

For the 1973–86 period, the archives of the Plateau, a microneighborhood of 136 single-family homes built in 1965–66, contain the notifications of transfer (or sale) that notaries submitted to its homeowners' association. They indicate the transaction date and sometimes the occupations of those leaving and arriving, as well as their age, place of birth, and address prior to the Poplars.

For the early period, we could supplement these archives with analysis of a sample of nominative data from the 1968 and 1975 censuses.

For the more recent period (1988–2005), we have the DIA database compiled from the municipal archives, described earlier in this introduction. These archives are exhaustive, but they are less rich than the previous ones for studying social characteristics.

The archives allow us to reconstruct a different version of the neighbor-hood's history that nuances the version most often heard in interviews, that of the "deterioration" of the neighborhood with the influx of "foreigners" (the "Turks") in the 1990s.[43] In contrast to this image of the harsh transfor-mation of a once-stable neighborhood, the archives suggest that the neigh-borhood served as a stepping-stone for some residents from the outset, and renewal is actually a permanent trait of the row houses.

Most of the initial buyers of the new row houses (between 1958 and 1964) were employed by large public and private enterprises in jobs rang-ing from skilled laborers to mid-level *cadres*. These "pioneers," as they refer to themselves, were a generation whose lifestyle left a lasting effect on the neighborhood. These households had left other parts of France to come to the Paris area, making them the first generation in their families to own a single-family home in metropolitan Paris, another fact reflected in the pio-neer label. When asked how they came to settle in Gonesse and the Poplars in particular, all the interviewed residents of this generation mentioned the dearth of new housing at the time, their financial limitations, and the need to grasp available opportunities: high-rise housing projects and this kind of row house were the only options they could afford. But the appeal of a single-family house was also in play to a certain extent, and nostalgic ref-erences to the neighborhood's former status went so far as calling it "chic":

> Mme Pageot: The Poplars used to be a chic neighborhood before. People were own-ers, all the little houses ... And then there were some people who lived in Paris and came on weekends. It was a sort of residential neighborhood. And I knew some peo-ple down there [*Gonesse center*]—it was more farmers, it wasn't as good. For young people down there, girls from the Poplars weren't for them. You said it like that at the time—the Poplars was already sort of a cut above.

Such references make the neighborhood seem like it was "sort of a cut above" the old downtown and the apartment complexes. Moreover, long-time residents today frequently describe the social position of pioneers and the neighborhood's early image as "lower *cadres*" (M and Mme Samson, M. Lenormand) or "middle classes" (M. and Mme Heurtin).

But is it possible that these residents, quick to embellish the past, tend to represent the neighborhood's early population as socially higher than it actually was? Using the resources at our disposal, we can get a relatively clear overview of the pioneers' occupations when they moved into the Poplars in the 1960s. The first generation was not a majority of *cadres*, not even mid-level ones. The occupation of office worker was most prevalent, for both men and women, and laborers and *cadres*/midlevel occupations formed the two main minorities above and below. If the image of a neighborhood of lower *cadres* does not entirely represent reality in the 1960s, this is because it designates the positions they aspired to more than their actual positions, reflecting their aspirations for advancement. These households dreamed of improving their living conditions, and the men and women we met never expressed the reticence or regret at having crossed over to white-collar work so often heard in laboring milieus. In fact, all of the women began their working lives in offices. Households that maintained a connection with manual labor—at least early in their careers—were often heterogamous: the husband was a skilled laborer and the wife an office worker. Often, the latter had pursued schooling longer, through the exam marking completion of middle school (BEPC; Brevet d'étude premier cycle) or even as far as the *baccalauréat,* while the husband's formal studies ended after receiving his primary school graduation certificate (*certificat d'études primaire*) or a short technical program degree. Such heterogamous alliances seem to be a fundamental impetus for these upward trajectories.

And last, all the pioneers we met had been young couples with two, three, or even four preschool-aged children when they moved into the neighborhood. This crops up again and again in interviews, along with the feeling of equality and similarity that we will return to later, as if the fact of being parents of small children, a characteristic immediately visible on the residential scene, eclipsed differences in socioeconomic status. Young parents with at least two children: this demographic characteristic is so obvious that one runs the risk of overlooking it, although it is crucial, as we shall see, for understanding how people live and socialize locally. Another similarity contributing to pioneers' feeling of homogeneity and equality is a widespread working-class background: the first residents all came from families of farmers, laborers, or small tradesmen. They all, men and women alike, experienced a socially upward trajectory relative to their parents. Some pioneers come from families with immigrant backgrounds (Portuguese or Italian), but all were born in France. Only a minority of couples is composed of a husband and a wife born in the same administrative department, adding up to only a quarter of all households (nine of thirty-eight). The fact that they are rarely from the same geographical area is thus an important characteristic: the migration experience and geographical distance from their parental families contributes to their seeing Gonesse as a space devoted to a life unlike the one they knew as children.

So it is clear that the microneighborhood of row houses favored the formation of a group of upwardly mobile households, brought together by common values and intense social interaction, and fostered their local rootedness—but this should not overshadow the steady replacement and renewal of the population living in the row houses. By the mid 1980s, nearly half the pioneers of the Plateau sector had sold their homes and moved out, a fact that contrasts with the oft-heard story of the long-stable neighborhood supposedly turned upside-down overnight by the arrival of families from Turkey in the 1990s. In fact, the row houses had quickly come to serve as transitional housing for a number of families who began to move on after a stabilization period of about five years. Several pioneer couples had rapidly resold their homes, explaining they left because they were looking for a "real house," meaning a free-standing house with a bigger yard. Such departures meant that from the very outset, this microneighborhood was a stepping-stone for some, and a place for others to lay down roots. Moving there in the 1960s made social ascension happen, but in the 1970s and 1980s, ascension happened through leaving the neighborhood. When neighbors thought to be equals move away to buy a better home elsewhere, does the neighborhood continue to function as a space of promotion?

Neighborhood demographics do not seem to have been deeply disturbed in this first phase of renewal. Interviews and archives show the new arrivals included laborers (skilled and unskilled), mid-level occupations, and a few *cadres*. Similarity reigned. New residents' demographic characteristics were more diverse: the row houses still attracted young couples with children, but also households of laborers nearing retirement who became homeowners late in their working lives. Another common trait was moving there from large public housing projects in and around Paris: either they grew up there in laboring families, or they had begun their adult residential paths there. This experience of living in the projects when their conditions went into decline is significant, both in terms of how they would relate to their new homes and neighborhood and how they would be seen by the well-settled pioneers, their new neighbors.

The row-house population continued to be renewed in the 1990s, and the aforementioned database on 1988–2005 sales allows some aspects to be substantiated.[44] First of all, there are more sales of row houses than any other kind of housing in the Poplars. In addition, we could identify newcomers' national origins based on their family names,[45] and whether they were coming from public housing based on their address. New arrivals came from nearby residential areas. Only 30 of 383 buyers were from departments outside the Ile-de-France region, and even they were from nearby departments such as the Oise. The rest were overwhelmingly from departments in the northern periphery of Paris, especially from towns neighboring Gonesse with a strong public housing presence and rising poverty. Buyers coming from Paris mainly came from the most working-class *arrondissements* (eighteenth, nineteenth, twentieth). In the 1990s, the row-house neighborhood became a space for first-time homeownership for families from working-class towns and cities near Gonesse, some of whom had been living in HLMs (*habitation à loyer modéré,* low-income subsidized housing, which is frequently built in large projects in urban peripheries). Buyers from elsewhere in Gonesse had either been living in an HLM neighborhood or were already living in the row houses, either as renters who went on to buy their homes or as children who grew up there and bought near their parents. These residential backgrounds are distinctly different from those of the pioneers, who mostly came from other parts of France. Families from the HLMs of working-class cities around Paris began to move in the late 1970s, but their arrival accelerated and became particularly visible in the 1990s.

The same seems to be true for the national and migratory backgrounds of the new arrivals. Analysis of the 431 buyers' family names shows first of all that although Turkish family names are numerous among newcomers between 1990 and 2005, their arrival was spread out: we are far from the brutal onslaught of an ethnic community bloc. The diversity of family names also reminds us that immigration from Turkey is hardly new, and far from homogeneous: Armenians, Kurds, and Chaldeans all have very different stories and paths. Some Armenian families had been living in the neighborhood or nearby for a long time, and the presence of Kurds is also product of a diffuse migration across metropolitan Paris. The Chaldean families came to France later, when a wave of repression in Turkey forced this neo-Aramaic-speaking Christian minority of the Chaldean Catholic Church to emigrate in the early 1980s. This situation made them eligible for political refugee status, and they were settled in metropolitan Paris or elsewhere in France. The Chaldean families' search for affordable housing suitable for very large families (they are traditionalist Catholics) brought them to the Poplars's row houses, but their housing progression is also in line with the gradual trajectory of leaving HLMs experienced by the preceding generation of arrivals, at a pace varying from family to family.

The arrival of Chaldean, Kurdish, and Armenian families is part of a larger neighborhood shift toward immigrant families or families with non-French backgrounds. These "Turkish families" (as they are referred to in the neighborhood) represent about a third of newcomers, but half of recent arrivals have family names from other foreign countries: the Maghreb predominates, but names also come from sub-Saharan Africa, Southeast Asia, Pakistan, southern and eastern Europe, and elsewhere.[46] These families (immigrant or from immigrant backgrounds, coming from elsewhere in the Ile-de-France region and many from HLMs) are the bulk of new row-house residents. They are clearly different from the pioneer families and are much more diverse in terms of age and social trajectory.

An overview with some profiles of these immigrant families would convey the variety of situations. Most of the Chaldean families already lived in metropolitan Paris (or elsewhere in France), most in a very run-down private housing complex in Clichy-sous-Bois in the department Seine-Saint-Denis, before buying a house in the Poplars. Initially the fathers were the only employed members of these households (most often as semi-skilled laborers), so home ownership became possible with the help of extended family, unlike the pioneers, who were supported by their employers.

> The Güneses were weavers in a mountain village in Turkey who came to France in 1985 and were granted political refugee status. They first lived with family in a very deteriorated neighborhood of a city in the outskirts of Paris, then for two years in an HLM in another part of France, where they received support as political refugees. Since the father couldn't find work, the family decided to go back to the Paris area so he could work in the garment industry. One of the father's sisters looked for housing for them before they came, a difficult task as there were eleven people to house (they had nine children). She found the row house, which they bought in 1991. Their neighbors, also Chaldean, helped them when they moved. The eldest son Paul, who at the time of our study had a DEUG degree (diplôme d'études universitaires générales, a two years of post-*baccalauréat* university study) in law and worked at a real estate agency, plans someday to buy a house nearby, but in a more prestigious town.

Most non-Chaldean families moved directly from HLMs in neighboring towns, often drawn to the Poplars by the relatively low cost without really knowing the neighborhood.

> The Bonfos migrated from Togo in the early 1980s, and bought a row house in 2001. He is a stock controller in a food business, and she is a nurse's aid in a retirement home. He had been living in Paris, and she in an HLM housing project in another town in the department; they began living together in her housing project in 1988. After the birth of their two children, they wanted to leave the deteriorating housing project and looked to buy in the area. Going through a real estate agency, they decided to move to the Poplars because they preferred a single-family home, and this one was within their means.

As these examples attest, many families from HLMs buy a row house because it is one of the only kinds of housing they can afford. Like the first generation of inhabitants, this purchase sometimes serves as a step in a residential progression bringing them from HLM to a single-family house.

> M. and Mme Piazza bought a row house in 1989. M. Piazza, whose grandfather was Italian, grew up in Sarcelles. He and his wife met there, while she was staying with her aunt who lived in the same apartment tower. He was a laborer for a tradesman in Paris, then a municipal worker for a town in the Val-d'Oise. She was an administrative employee in the city hall of another town, where she got regular promotions. They first lived in a low-income apartment building reserved for civil servants in Gonesse, then bought an apartment, which was followed by a row house. They sold it in 2005 to buy a "real house" with a bigger yard in the neighboring city of Arnouville.

As we can see, among these new residents, the fact of coming from an HLM, being an immigrant, or having foreign roots can span a wide range of situations. These situations all correspond, however, to trajectories of social ascension that progress thanks to the possibility of homeownership offered by the row houses. Some of these new households, like the Piazzas, can unquestionably be identified as little-middles: from working-class backgrounds, they have risen both professionally and residentially, distancing themselves from the working classes and placing them closer to the middle. But this is not the case for all newcomers: the Chaldean families, and some others as well, remain firmly in the categories of laborer, unskilled laborer, or small business owner, so becoming a homeowner does not necessarily mean everyone leaves the condition of laborer behind. It can consequently be said that the row houses were partly renewed from below in the 1990s.

At the same time, though, the Poplars as a whole was also being renewed from above, because of the construction of new subdivisions that would assume the role of new zones of social advancement with greater appeal to some families.

THE EMERGENCE OF NEW ZONES OF ASCENSION

Roughly 260 houses were built in the mid 1970s and mid 1980s, laid out in subdivisions meant to evoke villages. These houses were not very big, but their yards were rather large, and they have been inhabited by families with small children whose parents come mainly from working-class backgrounds and hold a variety of occupational positions—mid-level occupations and even some *cadres* along with laborers, basic employees, and small shopkeepers. The first residents of the 1970s subdivisions have trajectories rather similar to those of the first generation of row-house owners, a decade their senior. Interviews with several former residents of a small square named "Hamlet" dating from 1976 to 1980 revealed trajectories that neatly correspond to the position of the row house little-middles. The couples in late-1970s houses are characterized by upward social trajectories and low-level or no educational qualifications, whose mobility was due to careers in a single enterprise (especially for men) and accumulating real estate equity. Several lifestyle traits keep these socially rising families connected with the working classes. A significant number of them left upon retirement, many moving to other parts of France while others went on to have houses built on the Poplar's newer squares in the early 1980s, in all cases ceding their place to younger families. These new families were different from their immediate predecessors: many of them had lived in HLMs, were more likely to be from immigrant backgrounds (from French overseas departments or territories as well as the Maghreb, sub-Saharan Africa, or Asia), and had experienced a social ascension closely related to higher studies and employment as a civil servant.

In "Partridge Terrace," a subdivision we studied in depth, laborers, basic employees, mid-level occupations, and *cadres* all live together. The percentage of public employees is significant (at least half the couples contained at least one, according to the data). Two couples from the Terrace illustrate these characteristics well.

M Bensoussan is a (nonengineer) computing technician for a bank, and Mme Bensoussan is a schoolteacher in a neighboring working-class city. Both come from Algerian Jewish families that had respectively moved into the Cité du Nord housing project in Gonesse and to the nearby city of Sarcelles in 1962. M. Bensoussan's father worked as pharmaceutical preparer, and his mother was a homemaker. His parents also had a house built on Partridge Terrace, and left the Cité du Nord in 1986.

M and Mme Loiseau are both from farming families in the French overseas department of Martinique, where it is rare for young people to pursue schooling. Both of them completed middle school. He is a police brigadier, having first joined as a patrolman, and she was a civil servant (an administrative employee in the Ministry of Justice) after having held temporary positions in a variety of agencies. They lived in an HLM (like their siblings who also migrated to mainland France) before having a house built.

These couples achieved a significant ascent that unequivocally places them in the middle classes, and a minority of them (working as *cadres* and engineers) even approaches the upper classes. Within the neighborhood's internal stratification, village-style subdivision residents are thus an intermediate stratum, being situated (as one of the square's residents put it) "between the Turks and the golf," which is to say, between the row houses where the families from Turkey now live and the more upscale houses built near the golf course.

The so-called golf-course houses are the most recent addition to the neighborhood. They are larger than other houses in the neighborhood, so some teenaged residents have dubbed it Beverly Hills, and people living there are sometimes described as "rich" or "bourgeois." City hall and many residents alike have created a clear distinction between this zone and what many refer to as the "old Poplars."

As a result, one comes across well-off business-owners as well as high-level *cadres* with advanced degrees, and sometimes even couples of high-level *cadres*. Some of them are invested in local life and the schools, and their presence draws all "golf course" homeowners socially upward.

M and Mme Fayard are respectively a computing engineer and a doctor (general practitioner). She was in a private practice until 2004, when she became a school doctor. Her father was a skilled laborer, and his an engineer. They are about forty and have three sons who are doing well in Gonesse's public middle school and *lycée*.[47] Mme

Fayard is very active in the FCPE (Fédération des Conseils de Parents d'Elèves) a school parents' association that is considered left-leaning, and has been a Socialist municipal official since 2001. Originally from mining zones in eastern France, they both went to school in Nancy then left to work in greater Paris. After renting houses in the area, they had a large house with six rooms built on a 600-square-meter property they purchased in 1995.

Although this microneighborhood's population has a higher proportion of *cadres* than elsewhere in the Poplars, it is once again the diversity that matters. The upscale real-estate offerings appearing in the early 1990s did not reach the wealthy clientele they originally targeted. Some plans for deluxe subdivisions were converted into simpler versions, and some plots were sold as building lots for individual construction. It is likely that their proximity to an HLM housing project and the old row houses handicapped these elite projects. The everyday noise from the air traffic at nearby Charles de Gaulle airport may also have deterred affluent families from buying houses that were still rather expensive. As a result, many people in mid-level occupations and even some basic employees were able to move to this part of the neighborhood despite having thought they could never "aim that high," as Mme Germain put it. She grew up in Gonesse and has family ties there, and managed to buy a house in the "golf course" microneighborhood thanks to a significant upward professional ascension.

Mme Germain is forty-three and has always lived in Gonesse. Her parents were able to buy a small house thanks to her father's initiative, which got him internally promoted from his start as a basic employee. Her mother worked in a bank, stopped working, then resumed working (as a phone operator) upon the early death of her husband. Mme Germain left school at the end of *lycée* and worked as a bank employee like her two sisters. M. Germain is a customer service representative in a bank. He has a secondary-level vocational degree (a BEP, brevet d'études professionnelles) and was promoted internally. His father was a deliveryman (formerly an agricultural laborer), and his mother a child-care provider. He grew up in the Cité du Nord housing project, also in Gonesse. The Germains initially bought an apartment in a neighboring town, but after having three children they took out a loan to buy their house in 1996. The surface area of the house is 100 square meters, on a 300-square-meter property. Mme Germain is a member of the local FCPE (school parents' association).

Another share of the new homeowners comes directly from HLMs in metropolitan Paris. They are composed of couples, many of which are immigrants or children of immigrants and/or work as lower-level civil servants, who bought a house or had one built here to escape "the projects."

In 2003, Karima Dhif and her husband bought a house under market price because its first owners were divorcing and needed to sell quickly. The house had only eighty square meters of surface area, but the yard was rather big and Karima's sister Nadia and one of her coworkers also lived in the neighborhood. Karima and Nadia's parents are Algerian, and their father used to be a laborer. Karima left school upon completion of *lycée* and is an administrative employee in a university. Her husband, who is from Morocco, has a secondary-level vocational degree (BEP) and is a machinist for the metropolitan Paris train network, the RATP (Régie Autonome des Transports Parisiens). She grew up in an HLM in Bondy until her parents bought a house. When Karima and her husband married they moved into an HLM. With their parents' help and thanks to their status as public employees, they were able to get a mortgage to buy a house.

The arrival of these couples from HLMs, who often come from laboring and immigrant backgrounds, further diversifies this newly built microneighborhood that outsiders frequently describe as being full of *cadres*. Although these *cadres* are socially visible and valued within the neighborhood, the neighborhood is nonetheless still a zone of ascension, as much for families with roots in other less prestigious neighborhoods of Gonesse as for those coming from HLMs, so the people renewing the neighborhood's population are indeed little-middles. But as we shall see, their trajectories are very different from those of the row-house pioneers.

This sampling shows that, to the contrary of what many long-term residents say, the row-house neighborhood's history is not only one of an abrupt change in the 1990s when families from Turkey arrived. It is also the story of a slow diversification that began in the 1970s with the departure of some of the Poplars's earliest arrivals. These pioneers are indeed gradually replaced by families from housing projects in metropolitan Paris, who are often foreign—including the Chaldeans from Turkey—or from immigrant families and thought to downgrade the neighborhood. But at the same time, from the 1980s to the 2000s, the more costly houses in the newly built subdivisions would attract better-off families that elevate that microneighborhood's social status. These population changes, related to population renewal and new construction, spark some significant social moves within and out of the neighborhood, and are behind the constant social downclassing and reclassing that this book aims to comprehend. How does this mix of small homeowners born in France of French parents, from recent waves of immigration, and descended from older migrations living in housing projects coexist and live together in this residential neighborhood whose population has been in constant renewal since the 1970s? How do these residents of diverse origins perceive each other, and how to they relate to each other in everyday life? How important is ethnic belonging, along with demographic and socioeconomic characteristics, in these perceptions and relations? What activities and groups of people prompt neighbors to lend each other a hand or, to the contrary, express hostility or rejection?

A COLLECTIVE ETHNOGRAPHIC STUDY
OF SMALL HOMEOWNERS

Study of the city of Gonesse began in 2003–4, as part of a program to train students in urban ethnography. A member of the teaching team had grown up there and knew the city well, prompting us to chose it as a field site. In its second year, 2004–5, the study focused on the social trajectories of people living in the Poplars neighborhood as well as their residential practices and neighborly relations. The researcher-student team tightened in 2005–6, then was reduced to the authors of this book in 2006–7.[48] Research in the neighborhood itself thus took place over the course of nearly four years and involved several stays during which we were housed in the neighborhood and additional periodic visits to conduct interviews or observe local events.

It was not easy to contact residents of the Poplars, or to convince them to talk with researchers. The youngest households—dual-income couples—are not home very much because of their long work days and/or commuting times, and when they are, they prefer family activities: one woman we telephoned several times ended up replying that she is only available weekends, and weekends are "for family life." The oldest residents—retirees who are home most of the time—are (as we will see) unhappy with how the neighborhood has developed and seem suspicious or disillusioned when asked to talk about their house and neighborhood today. And more generally speaking, these homeowners trying to be "like everyone else" have trouble seeing how their stories or lifestyles could interest researchers and students from Paris. Although they are prepared to decry the neighborhood's "problems," they are less eager to speak of themselves as individuals.

We were ultimately able to make contact with the network of longest-term residents by using the contacts of the teaching team member who had grown up in the Poplars and whose family still lived there, consisting of old neighbors and friends that went to the same recreational association. Being able to introduce ourselves as having connections with a family that had been in the neighborhood since the beginning was an open-sesame: the friendships and relationships of mutual aid tying these longtime residents together made them more willing to grant us interviews.

This connection with the group of long-term residents explains why the research addressed them more than the newcomers. Of course, we still worked to make contacts among more recent arrivals, especially with the families from Turkey, but research with them proved to be much more difficult—because of the language barrier, obviously, but for other reasons as well. In interview situations, they assumed the role of community representatives from the outset, and tried incessantly to counter the stigmatizing stereotypes that tarnished their community's reputation; they avoided our questions about domestic practices and personal histories to give an abstract collective image of a united, respectable, and well-integrated community.

To reach the youngest couples living in the most recent part of the neighborhood (the New Poplars), we began with the school parents' associations: the interest these parents show in schools and their children's education made them more likely to agree to invite Parisian researchers and/or students in their homes, because we were seen as representing the world of education they valued. A fortuitous chance encounter with a former student who had grown up in a Poplars subdivision and was still living there finally put us in touch with several "suburban youth" through his friendship and neighborly networks.

Once we had started pursuing these initial networks, our initial interviewees put us in touch with other homeowners, allowing us to gradually expand our contacts in a common ethnographic sampling technique.

The mayor of Gonesse was favorable to our study from the very beginning, if only because the Poplars "was a problem" for him: tensions between neighbors arising from how the population was developing, the increase in petty crime, the rising vote for the extreme-right political party Front National, and some households' socioeconomic insecurity led the city to designate this neighborhood as a "city contract" area (generally reserved for public housing neighborhoods) so it could benefit from state-sponsored "city policy,"[49] thus allowing it to intervene. The mayor put us in contact with a variety of administrative services, but he and his agents made only the slightest effort to influence our choice of residents to interview. In interviews, however, we did often have the feeling that the residents associated us with Gonesse city hall (in addition to Paris and the university) because the complaints and demands scattered throughout interviews often seemed to be aimed past us, at local authorities.

Interviewees often think of residential practices as too mundane and uninteresting to discuss them readily and at length in recorded interview situations. The choice to interview in pairs allowed us to minimize this problem by converting the interview into a tour of the house with one of us taking photographs: drawing our attention to particular objects and remarking on various interior and exterior arrangements led the people we interviewed to speak more explicitly and in greater detail of their residential history and neighborhood life today. The long interviews were then supplemented by observations of their houses as well as the surrounding streets and businesses. When we returned to the field without students at various times between 2005 and 2007, we were put up by neighborhood residents, which gave us further opportunities for observation and also allowed us to see some residents regularly, making them allies in our study (Isabelle Fayart, physician; Paul Günes, university student from a Chaldean family; Paulette Sanchez, a row-house resident; Thomas Loiseau, university student living in one of the more recent subdivisions). We also attended local political and social events: neighborhood picnics, monthly neighborhood board meetings from October 2005 to June 2006, neighborhood council meetings,[50] the presidential election of April 2007, a public meeting city hall held for residents of the Poplars and the Cité du Nord after incidents between young people from the two neighborhoods. Following the 2008 French municipal elections, which were marked by a declared desire to open politics to "visible minorities," we conducted another study in 2008–9 on Poplars residents who ran in this election.

Although the ethnographic rule of thumb holds that place names and the names of people should be changed when research findings are made public, in this case we chose to keep the actual city name, Gonesse. The need to contextualize our interviews and observations by relating the urban, economic, and social characteristics of the city made any effort to keep it anonymous useless, as anyone with the slightest knowledge of the Parisian metropolitan area could easily identify it. Retaining the real name moreover facilitates potentially fruitful comparisons and dialogue with geographers and urban sociologists, who do not generally hide place names. Nevertheless, the personal nature of the data acquired through interviews meant that we had to make it untraceable: the names of the neighborhood, streets, and schools have been changed, as well as the names of the people we spoke with, of course.

To conclude this introduction to the study and our argument for ethnographic methods in studying the class structure of contemporary France, we wish to stress how scientifically and politically important it is to use this research method to study the relationship that little-middles, these homeowners in modest social ascension, have with politics today. Every election cycle, local or national, prompts a mass of commentary on "modest suburban homeowners" as a group. The 2002 presidential election gave nationwide visibility to the suburban vote for the Front National, which is simplistically described as a vote by relegated "poor whites" living outside large cities, despite the fact that many residential neighborhood homeowners are now immigrants and people from immigrant backgrounds,[51] their residential trajectories are hardly in mass decline, and their voting preferences actually vary widely. The monograph format will allow us to connect political behavior to the neighborhood's social history as well as the personal histories of the families living there. After characterizing how neighbors relate to each other and the form of social mobility that unites them, and demonstrating that the conditions that make these little social ascensions possible get harder for each successive generation, in the conclusion we will endeavor to describe and understand how these little-middles vote, and how they relate to local politics.

NOTES

1. On the occasion of the English-language edition of our book (originally published in French in 2008), we have rewritten the introduction, integrating a subsequently published analysis: M Cartier, I Coutant, O Masclet, and Y Siblot, "From the Petite Bourgeoisie to the Little-Middles: An Invitation to Put Small Social Mobility into Question," in *The Routledge Companion to Bourdieu's "Distinction,"* ed. P Coulangeon and J Duval (Oxford, 2014), 63–77.

2. L Chauvel, *Le destin des générations. Structure sociale et cohortes en France au XXe siècle* (Paris, 1998); L Chauvel, "Le retour des classes sociales," *Revue de l'OFCE* 79 (2001): 315–59; P Coulangeon, *Les métamorphoses de la distinction. Inégalités culturelles dans la France d'aujourd'hui* (Paris, 2011); T Piketty, *Capital in the Twenty-First Century,* trans. A Goldhammer (Cambridge, MA, 2014).

3. S Beaud and M Pialoux, *Retour sur la condition ouvrière* (Paris, 1999).

4. S Beaud and M Pialoux, *Violences urbaines, violence sociale* (Paris, 2003).

5. I Backouche, F Ripoll, S Tissot, and V Veschambre, *La dimension spatiale des inégalités. Regards croisés des sciences sociales* (Rennes, 2011).

6. W Wilson, *The Truly Disadvantaged: The Inner City, the Underclass, and Public Policy* (Chicago, 1987); W Wilson, *When Work Disappears: The World of the New Urban Poor* (New York, 1997).

7. To cite but one prominent example from anthropology: P Bourgois, *In Search of Respect: Selling Crack in El Barrio* (New York, 1995).

8. However, an array of studies have shown the importance of homeownership to self-esteem and respectability, as much in the American working classes (D Halle, *America's Working Man: Work, Home and Politics among Blue Collar Property-Owners* (Chicago, 1984) as in the middle classes (K Newman, *Falling from Grace: Downward Mobility in the Age of Affluence* (New York, 1988). Gated communities have also been subject of recent studies, such as S Low's *Behind the Gates: Life, Security and the Pursuit of Happiness in Fortress America* (New York, 2003).

9. N Townsend, *The Package Deal* (Philadelphia, PA, 2002), 142; H Gans, *The Levittowners: Ways of Life and Politics in a New Suburban Community* (New York, 1982).

10. M Pattillo-McCoy, *Black Picket Fences: Privilege and Peril among the Black Middle Class* (Chicago, 1999).

11. We chose to retain the French term *banlieue* in this text to avoid confusion with the connotations associated with the English-language word "suburb," though both technically refer to areas in the urban periphery. While in the United States, a suburb evokes the image of tidy lines of houses and neatly trimmed lawns (because of the American relationship to urbanization), in France *banlieue* raises the image of high-rise low-income housing projects (often referred to as *cités*) and the tensions Americans associate with the term *inner city* or *housing projects*. We have accordingly limited using *suburb* to cases with a more middle-class, single-family housing association, preferring the more neutral words *periphery* or *periurban* (where the urban edge mingles with farmland) for the geographical space surrounding the city itself.

12. The following is a nonexhaustive sampler of the many references on the subject: J Chamboredon and M Lemaire, "Proximité spatiale et distance sociale," *Revue française de sociologie* XI, no.1 (1970): 3–33; J Laé and N Murard, *L'argent des pauvres* (Paris, 1985); F Dubet, *La galère. Jeunes en survie* (Paris, 1987); O Masclet, *La*

gauche et les cités. Enquête sur un rendez-vous manqué (Paris, 2006); D Lapeyronnie, *Ghetto urbain. Ségrégation, violence, pauvreté en France aujourd'hui* (Paris, 2008).

13. C Pétonnet studies transitional housing projects; C Pétonnet, *On est tous dans le brouillard. Ethnologie des banlieues* (Paris, 1979); G Althabe studies neighborly relations in a housing project in the city of Nantes; G Althabe, "La résidence comme enjeu," in *Urbanisation et enjeux quotidiens. Terrains ethnologiques dans la France actuelle,* ed. G Althabe, C Marcadet, M de la Pradelle, and M Sélim (Paris, 1993), 11–69.

14. The riots were set off by the electrocution of two young *banlieue* residents who hid from police pursuit in an electrical station. The ensuing uprising in *banlieue* across the country made international news and shook French society in their exposure of the tense and harsh living conditions in French public housing projects; for discussion, see D Fassin, "Riots in France and Silent Anthropologists," *Anthropology Today* 22, no. 1 (2006): 1–3; S Terrio, "Who Are the Rioters in France," *Anthropology News* 27, no. 1 (2006): 4–5.

15. For example, H Lagrange and M Oberti, eds, *Émeutes urbaines et protestations. Une singularité française* (Paris, 2006).

16. Two recent publications are good illustrations of this focus: B Epstein, *Collective Terms: Race, Culture, and Community in a State-Planned City in France* (New York, 2011); J Selby, *Questioning French Secularism: Gender Politics and Islam in a Parisian Suburb* (New York, 2012).

17. N Haumont, *Les pavillonnaires: étude psychosociologique d'un mode d'habitat* (Paris, 2001). See also H Raymond, N Haumont, MG Dezès, and A Haumont, *L'habitat pavillonnaire* (Paris, 2001).

18. S Magri, "Le pavillon stigmatisé. Grands ensembles et maisons individuelles dans la sociologie des années 1950 à 1970," *L'Année sociologique* 58, no. 1 (2008): 171–202.

19. A Fourcaut, *Bobigny, banlieue rouge* (Paris, 1986). See also A Fourcaut, *La banlieue en morceaux. La crise des lotissements défectueux en France dans l'entre-deux-guerres* (Paris, 2000).

20. A Faure, ed., *Les premiers banlieusards* (Paris, 1991). In the United States in the 1960s, the Levittowners, who were quite focused on their houses as a unique space of freedom, nonetheless proved to be more "in the world" than their parents and grandparents had been: they trusted their neighbors and joined them in civic and social activities (Gans, *The Levittowners*).

21. M Jaillet, *Les pavillonneurs* (Paris, 1984); P Bourdieu, *Les structures sociales de l'économie* (Paris, 2000).

22. M Berger, *Les Périurbains de Paris: De la ville dense à la métropole éclatée* (Paris, 2004).

23. D Pinson and S Thomann, *La maison en ses territoires. De la villa à la ville diffuse* (Paris, 2001); E Charmes, "Entre ouverture et fermeture: les rapports à autrui dans les tissus périurbains," in *La société des voisins,* ed. B Haumont and A Morel (Paris, 2005).

24. C Bonvalet and A Gotman, eds, *Le logement une affaire de famille* (Paris, 1993); Y Grafmeyer and F Dansereau, *Trajectoires familiales et espaces de vie en milieu urbain* (Paris, 1998).

25. M Verret, *L'espace ouvrier* (Paris, 1979); B Légé, "Les castors de la Monnaie," *Terrain* 9 (1987): 34–39; D Maison, "Pionniers de l'accession," *Les Annales de la Recherche Urbaine* 65 (1993): 46–53.

26. See "Petits et grands déplacements sociaux," chapter 12 in B Lahire, *La Culture des individus* (Paris, 2004), 411–70.

27. C Peugny, *Le déclassement* (Paris, 2009).

28. Our work is very similar to that of anthropologist K Newman, who works to show the experience of downclassing among middle-class men and women, and how they interpret and react to the experience (Newman, *Falling from Grace*).

29. R Hoggart, *The Uses of Literacy: Aspects of Working Class Life* (London, 1957).

30. P Bourdieu, *Distinction: A Social Critique of the Judgment of Taste*, trans. Richard Nice (Cambridge, MA, 1984).

31. On greater Manchester, England, see "Local Habitus and Working-Class Culture," chapter 5 in M Savage, G Bagnall, and B Longhurst, eds, *Rethinking Class: Culture, Identities and Lifestyle* (New York, 2008), 95–121; on Porto, Portugal, see V Borges Pereira, *Classes e Culturas de Classe das Famílias Portuenses. Classes sociais e "modalidades de estilização da vida" na cidade do Porto* (Porto, 2005).

32. Two former colleagues of Pierre Bourdieu formulated this criticism a couple years after the publication of *Distinction,* in a seminar on the sociology of the working classes at the Ecole des Hautes Etudes en Sciences Sociales (EHESS) in 1982 (see C Grignon and J Passeron, *Le Savant et le populaire. Misérabilisme et populisme en sociologie et en littérature* (Paris, 1989). Anthropologists of working-class cultures have voiced similar critiques of the Bourdieusian approach to dominated groups. For example, see F Weber's research on the positive taste for activity among rural laborers; F Weber, *Le Travail à côté* (Paris, 1989), and D Reed-Danahay's analysis of her study on how farming and laboring families related to the school system in a rural village in the Auvergne region in the early 1980s (D Reed-Danahay, *Education and Identity in Rural France* (Cambridge, U.K., 1996).

33. After studying forms of family life and gender roles among laborers in the Nord-Pas-de-Calais region of France in a long-term ethnographic study (O Schwartz, *Le monde privé des ouvriers. Hommes et femmes du Nord* (Paris, 1990), Schwartz conducted an ethnographic study of bus drivers in metropolitan Paris in which he paid particular attention to how the cultural boundaries between the working and middle classes are reformed. He showed, for example, how the fact of holding a service job may partly change how men with low job skills conceive of virility, by favoring their apprenticeship in psychologically orthodox ways of behaving and speaking; Schwartz, "La pénétration de la 'culture psychologique de masse' dans un groupe populaire: paroles de conducteurs de bus," *Sociologie* 2, no. 4 (2011): 345–61.

34. O Schwartz, "Does France Still Have a Class Society? Three Observations about Contemporary French Society," *La Vie des idées* (2014), http://www.booksand ideas.net/Does-France-Still-Have-a-Class.html.

35. Bourdieu, *Distinction,* 318.

36. For a summary of sociopolitical debates on the petite bourgeoisie and the middle strata in the 1970s, see S Bosc, *Sociologie des classes moyennes* (Paris, 2008).

37. Employment categories reflect the categories of INSEE (the French census), which do not always have a simple equivalent in other census systems. Most relevant here are "basic employee" and "*cadre.*" According to the French census, an *employé* (translated as basic employee) is a vaguely defined category of low- to nonskilled workers, excluding laborers, that includes sales clerks, secretaries, domestic workers, hospital aids, firemen, police, and military. We retain the French term *cadre* according to the usage in the English translation of L Boltanski's sociological treat-

ment of this occupational category, akin to—but not the same as—a "white collar worker" in American English. *Cadres* are recognized both in the French census and in common usage as being persons occupying a range of jobs from low technician positions to upper executive, with associated job security, benefits, and social status. See L Boltanski, *The Making of a Class: Cadres in French Society,* trans. A Goldhammer (Cambridge, U.K., 1987).

38. E Préteceille, *La division sociale de l'espace francilien. Typologie socio-professionnelle 1999 et transformation de l'espace résidentiel 1990–1999* (Paris, 2003).

39. T Saint-Julien, J-C François, H Mathieu, and A Ribardière, *Les disparités des revenus des ménages franciliens en 1999. Approches intercommunales et infracommunales et évolution des différenciations intercommunales (1990–1999),* unpublished report for the DRIEF (Paris, 2003).

40. The *baccalauréat* (commonly known as the *bac*) is a diploma marking successful completion of secondary schooling, granted upon passage of a rigorous annual nationwide examination. It is a prerequisite for academic-track university studies, but not necessarily for further vocational training. There are currently four specializations: science (the most prestigeous), economics and social sciences, literature, and technology (the least valued).

41. Gonesse's urbanization occurred at the same pace as that of Wissous, the village studied in the late 1950s by anthropologists R and B Anderson. While they were more concerned with gathering older residents' recollections of fading rural conditions, we are interested in the perspective of the new arrivals who began the urbanization of these old Ile-de-France villages; RT Anderson and BG Anderson, *Bus Stop for Paris: The Transformation of a French Village* (Garden City, NY, 1965).

42. J Chamboredon, "Construction sociale des populations," in *Histoire de la France urbaine,* ed. M Roncayolo (Paris, 1985), 467–501.

43. The term "the Turks" is commonly used in the Poplars to refer to a diverse population including a variety of groups from Turkey as well as people from other backgrounds, which prompts us to use the term with quotes when evoking local usage and perception of "foreign" (as opposed to "French") neighbors. We likewise sometimes use "foreign" with caution, because its usage corresponds more with perception of difference than actual nationality or even place of birth, further accentuated by the more fluid meaning of its equivalent in French (*étranger*), which can also designate "outsider." The locally used term "the French" is also problematic, since some of the pioneering longtime residents have non-French origins (Italian, Portuguese) but identify and are fully accepted as French by other pioneers, while some of the newcomer "foreigners" are actually native-born French citizens. We thus use these three terms in quotation marks to describe these group dynamics in local terms without subscribing to their inaccurate and polarizing representations.

44. There is no information on buyers for 1988 and 1989, so the analysis concerns 449 sales that took place between 1990 and 2005. As some information is lacking, we only know 383 prior addresses and 431 buyers' family names.

45. It is sometimes difficult to identify the geographical origins of family names, and obviously they say nothing of the buyers' nationalities, birthplaces, or migratory paths. Here we identified French family names and foreign ones, sorted into four broad categories: European (Portugal, Italy, Yugoslavia …), Turkish (including Kurdish, Armenian, and Chaldean), Arab (for the most part from the Maghreb), and other (sub-Saharan Africa, Asia, etc.).

46. This great diversity of cultural and ethnic backgrounds is typical of many neighborhoods in France, especially in greater Paris's public housing and housing development neighborhoods. For example, B Epstein encountered a similar ethnic and cultural mix in the public housing neighborhood she studied in Cergy Pontoise (Epstein, *Collective Terms*).

47. We chose to retain the French word *lycée* to highlight the great difference between "high school" in the United States and the French system. *Lycée généraux* (which, following common usage, we will refer to simply as *lycée*) are fairly rigorous academic-track schools where most students aim to take an academic *baccalauréat* in order to attend university, whereas students pursuing vocational tracks attend lower-status *lycée professionel* ("vocational *lycée*"), which prepares them for a manual trade, and in some cases a vocational *baccalauréat*. The vast majority of French youth attend one kind of *lycée* or another, but it is not required and they may opt for lower-level vocational training instead.

48. Appendix 1 contains the list of interviews cited in the book, as well as the names of the researchers that conducted them. Appendix 2 details additional data sources that do not fit into the bibliographical format.

49. The city policy developed in France since the 1990s consists of a collection of state actions aiming to renew certain so-called "sensitive" urban neighborhoods.

50. Neighborhood councils and boards are bodies aiming to get ordinary citizens to participate in the discussion of city decision-making that concerns the public. Of varying forms and names, these bodies for local citizen participation appeared in France in the late 1990s.

51. A Lambert, *"Tous propriétaires!" L'envers du décor pavillonnaire* (Paris, 2015).

1

THE "GOOD OLD DAYS"

Following World War II, France experienced a severe housing crisis and dramatic demographic growth due in part to immigration but largely to a high birthrate supported by an ambitious family policy. The 1939 family code had significantly increased the first-child bonus and family allowance (*allocations familiales*), an annual per-child subsidy sent to all parents regardless of income level. The early 1950s ushered in a proactive policy for the construction of publicly owned rental properties, low-income subsidized housing, and other inexpensive lodgings. Big companies had to contribute to "1% Housing," a program that became mandatory in 1953 requiring them to invest 1 percent of total payroll in employee housing, either by direct contribution to construction or financing loans. Apartment complexes and housing projects sprang up on the outskirts of cities, and most of all around Paris. The working and middle classes mingled in these modern high-rise buildings, so the Parisian periphery was not as segregated then as it is today. These housing projects soon drew criticism, however, for their imposing outlines and repetitive forms as well as their shoddy interior construction. Housing policy shifted from supporting the construction of multifamily buildings (through construction subsidies known as *aide à la pierre*) in the late 1970s to individualized housing assistance and property ownership support for the working classes (called *aide à la personne,* personal assistance).[1]

A time of intense urbanization, the 1950s and 1960s also saw salaried employment strengthen in a context of strong economic growth.[2] The contracts of all employees, regardless of employer, were reinforced by new rights and assurances: the program bundling health insurance and retirement, called Social Security, in 1945; a guaranteed minimum wage in 1950 (first known as the SMIG (salaire minimum interprofessionnel garanti), with some modifications it became the SMIC (salaire minimum interprofessionnel de croissance) in 1970); the rights to unemployment benefits in 1958, continuing job training in 1971, and monthly pay in 1978. The improvement of modest social categories' living conditions and the proliferation of possibilities for upward social mobility allowed people to project potential futures, raising aspirations of homeownership for some. Although most laborers and basic employees were still renters in 1973, an increasing number had access to ownership: 36.6 percent of laborers and 34.4 percent of basic employees were homeowners, as compared with 60.9 percent of industrial and commercial business owners and 50.6 percent of *cadres* and professionals.[3]

Numerous sociological studies were conducted during this period of rapid economic and urban growth in 1950s through 1970s France. In the same spirit as Young and Willmott in England and Gans in the United States,[4] researchers wanted to provide useful data to city planners building new forms of housing. The research plan often consisted of comparing social life in the old condemned neighborhoods of large cities to that in the new suburban neighborhoods to show the transformations in a supposedly traditional lifestyle.[5] Such research in France found the cohabitation of laborers and middle classes in these new socially heterogeneous neighborhoods multiplied social differences, heightening tensions between groups artificially assembled in the same space.[6] The rare studies devoted to new neighborhoods of single-family homes persisted in affiliating themselves with the petit-bourgeois ideology of the laborer-homeowner and his "turning inward on the house."[7] This figure of the petit-bourgeois owner of a modest single-family home, borne of an intellectual and political context marked by Marxism, communism, and the glorification of multifamily housing, would be taken up later by Pierre Bourdieu, once the single-family house had become the priority of French housing policy: "turning inward into one's home and weakened (if not broken) social ties are indeed the trademarks of the modest homeowner, old or new."[8]

The development of the Poplars neighborhood in Gonesse, starting with the construction of 644 row houses between 1958 and 1966, is part of this dual trend toward urbanization and employment stabilization (although it consisted of individual houses for first-time ownership instead of the more common rental apartments), and it attracted households of basic employees and laborers in large public or private enterprises with small children. From laboring and/or farming families, the first generation to own a new house in a new neighborhood in metropolitan Paris with a new lifestyle to be invented, they see themselves as pioneers. So what did the social life in this neighborhood of row houses sheltering great occupational diversity look like in the 1960s? Sociological research from the period leads one to think that it was marked by class divisions and tensions, individualism, and everyone turning inward, focused on their own houses and households—but row-house pioneers' accounts today depict an intense and happy social life instead. Should this be interpreted as a trick of memory and nostalgia? Fueled by the work of historians showing that laborers and basic employees' accession to single-family homes does not automatically engender crumbling sociability and a break with the values of equality and social justice,[9] we instead chose to take residents' proffered hypothesis of an intense social life seriously. The question then is how the Poplars, a new neighborhood of adjoining houses attracting midlevel white-collar workers and laborers alike, could have been the basis for such an intense social life.

Despite occupational differences, these families formed a relatively united group on the domestic and local scene because of their very similar social backgrounds, ages, and family situations: this chapter starts with the formation of this group, its values, and its practices. It will demonstrate that the kind of housing (three-level adjoined houses) worked both as a constraint and a resource in the process. It fostered the emergence of what could be called a "local domestic culture," combining how houses were used, "ways of living," and forms of sociability.[10] Starting in the late 1970s, the Poplar's population was refreshed by the arrival of new first-time buyers of modest homes, but with more diverse demographic characteristics (age, family situation), with consequences for the initial resident group and the local domestic culture they had invented. By detailing how this culture decomposed, we show how a neighborhood for upward mobility can also become one for demotion.

THE ROW-HOUSE PIONEERS:
AN EGALITARIAN ENVIRONMENT

Many of the pioneers stress the feeling of equality that reigned among them, and the fact that the differences of occupational status were barely perceptible in neighborly relations. The variety of occupations could well have engendered an ambiance of social competition and jealousy, neighbors judging each other on their status and their resources. Households like the Samsons, where only the husband worked (as a semi-skilled laborer at Citroën), are, in terms of socioeconomic status, far from the minority of lower *cadres* in the neighborhood. And yet even these families are insistent that neighbors all got along and played down differences among them.

Interviewer: And the neighbors when you got here, they were in the same situation as you?

Mme Samson: Well, the same, more or less, we were … There weren't many people much better off than us, really.

M. Samson: Well, there were some who were in maybe better situations.

Mme Samson: Not many. The Poiriers and the Brissets, yes, but the Dubois and all them. No, it was all little people like us. No, it was all humble people.

M. Samson: But those in a better situation never made out that we were inferior to them.

Mme Samson: We are still very good friends with them. And no one ever made us feel like we were laborers.

How can laborers, low-level employees, teachers, and engineers treat each other as equals on the residential scene? Even if this equality is more proclaimed than real, how is it that the very people who could have been kept at a distance as the most modest of the neighborhood should feel it so strongly?

Careful Spending

Behind the variety of occupations, there were indeed differences in financial resources from the very beginning that were likely to result in immediately recognizable consumption practices on the residential scene: whether a household owned a car or not, and/or how rapidly they acquired a color television. The variety of ways people financed the purchase of a home also testifies to such objective resource inequalities: some households, like the Bouchers and the Morins, had no savings to put toward a down payment, while others already had some money set aside. This is quite unlike the claim to equality typical of traditional working-class neighborhoods: an objective reality so long as the differences in conditions are minimal, it is also a moral norm maintained through accusations of pride and jealousy and by conserving a closed in-group and class solidarity.[11] At the Poplars, the environment of equality came from the respect for and encouragement of plans and strategies for individual achievement.

Even though the occupational positions and the financial resources are varied, these families have the same relationship to money and expenditures. All the pioneering couples, whether laborer or engineer, made a considered choice to buy this kind of inexpensive single-family residence in the poorly reputed northern Parisian *banlieue* because its three stories and shared walls resembled apartment living.

"Something in our means," "You shouldn't be too picky": such formulations indicate a prudent and realistic economic disposition, which was certainly quite widespread at the time and especially among the working classes. But what is particularly interesting is seeing them continue in couples trying to leave the working-class position of their families of origin, through home ownership in a neighborhood of low-level employees through mid-level *cadres*. Often, as mentioned earlier, this reasonable choice was encouraged by employers who gave them help in the form of loans for all or part of their down payment, or served as guarantor of their loan. "The directors, actually, directed us here!" quipped M. Samson, a semi-skilled laborer at Citroën. His words equally apply to bank employees and salaried employees of public-sector firms that were also implementing policies to favor property ownership for their employees while at the same time inducing them to stay in their place and show restraint and modesty. Neighborhood pioneers did not seem to think property ownership was a risky venture, as it required neither relational activism nor complex strategies. They often followed colleagues' advice and were guided by assistance offered by their employers.

The feeling of equality aroused by neighborly relations is related to their common characteristics, namely, being young parents and being in debt, both characteristic of a material and moral family mobilization that is found equally among manual laborers and midlevel *cadres*.[12] The variety of occupations and financial resources is indeed initially obscured by the fact that everyone took out a loan—usually over twenty years—and had to show restraint in their expenditures. This was the period when possession and use of a bank account for managing financial resources became widespread among the French working classes.[13] With several bank employees in the neighborhood, it is likely that they contributed to the circulation of bank-based savings and credit practices.

At the same time, this well-informed group still respected moderation and the memory of frugality from their working-class upbringings. Although they adopted the norm of credit and debt, new in comparison with their parents and the classic working-class culture that marked their childhood, it was often exclusively for housing. The Samsons explain that they accepted going into debt for housing, but refused any other form of credit for consumption (for a car or household furnishings, for example), which was a common practice in *cadre* households in the 1970s. The only time they bent the rule, Mme Samson emphasizes, was the purchase of a color television on credit in 1965, justified by the fact that she was home alone several nights a week while her husband worked the three-to-eight shift at Citroën.

Unlike research findings from many other new neighborhood developments, a new house in the Poplars does not seem to have led to additional expenses in an atmosphere of social competition.[14] Spending is neither immediate nor ostentatious in these families, most of which have higher incomes than the Samsons, but discretely spread out over time and carefully planned. The constraint of property acquisition meant that houses were only gradually furnished and equipped. Interviewees report that loan reimbursements were a third of their income, including family allowances (*allocations familiales*); such a "rent-to-income ratio" signified a non-negligible financial engagement for pioneers. Household revenues were reduced to a single income when wives put their economic activities on hold, which usually happened around the time of home purchase and the birth of a second or third child. The couples we met stressed the paucity of this single income since the husbands were just starting their careers.

Yet despite the fact that reimbursing a twenty-year loan on a single income demands tight management of the family budget, the interviews did not emphasize privation. There is barely any mention of working overtime or taking on side jobs to supplement income and pay for ownership, as is often the case for new property owners from the working classes.[15] The Pageots and the Samsons describe the early years, when they economized by not going out (to the movies, theater) and not going away on vacation. The Samsons went without certain expensive foods, reserving them for the children, and contented themselves with Formica furniture, but their greatest savings was remaining carless for nearly ten years after buying their home at the Poplars, which seems rather rare in the neighborhood (M. Samson carpooled to Saint-Ouen with friends, then went by scooter). Even though they remember that it was "very hard at the beginning" and they "restrained themselves," they refuse to use the term "sacrifice" in describing these restrictive practices ("we were used to it"). The Pageots speak in similar terms.

The limited references to the theme of privation might be connected to the reasonable level of debt these households took on, and that the economizing effort was concentrated into the first years of accession for households needing short-term supplementary loans for their down payments. In addition, all pioneering households' home buying benefitted from the inflation of the 1970s and 1980s, regardless of their resources at the outset, and many of them proudly declared that their payments were "practically nothing" as their loans drew to an end.

These households' economic dispositions are thus marked by the will to have better than their parents but also by the limitation of desires and ambitions. Worried about her son who had just contracted a bridge loan to buy a new house, Mme Samson said that he told her "You taught us to live with what we have." And her husband added, "They are like we raised them, they don't take on more than they can handle." Such modest aspirations are far from being limited to the Poplars's semi-skilled laborers, as we observed them also among many neighbors working as midlevel *cadres,* floor supervisors, and engineers, and *a fortiori* among those who stayed on in the neighborhood when others moved out in the 1970s.

There are many convergent socialization experiences behind these dispositions. The first is growing up in a working-class family, either industrial or agricultural, where you learned early and well to track and moderate spending, choose necessities over luxuries, and make do with what you have.[16] None of the pioneers we met came from a family that owned its housing. The elder M. Heurtin started working at age fourteen as an agricultural laborer before becoming a worker at the national gas company and buying a home at the Poplars in 1968, and his son emphasizes the exploitation and dispossession that marked the condition of his parents' original social milieu. In the quote that follows, he helps us understand the dramatic lifestyle change and new relationship with material goods experienced by his generation that had migrated to the Paris region, found secure employment, and achieved property ownership. It also illustrates the legacies pioneers retain from their upbringings in rural or laboring families.

> Not everyone had the means to buy. No one in the farming milieu owned like that. That came later. It was a system, a "company store" kind of system, where the farm owners had a variety of lodgings where they housed their workers. It's just that when they retired they had to find someplace to live because from then on, they weren't housed by the boss anymore. The Boss with a capital B! And on top of that the boss at the time was a baron or something like that, a senator of the Aisne [*administrative department*], a dignitary. They called him The Great—it was back in the days when you still invited the boss, the curate, the local mayor to baptisms, weddings, et cetera. ... The boss exploited everyone. And the women all worked in the farmyard, sorting potatoes. I can still see myself in the middle of hoeing the forage beets—an exhausting, draining job, for kilometers. My July and August vacations, I'd go past them to gather potatoes, so I remember. The whole "become a homeowner" thing was unimaginable. All the people who stayed in the Aisne were renters, it was another life.

In addition to the fact that most of pioneers had acquired economical habits from their working-class backgrounds, the fact that the majority of interviewed households had been socialized Roman Catholic also appears to be significant, all the more so as it was maintained and transmitted in the 1970s through women's engagement in parish activities, as seen later. This Catholic upbringing favors both a realistic and measured relationship with money and modest social ambitions.

Moreover, the effects of personnel management policies implemented in large public or private companies in the 1960s and 1970s should not be overlooked. Most of the men's careers were dependent on internal promotion, so they had to exhibit conformity with their employers' expectations. It was also at work, in the 1960s—at the bank, the electric and gas company, or the postal, telephone, and telegraph service—that pioneers were exposed to the ideas and financial means allowing them to consider prudent debt and limiting spending (living within one's means) to be a reasonable choice.[17]

To conclude, in addition to moderating spending and the absence of ostentatious consumption practices, neighbors also shared household belongings that were relatively rare at the time, which itself contributed to a sense of equality. The arrival of the first color televisions in a few households (the Bergers and the Morins on Alouette Place, for example) often meant neighbors used it together, instead of sparking gossip, jealousy, and avoidance. Mme Morin happily recalls the boys of Alouette Place coming to watch television at her house, and inversely Mme Pageot remembers that the children across the street came to get her when there was "something to watch." In addition, families with secondary homes (a family house in their home department, a camper in the countryside around Paris) shared them, if not with the neighbors then at least with their children, who were invited as playmates for their own children for weekends and vacations (the Sanchezes and Bergers did this, as did the Boyers and the Rodriguezes). The same kinds of collective use developed around the telephone:

> M. Boyer: When we got a telephone, we gave out our number.
> Interviewer: And people came to your place to make calls?
> Mme Boyer: Right, mostly Mme Besse, because she had several brothers and sisters and they'd call her here. So I'd put the phone down, I'd cross [*the street*], and she'd come answer.

And even when residents perceived these inequalities of possessions and status, that perception was expressed in terms other than competition or distinction. Whereas in old working-class neighborhoods possession of rare things was immediately interpreted as "putting on airs" or "being stuck-up,"[18] in this neighborhood of rising employees and midlevel *cadres,* such material inequalities were accepted because they were thought to be temporary. The only inequality the less well-off households usually felt was in the pace of acquisition since they, too, were in social ascension.

To take full account of the mechanisms producing this environment of equality, lynchpin of the formation of the pioneer group and its domestic culture, we must return to the material framework of housing. Row houses, standardization, and adjoining walls are indeed primarily constraints made necessary by modest financial resources in what was a tight housing market in greater Paris. Drawn to individual homes, most pioneers bought row houses because it was the best they could afford. But they appropriated and transformed this constraint into a material symbol of equality. In fact, these single-family homes were initially managed as a common interest development, also known as a co-ownership, with rather strict rules concerning common spaces and the exterior of buildings: the same materials and same paint for the front garden gates, same color for the façades, same tile for the roofs. Co-ownership seemed to have worked for a decade or so, the pioneers conforming to the collective norms. Many households demonstrated respect for co-ownership norms in the name of equality.

Mme Samson: I liked it a lot, because everyone had his own little privet hedges. Everything was painted the same, because at the time there was a sort of board, which was dissolved later ... But all the garage doors had to be painted with the same paint, the shutters, everything. I thought it was cute. And then, gradually there was no more board, so everyone does whatever he wants! And so I think it looks slummy now. It's more the style of a little housing project.... Before, the front doors were grey, the garage doors were dark green; I thought that everyone was the same, it was ...

M. Samson: Yes, but on the other hand, well uh, that way [*today*], everyone has his own personality.

Interviewer: Yes, that way everyone can personalize his house.

Mme Samson: Yes, its good for small, low houses like that. But when you're in a row, not everyone has the means to re-do the roof at the same time, to re-stucco the exterior. So everyone does it when he can, and it's not the same shades anymore, it's not the same. When it's in a row, it should be uniform.... Before, it really looked like a little village, a little bit like in America or England, I have the impression—I've never been but based on what I've seen on TV—all the same style, a little bit, except for little trees, flowers.

Mme Samson explains her attachment to these collective norms beyond taste judgments ("it was cute"): co-ownership rules requiring standard façades and exterior elements prevented the excessive display of very real differences in means. Where co-ownership rules are concerned, attachment to being "all the same" implies not only individual docility and submission to the rules, but also a preference that everyone be subject to rules that neutralize status differences.

Of course from the Poplars's earliest days, there were recalcitrant residents who wanted to live independently and free of collective norms in what had indeed been sold as single-family housing. But accounts from residents like M. Berger, who managed the Plateau's co-ownership association for ten years, also make it very clear that the pioneers responsible for enforcing co-ownership rules could at least tarnish the reputation of the noncompliant, even if they could not always force them to comply.

M. Berger: The problem is that people in this kind of situation don't feel like they are co-owners.... So people shouldn't have touched the fences because they were commonly owned, but people started making their own fences. We were able to maintain more or less acceptable fences.

Interviewer: What you have at the beginning, little wooden gates?

M. Berger: Little wooden gates with a knee-high metal fence. Well, there are some people who built little walls. So long as it was the same height, it was fine, but there was one who was really imprisoned, he built walls two meters high. We made him take them down.

Interviewer: And the two-meter walls, that was at the very beginning, even in the 1970s?

M. Berger: Yes, pretty quickly. He wanted to be all at home, he didn't want to be bothered. . . . We sent him a letter telling him to kindly take down his wall, that the co-ownership regulations did not permit him to make his own co-ownership rules.

As with the kind of housing (in rows), for several years the construction quality favored this material appearance of equality since there was no need for "major work"; pioneers spoke with one voice in describing an affordable but sturdy and well-finished construction. Shared walls and narrow yards moreover limited the possibility to add on, which co-ownership regulation forbade anyway.

The neighborly relations developing between these homes from the 1960s onward were not, then, distinguished by social competition and individualism. The uniformity of economic dispositions (marked by modest aspirations and the desire to improve material living conditions) in a physical setting comprised of attached houses (individual housing subject to collective norms) led to an environment of equality that accepted inequality of possessions. It is not, in this case, a matter of *equality of conditions* (as found in laborer's families, typified by the residential conditions of miners in the French Nord-Pas-de-Calais region[19]) but on *equality of social ambitions*. This atmosphere was enhanced by a certain familial morality that made intense sociability possible between residents of the Poplars.

Traditional but Relaxed Family and Domestic Norms

The Poplars's pioneers were young couples in which both members were working when they met and married in the late 1950s or early 1960s. At best, the husband was a midlevel *cadre,* most often a clerical employee, and less often a laborer. Most of the wives who worked were clerical employees. Based on these occupations, early access to private homeownership (between twenty-five and thirty years of age), their working-class social backgrounds, and how they describe their residential history, they are united in their hope for social promotion and their desire to live differently than their parents. Given the broader trends in French society in the three prosperous decades after the war, we could readily expect these pioneers, like many basic employees of the time, to be devoted practitioners of female employment and restrained fertility.[20] But this is far from being the case, and moreover, they bought these houses with three or four bedrooms and a little greenery precisely because they had (or wanted) several children. For all that, they do not want their families to be too big, and although the wives stopped working, they sometimes resumed work when the children were grown.

Consequently, these pioneering families and their domestic practices feature composite norms. Most stem from what could be simplistically termed as a traditional model, but others tend to the more modern.[21] Should we speak of the "laborer" model identified by studies between the 1950s and 1980s, and a "middle-class" model from the sociology of French families in the 1980s and 2000s?[22] O Schwartz warns us against the tendency to rush to attribute a single kind of "family norm" to social groups (especially concerning how children are raised).[23]

First of all, these pioneering families seem to have believed that the obvious vocation of the couple was having multiple children. They had children as soon as they got married, in the 1960s, and in many cases while still living in uncomfortable housing conditions. Far from strictly limiting births, most of these couples had two or more children, and references to large families were recurrent. Mme Boucher remembers: "We all had three or four kids, something like that. There were several families, four children, yes, it was relatively common."

But quantifying pioneering households' fertility nuances the images conveyed by interview-based research. To put the interviews in perspective, we analyzed a sample from the 1968 census, which is of admittedly limited utility since it is only a snapshot and does not include children not yet born or having already left home. Analysis of informants' family situations and the 1968 census sample nonetheless show that the norm for children was around two per household, and families with more four or more were rare (see tables 1.1, 1.2).

Fertility may not be tightly restricted in the studied households, but it is controlled. For couples coming from very large sibling groups themselves, having two or three children is already limiting births, and families with more than four children was still commonplace in working-class milieus in the 1960s. In fact, the theme of controlled fertility is embedded in Mme Samson's reaction to her new Chaldean neighbors' behavior; she feels sorry for the mother, who has nine children to care for, and is angry with the priest who discourages use of contraception.

Our interviewees' overestimation of the proportion of families with three or four children above all reveals that children, even in

TABLE 1.1. The number of children by couple living at the Poplars prior to 1975.

Berger	2
Boyer	1
Boucher	3
Dumesnil	2
Heurtin (elder)	4
Heurtin (younger)	4
Legris	2
Lenormand	4
Morin	3
Pageot	2
Sanchez	4
Samson	3

Source: Interviews.

TABLE 1.2. The fertility of the thirty-seven households of Ibis Avenue, 1968 census.

No children	5
One child	9
Two children	14
Three children	6
Four children	3
Five or more children	0

Source: Nominative lists, 1968 census.

quantity, were widely appreciated in the neighborhood, and through them, so was family life. On this path of modest social advancement, family life is valued no less than working life and its possibilities for success and satisfaction. Parents often justified the purchase of an individual home with a yard on the grounds that it was better for the children (possibility for teenagers to have their own rooms and for children to move freely and play outdoors).

This high regard for children goes hand in hand with another major trait of the family morphology of Poplars pioneers: a strong sexual division of roles, where women leave the workforce. They devote themselves to raising the children and taking care of the house, although many of them worked previously, usually as basic employees (in offices, retail, hospitals) and sometimes as laborers. Among our informants, this was so for Mme Samson (who worked at a bank), Mme Morin (who was a stenographer), Mme Lenormand (nurse's aid), Mme Boucher (laboratory assistant), and Mme Pageot (secretary). All of them explain that they made the "choice" to stop working.

We must not forget that it was commonplace for women of this generation to stop working with the birth of children: in the 1962 census, the employment participation rate for women between twenty-five and forty-nine was 41.5 percent (26.1 percent for women with two children under sixteen and 15.9 percent for women with three or more children under sixteen).[24] Mme Morin emphasized this, saying she was part of a "generation where women stayed home and raised their children." Residents of the Poplars, then, largely adhered to the traditional and widespread familial norm of the time wherein child care fell to women: the job of mother was full-time and not split with paid employment. Interviewees evoked an array of justifications for "choosing" housewife status, ranging from financial calculations (the high cost of child care) and men's reservations about women's employment (Mme Samson said that "it's hard for a man to send his wife off to work") to a myriad of practical limitations: no driver's license, only one car, impractical public transportation, schools too far away, the number of children, insufficient facilities, and financial assistance issues.

We are indeed far from the familial norms valued by the couples Catherine Bidou described as the "new middle classes" during the same period. Coming from generations very close to those of Poplars pioneers, in most couples, both husband and wife were employed as teachers, social workers, health care professionals, or clerical workers. Described as "everyday adventurers," they defended the principles of shared domestic work and symmetrical gender roles (although they did not always apply them).[25] And yet for other women of these generations, such as rural female laborers, the choice of mothering work is an obvious one and needs no justification; the Poplars's pioneering women seem to have felt the same.

If this is so, then why do they justify their decision? It might be a consequence of the interview setting and the presence of younger women who
(like their own daughters) embody today's widespread norm to combine
maternal and paid work. The need to justify their choice may also indicate
that the norm of women continuing employment while raising young children was already known and imaginable in this Parisian suburb: data from
the 1968 census shows that of thirty-eight households, sixteen women (40
percent) were employed, twelve as office workers. Moreover, we must not
forget that several of these women who stopped work were as qualified as
their husbands, if not more so: Mme Samson proudly pointed out that she
had a *brevet*, "the equivalent of the *bac* at the time," while her husband (who
was an agricultural laborer at fourteen and the youngest of eight children)
"only had the *certificat*."[26] We discern the same disparity in educational levels in the following description by Mme Pageot, who stopped working at the
birth of her first son in 1961:

> Interviewer: And your husband, does he have any particular diplomas?
> Mme Pageot: None at all. His parents were farmers. There were four children, they
> had ten cows. They started working in the fields at fourteen, y'know! It was a one-
> room school, from age five to fourteen, then he did that at home. After, he worked
> in a forest planting pine trees, and then he was in the regiment [*for his mandatory
> military service*]....
> Interviewer: And did you continue your studies?
> Mme Pageot: I got a first-degree commercial *brevet*. And then there was the second
> degree, so I went to supplementary classes in Saint-Denis. I was there four years,
> and then the last year I went to Paris for the second part, I mean, it was six months
> because after that there were three months of internship. During vacations, I
> worked for the postal service.

Many studies have identified this form of conjugal heterogamy as a trait
associated with trajectories of social ascension in the working classes.[27] In
many cases, it seems to favor the presence of composite familial norms. Mme
Samson thus shares her husband's high esteem for his mother, a housewife
he holds up as a model: although she could not read, she was generous, welcoming, and "strong." But Mme Samson (our informant) encouraged her
daughters to pursue an education and wished that her husband and children
would help with housework, a conceivable possibility for her generation (although it is not put into practice). The idea that women could keep working
was already present in the neighborhood and incarnated by some neighbors;
it introduced some distance from traditional roles, even if they still deter-
mined practices.

This same blend of traditional and contemporary inclinations is found in
uses of the house (in the division of the domestic space as-such, as well as interior and exterior activities). The house, at least its main rooms (especially

the second-floor kitchen and living/dining room), seems to be a space under feminine control, while there is a more masculine appropriation of external domestic spaces (garage, yard), as M. Samson explains:

> M. Samson: I'm there all the time, if not in the yard, in the garage! ... My wife used to say, "Where were you? I haven't seen you all day!" (*laughs*) I come back up to eat. But I can't stay ... What am I supposed to do up there? Read? Bleh. Around three o'clock my butt hurts! (*laughs*)
> Interviewer: Sure, so you tinker around, there or in the yard.
> M. Samson: Right, I invent! ...
> Interviewer: Has retirement changed anything, or was it already like that before?
> M. Samson: Ah, it was like that before.
> Interviewer: Were your weekends before you retired, were they already ... You were in your own place?
> M. Samson: Ah, yes, yes, and then, when I was working, every Sunday I'd wash my floor [*in the garage*] (*laughs*).

Lest we lead anyone to think that this sexual division of the domestic space is only typical among laborers, we will also quote an interview with M. Lenormand, who was an engineer (after having taken night classes while working at the electrical company) when he moved into the Poplars with his wife and three children. They chose it because there was an opportunity to buy an extra garage and take a home "at the end of the row," with only one shared wall. His fondness for gardening, like home repair and tinkering in a masculine domestic space (more of a workshop than a simple bench), is shared with M. Samson, who is a semi-skilled laborer.

> M. Lenormand: When you're in housing like the Poplars, there was really a certain kind of appeal, when you're young ... We still had five rooms, because we thought about having another child. There was that, and then having a garage was really appealing, to shelter the car. And I was quite the handyman at the time, interested in having a bench and what I needed to work in my garage. That's where the idea for a second garage came from, which let me convert my first garage into a workshop. And living on the second floor is nice, it gets you off the ground, there's only the stepladder for stairs, which is kind of steep. But when you're young it doesn't seem like it, you go up and down them fast. And then the rooms up there, with a bathroom and three bedrooms, it was well designed. Plus, from top to bottom, it's all yours.
> Interviewer: And then there's the yard.
> M. Lenormand: There's the yard, and I did yard work.

So the local domestic culture that developed here in the 1960s and 1970s is indeed marked by a traditional gendered division of roles and spaces. This division, however, is partial, flexible, and supplemented by the existence of spaces and activities notable for the presence of both sexes. Although men do the gardening and yard maintenance, it is also a space for children to play, and thus a space mothers spend time in and appropriate as well. Nearly all the houses had small yards, making them subject to negotiations between parents on topics such as whether the vegetable garden should be sacrificed for a sandbox so the children could play in the yard instead of in the street.

Just like the yards, the parks and avenues that also served as playgrounds were spaces for family more than for men or women. Interviews demonstrate the significance of children (in budgets as well as in domestic and common spaces) through stories rejoicing in the intensity of childhood sociability at the Poplars in the 1970s. The families we met regularly gave the row houses' ground-floor bedrooms to children, giving teenagers independence and freedom of movement that the parents had never known. The pioneers were united in common values and dispositions, especially a great appreciation for children and their well-being, cautious spending, ambition, and the desire for social promotion. It is thus striking to see how critical Mme Samson and Mme Sanchez are today of gender relations among their new Chaldean neighbors:

> Mme Samson: You have the impression, though, that the father's the boss. The children are children, the wife's the wife.... He's still the head of the family. They are really nice, but they live like our parents, our grandparents lived a hundred years ago, y'know! The wife, she's still the wife.

Mme Sanchez is astonished to see her Togolese neighbors' yard used only by the husband and his friends, and never by the wife. Neither she nor the children join the exclusively male cookouts or shared drinks. In her and Mme Samson's reactions, we can detect the composite nature of familial relations that they themselves have known: their household arrangements and life courses contain major characteristics of the traditional family model built around the gendered division of roles, but they also express some more modern elements, privileging children's activities and well-being and a partially mixed sociability between men and women.

THE "GOOD OLD DAYS": A LIVELY NEIGHBORHOOD WITH AN INTENSE SOCIAL LIFE AMONG FAMILIES

Pioneers' stories reveal the intensity of the forms of sociability that developed in the neighborhood in the 1960s and 1970s. Whether this social life was formal (through associations) or informal, children were their primary impetus and foundation; this social scene was also a place for raising children and transmitting values and norms from parents to children, and probably between families as well. They are at the heart of collective appropriation of the neighborhood, which is turned into a "village in the city," a "little village." These conventional expressions demonstrate the extent to which residents appreciate the fact that neighbors knew each other so well, in a local, dense, and protective mutual acquaintanceship. Even more than the house, in fact, the neighborhood functions simultaneously as a protective and emancipating space for the pioneers, because it fostered the happy experience of a lifestyle different than the one these men and women knew growing up.

Children as the Starting Point for Men's and Women's Sociability

Speaking of 1950s-era Bethnal Green, an old East London working-class neighborhood, Young and Willmott noted that residential seniority and proximity to the extended family explained the intensity of its local social life. The Poplars's situation is radically different because social life instead seems to rise precisely from the lack of residential seniority and a common collective "pioneering," "conquering" spirit (to use terms used by some interviewees). One of the important characteristics of this neighborhood in the 1960s was the very fact that the pioneers did not initially have ties there, especially no family, since nearly all had come from central Paris or elsewhere in France. Some came from neighboring towns, like the Bouchers who grew up in Garges-lès-Gonesse, and some lived for a few years in the neighboring housing projects, like the Lenormands, but none had any family in the neighborhood.

In the newly built neighborhood, which took in a large population of children but initially lacked any child-specific equipment, child-centered activities were the major source of intense formal and informal social exchange:

> M. Lenormand: So, you see, we found ourselves there with a population, we were all more or less in the same ballpark, age-wise. With school-age kids. On top of that there were a ton of problems: there weren't enough schools yet, there wasn't the new school. So immediately we made connections.
> Interviewer: Through the school?
> M. Lenormand: The school was an important link between residents. We had to make a real effort with the school problems. Our children were supposed to go to Cité du Nord, which was built in the early 1960s. And Cité du Nord had really beautiful schools—they still are beautiful, actually, but for the time they were really beautiful. We got together—especially this part of the Poplars—to form a parents' association, to stand up for ourselves and, already, fight city hall. And we got school bussing. At the time, the railway here [he points on a map], the footbridge didn't exist. The little bridge wasn't built yet. We had a ton of problems, kids who went under the fences because there weren't the walls that are there today. They'd cross the railroad tracks to go to school! That went on for quite a while, then we got them to make a path. That was the first step. Then we got a bus. At the beginning the parents worked together to drive the kids. And the other thing is that being

in co-ownership made it so the neighborhood bonded between people. They had common interests. And then the sports, et cetera. We kind of built our little village in the city, as it were. And that was the good old days at the Poplars.

Interviewer: You were involved in basketball?

M. Lenormand: No, that was M. Morin. I was involved in scouting, because I used to be a scout. I led the scouts—we had a space at the station. We got the kids together on Sunday to go for a walk.

This account includes several forms of sociability that crisscrossed the neighborhood and that partially differentiated it from working-class neighborhoods, for men in particular. One significant difference is the apparent lack of a masculine sociability based in café-bars, although café-bars were central to Parisian working-class neighborhood life at the time[28]: no row-house resident mentioned nearby café-bars as meeting places, and the only informant to evoke going to a café-bar, a municipal worker living in an apartment at the edge of the Poplars, went to an adjacent neighborhood. Instead, masculine sociability largely coalesced around the house and raising the children.

Indeed, men appropriated their houses and neighborhood through the exchange of tools and help, as well as through their collective submission to the co-ownership rules. The co-ownership system helped unite homeowners around a common interest, not to mention simply giving them the opportunity to get to know each other; indeed the co-owners' board is sometimes cited as a place where people first met in the early years (Mme Berger mentions the husbands' evening meetings). Relations of friendship and mutual help also frequently developed around home repair and various projects. M. and Mme Heurtin, who both grew up in the neighborhood, described such relationships in some detail.

Mme Heurtin: People helped each other out. His father, since he was a handyman and mine wasn't at all handy, obviously they'd help each other out. Dad always had some scheme to get, I don't know, some wine, some stuff, there was a sort of exchange of skills, of help, like that.

M. Heurtin: My father was a plumber, so he maintained all the water heaters here.

Interviewer: It was a side job, under the table?

M. Heurtin: No, it was just like that, when people had a problem they'd call. Like I do with M. P, who's more handy than I am. The gentleman who was electrician, when we had an electrical problem: "Hey, you wouldn't have a few free minutes?" Each one, according to his knowledge, chipped in, it happened naturally.

...

M. Heurtin: At the time we had an owners' board and we owned the public way. Everyone took turns doing the maintenance. At the time, for example, we bought a lawn mower together, and every weekend someone would go mow the lawn. Each one of the co-owners would go mow the shared lawn.

Mme Heurtin: We even bought rose bushes in common.

Moreover, men's associative engagement was initially turned toward the children and family: Scouting for M. Lenormand, whose own children were scouts; the basketball club for M. Morin, who directed it for a long time and whose two children were active members, and for M. Boucher, who was basketball coach; soccer for the Legrises and the Sanchezes, where the fathers actively supported their children. Today, it is difficult to analyze the norms the parents, as coaches, assistants, and/or spectators, may have emphasized or passed along through these athletic activities, which could have included leisurely diversion, the pleasure of the game, the morality of effort, physical discipline, and the spirit of individual or team competition. But it is essential to point out that the young parents of the Poplars all went to athletic activities with their children, which further reinforced sociability among children and teens as well as adults, and among men in particular.

Women's accounts confirm what men reported, while shedding light on distinct forms of feminine sociability. Like the men, women speak with one, joyful voice of the intensity of childhood play and adult sociability at the Poplars. As several informants let us understand in what follows, the work of looking after children (driving them to school, watching over their play) was behind lasting friendships between women.

Having observed the solidity of these women's friendships dating to when they were young stay-at-home mothers, we cannot equate domestic work in the early days of the Poplars with isolation, being stuck at home, and an absence of social contact as they are in other settings. Just like personal friendships, women's engagement in various associations connected with the church (such as catechism and Secours Catholique, a Catholic antipoverty charity) or school (volunteering at the library, parents' association) also had a liberating effect. Several women, like Mme Boucher, volunteered at the Cité du Nord social and cultural center, for example. Here again, they first got involved in volunteer organizations through the children, and these associations would later help them adjust as their children's increasing independence made motherhood less demanding and less gratifying. This is how Mme Morin associates women's domestic work with sociability, to the contrary of women's employment and the impossibility of having "a life in common":

Mme Morin: Everyone knew each other, through the school where we'd go pick up the children. It's obvious, one thing leads to another. And then, life wasn't the same. You've got to admit that a young woman today, who has children, who goes to work in Paris, who takes the train at 7:30 in the morning—when there are trains, because today it's a mess—she works her day, she comes home at 6:30, 7 o'clock, you can't really have a life in common like that. You can't have the same relationships.... Women were more involved in associations. We were everywhere, at the school, the hospital. But we didn't work, it's not the same thing.

These ties dating back to the neighborhood's early history would act as a resource for maintaining a positive female identity as these women gradually lost many of the activities and rewards associated with the status of young mother as they aged, and even more so for those who divorced. These volunteer activities and the resultant acquaintance networks sometimes proved useful in finding a job: some of them watched friends' children to supplement their household income, and women would keep one another informed of opportunities and help each other out. They were also useful when some needed to resume full-time employment: after volunteering at a municipal social and cultural center, Mme Boucher was offered a job as librarian when her husband lost his job; after her divorce Mme Sanchez could apply for a secretarial position because she had learned to type to help the parents' association.[29]

So paradoxically, the renewal of the traditional division of gender roles in this setting also had a liberating effect for women. Furthermore, despite the divisions in where and how men and women socialized, neighborhood social life mixed genders and generations in a lifestyle with shared norms that assured that getting along took precedence over political differences.

Shared Forms of Family Sociability Stronger than Political Divisions

The account of the formal ways in which pioneers socialized tends to mask the fact that they were not entirely uniform and universal. There were several coexisting networks in the neighborhood, typified by differing political sensibilities, from a rather conservative pole to another more rooted in the left. Without getting into the analysis of some residents' activist practices or the structure of the Poplars's voting patterns (strongly split between the left and right in the 1960s and 1970s, as the analysis in chapter 5 discusses in detail), we would like to focus here on the variety of pioneers' associative, religious, and political engagements.

For a start, M. Lenormand's and M. Morin's investment in youth and athletic associations drew them into municipal political engagement.

> M. Morin: Because I liked sports, I'd put together the basketball club in Gonesse. We first played among the old-timers, then later I made youth teams, and that's how I came to know lots and lots of people. That's also how I became well known without meaning to, because after that, M. Février and M. Lenormand showed up at my house, telling me that it would be great if I joined the team of municipal officials. So that's how I got to city hall, through sports. A lot of people must have known us, there were a lot of kids in basketball.

In 1971, they both ran on an initially apolitical slate and became members of the municipal council under mayor M. Février, an arrangement that lasted until 1995. In the interim, the slate's base moved farther to the right. In 1989, M. Morin and M. Lenormand were second and third deputy mayor. They are known for their political engagement in the neighborhood, and some residents, including the Bouchers and M. Piazza, appreciate them for it. They both send their children to a private Catholic school in a neighboring town, as do several other neighborhood parents such as the Pageots.

There is a left-leaning network centered on the school parents' association (FCPE), an organization in support of the public school with many members from the neighborhood. M. Sanchez, its president in the 1970s, was in the CFDT[30] union while his wife, Mme Sanchez, has been a member of the Socialist Party since 1971. Although many members of the parents' association are not very political, the generally left-leaning organization also has some members and sympathizers of the Communist Party.

The Catholic Church is another, more politically heterogeneous, social nexus in the neighborhood that has a variety of ways of socializing. M. Lenormand remembers discussion groups among parishioners at the church in an adjacent neighborhood in the 1960s, and the Bergers and Mme Vallès spoke of catechism classes. Several families send their children to the church-associated scouting group, and women like Mme Samson and Mme Boyer volunteer at Secours Catholique, a charity to help the poor. These parish activities were fostered by the presence of a chapel from the Poplars's very inception. According to M. Berger, who was on the parish council, Sunday mass and First Communion ceremonies were held there throughout the 1970s. The priest asked Mme Berger to hold catechism classes in her home, and she cited three other neighborhood women who did the same; she estimates that about 160 children participated every year.

Neighborhood competition between people with left- and right-leaning political affiliations could be strong at times, especially during the 1971 and 1977 municipal elections, when the unaffiliated candidate squeaked by over the joint Communist/Socialist slate, but it does not seem to have created very strong divisions in daily life. This is another clear difference with the aforementioned "everyday adventurers" of the same generation that Catherine Bidou studied. Although the suburban development residents she studied, largely teachers, social workers, or middle managers, were also very invested in associations, theirs were mostly for adult cultural activities or environmental activism, or third-world solidarity. Left-leaning tendencies, often closest to the Socialist Party, were quite diverse and created tensions with people from rural backgrounds.[31]

But in the Poplars, the most engaged on both sides recollect the periods of political campaigns with amusement, stressing that it did not disrupt good neighborly relations. So Mme Sanchez, a member of the Socialist Party also invested in the FCPE, and Mme Morin, wife of the right-leaning deputy mayor, have always gotten along quite well, and they are also on very good terms with Mme Berger, who is very active in the parish. Mme Sanchez says she "never knew how the Bergers voted" that they are true "friends." The parents' association held very animated parties on a large empty plot at the end of every school year that brought together a wide range of parents, not just members of the FCPE. Discretion about voting preferences, like avoiding political discussions, ensured a minimum of conflict despite very different orientations and engagements.

Networks of all orientations were nonetheless built on very similar bases: a sociability that began with the children, the family, and neighborhood life. Other than their differing political positions, the pioneers had very similar familial and neighborly norms—in other words, the same local domestic culture.

Families especially shared the same principles for raising their children, expressed through mothers' fondness for overseeing children's play and fathers' attachment to athletic activities, described by Mme Legris:

Interviewer: So what exactly were you involved in?

Mme Legris: Taking care, you know, of the children. I was pretty involved in catechism, too. And my husband took charge of soccer, he brought the kids to soccer. He wasn't a coach, but he drove them. But that wasn't in Gonesse, soccer was in Arnouville.

Interviewer: Where was catechism?

Mme Legris: At the Poplars—there's a gym there now.

Interviewer: Oh right, it used to be a chapel!

Mme Legris: Right, it used to be a chapel. It happened there, once a week. It was nice, we had the boys and girls, school pals, it was nice.... We have good memories. When they talk about their childhood at the Poplars, along with the fields, it's timeless.

Interviewer: On the square with the gymnasium?

Mme Legris: Right, that's it. It was great, we'd take out our bikes before going back to school, we'd ride bikes around the field. It's true, for the kids it was ... They ate and then there was an hour to have fun before going back to school.... They're really happy when they talk ... Yes, they had a nice childhood. They played outside, they weren't shut up in the house. The Poplars's little yards, the kids came, it was full of them.

Social occasions between families were also settings for spreading new family norms. For example, the neighborhood's common spaces that served as playgrounds for the children were also places for experimenting with new, more egalitarian relations between generations in the same family. The Morins recall how young parents on Alouette Place would sometimes join in children's play.

M. Morin: From May, June, late at night, it wasn't rare to see—at least one representa-
tive of the twelve on the place—and it was water-hose fights, worse than the kids!
There were games of *boules,* volleyball, there was a great ambiance.
Mme Morin: It's a shame. The youngest aren't going to experience that.

At the same time, although one could imagine pioneers breaking away or
taking a distance from their parents and their lifestyle, we can see a variety
of ways in which they maintained close relationships and proximity between
the conjugal and extended families. Many of the interviewed couples would
take in their elderly parents for several years (M. and Mme Sanchez, M.
and Mme Samson, M. and Mme Heurtin, Mme Boucher). The ground-floor
room—well separated from the rest of the house—allows them to maintain
some separation and autonomy between the generations. Other couples—
the Lenormands in particular—speak of an elderly relative living in an apartment in the Cité du Nord, a stone's throw away from the Poplars. Moreover,
we find cases of siblings (M. Legris and his sister, Mme Pageot, the Sanchez
brothers) who moved into the row houses within a few years of each other.
In all these instances, the proximity of extended family multiplied opportunities for sociability.

Political divisions thus seemed to be secondary to neighborly relations,
and the desire to maintain good relations took the upper hand and inspired
mutual tolerance, a will that seems to have expressed itself in other domains
as well. Despite what some of our informants say, it seems very likely that
the Poplars was not merely lively in the 1970s, it must have been downright
noisy with so many children playing freely in its squares and yards. Several
accounts also indicate that some of the big garages that had attracted so
many men to the row houses were being used for potentially noisy activities
such as cabinetry. From the beginning, the poor soundproofing of these otherwise well-built and comfortable houses would confront the pioneers with
the noise of their neighbors. But the local domestic culture built on the same
ambitions and intense familial sociability also produced a tolerance for the
noise of children and neighbors. The strength of the group permitted calls
to order and made them effective. That is, in most cases: M. Manzani, who
garnered the reputation of bad neighbor and got on the wrong side of the
eleven other homeowners on Alouette Place, was intolerant of children and
would stop them from playing.

Many interviews mentioned the little alleys that connected the neighborhood's streets and squares with a pathway between the row houses' yards,
used by children and adults alike:

There's still something I think needs to be pointed out—before, there were lots of little
paths. There are the houses, and behind them more or less big yards. Before, between
subdivisions, there were little trails, and it was really pleasant taking these little paths.

It gave it charm. And the kids loved taking the little paths going to catechism, they chased each other, waited for each other, played hide-and-seek, but now ... Well, it's not unique to the Poplars, a lot are closed. I really liked it, myself—you'd cross a street and presto, you'd take the little path. The trails'd come on little clearings that made it a little ... not "countryside," I don't want to exaggerate, but far from the city. (Mme Legris)

Might these little paths and the shared affection for them be interpreted as a sort of material symbol of the freedom of movement and the intensity of exchanges between families?

We have one final and decisive observation. What could be a better confirmation of the development of a local domestic culture and the establishment of collective local roots than the continued presence (even temporary) of former neighborhood children, now adults, and the formation of couples among them? The Heurtins are the perfect example. Both moved into the neighborhood with their families in 1968, when they were twelve, and met through all the aforementioned play on the square where their respective families lived. They got married in 1977, and in 1982 bought Mme Heurtin's parents' row house, where they lived until 2002.

Mme Heurtin: There were several weddings on the square. There was us, and there was also the Mollet's son with the Poinsot's daughter....
Interviewer: And so, where did you meet—Victor Cousin square?
M. Heurtin: Absolutely! By playing some of the same games.... What did we play? Dodgeball, hopscotch ... There was the tennis court that was behind. And then later, we'd grown up, we talked late at night in the square. There was an atmosphere ...
Mme Heurtin: But not late at night like today—it was exceptional at the time! ... There was a collective spirit. My brothers played, the same, with the other children, because the families were all the same ages. And then, there was a warmth, I mean ...
Interviewer: Did you have picnics?
Mme Heurtin: Yes, there were snack-times, birthdays. There were parties! ... And there were amazing Christmases when we all got together on the square, everyone! There were fantastic Christmases. We'd all go out, and end up at someone's house. It happened at New Years, too.

URBANIZATION, MOVING AWAY, AND AGING: THE RETURN OF INEQUALITY

In interviews with residents of the Poplars and even more so with people in city government, the large-scale arrival of migrants from Turkey appears as the major event marking the neighborhood's history. This image is nonetheless incomplete because, as we have shown, the neighborhood's renewal actually began in the late 1970s. In this next section, we aim to show that the disintegration of the local domestic culture invented by the pioneering group was an equally decisive factor. To understand the relations that the few remaining pioneer couples in the Poplars have with their neighbors of foreign backgrounds—which we address in chapter 4—we must first of all explore what it means to grow older in this little neighborhood in transformation. By shedding light on the mechanisms behind the disintegration of the pioneer group's local domestic culture, we show how a neighborhood of social promotion can become a neighborhood of downward mobility.

Increasing Housing Density and the Development's Degradation

In all of our interviews, pioneers and households who arrived in the early 1980s alike indicated that that "rural" setting (fields, empty lots) was one of the reasons they moved to Gonesse and are so attached to the Poplars.

Although the golf course still offers a green vista today, the setting is entirely changed from the old fields that parents and children alike could use as they wished, be it for walks or gleaning onions and potatoes. The history of the Poplars is the history of the dense urbanization of an area that in the early 1960s "looked like the country" before the open land gradually disappeared. M. Berger regrets the overcrowding resulting from the construction of a housing development in the 1980s:

> The town looked at the cash it ... They didn't even leave a strip of grass between the lots! Because before, there were fields, y'know. They didn't even leave a strip for the kids to play. No, they put them together, one house practically touching the one behind it. There's just a road that separates ... no, it's no good—well, it isn't!

And the interview with the Samsons quoted below makes us consider the consequences of the disappearance of open land. It could be appropriated by all ages precisely because it had no predetermined and prescribed uses:

> Mme Samson: There was the field there before, where they put the gymnasium. Our children ... I was left in peace! Every Wednesday they were out on that field playing soccer. One of them, our second one, even had a little garden in a corner—he even grew strawberries.... He planted himself a little pine tree and made himself a little garden in a corner no one could see. And other than that, they played soccer. That attracted people, you know, people came to see the game.
> Interviewer: And it isn't like that any more?
> Mme Samson: No. We were a little bit angry with the municipality about that at the time.

The disappearance of these fields was the disappearance of a means of appropriating the space. In these words, we also sense that the dense urbanization of the district made the open spaces for children's games disappear (the beloved little paths also suffered the same fate). In addition to the disappearance of free lots and fields, the noise of aircraft taking off and landing at nearby Charles de Gaulle Airport has increased dramatically over the period: it henceforth sets a daily rhythm, and the nuisance is bad enough that a public abatement subsidy was made available to residents to install double-glazed windows for free.

We discovered that Mme Boyer had made several photo albums documenting the history of the transformation of the Poplars, Gonesse, and Arnouville, which she brought out to show us a picture of the plot where a new primary school had been built in the late 1990s. She had found some old postcards and took pictures of the same places today to keep track of the changes to the neighborhood and surroundings. Residents' interest in these changes is proportional to the extent of their attachment to these northern periurban spaces.

For this generation of inhabitants that had found a transitional space between city and country in greater Paris, residential life was deeply affected by intense lifestyle urbanization and the loss of common areas (open plots, little paths) that responded to dreams of and taste for the country. And along with the transformation of the material setting, the foundations of the local domestic culture would also come to be shaken by the departure of some of their peers from the neighborhood.

Departures in the 1970s and 1980s, and What They Meant

In the introduction, we mentioned the fact that some pioneers resold their row houses soon after purchase (starting in the 1970s) to move to a "real house": those who left were partly the pioneers in the highest social positions, but not exclusively. In the interviews, these first departures are often mentioned in passing, and associated with retirement and returning to their home regions. Only further prompts for more detail made the interviewed couples remember that some neighbors had quickly moved on to a bigger, free-standing house upon getting a promotion, sometimes only moving as far as adjacent Arnouville.

> Interviewer: And the people who moved in in 1966, how long did they stay, in general? It varied, but did some leave quickly, like that family there ... ?
> Mme Boyer: They left in '87.
> Interviewer: Oh yes, they stayed a long time.
> Mme Boyer: Yes. Well, that pretty much matches up with some people reaching retirement age, to say, well, on retirement we'll go someplace else.
> Interviewer: And who lived where the P's live?
> Mme Boyer: Oh, I don't remember them either, because ... In the order, I couldn't really say who left first, maybe around '84?

Interviewer: And next to the C's?

Mme Boyer: Before there was T, and before them was M, who worked at [*the electric company*] too. But they were among the first to leave. There was also L, just next door, who also worked at [*the electric company*], and both of them were among the first to go.

Interviewer: There was a police inspector living around here, with long hair …

Mme Boyer: But he wasn't the first, either … It changed a lot across the street … It's at least the fifth or sixth. (*Speaking to her husband*) Do you remember when M left? You remember?

M. Boyer: 1976.

Interviewer: So, around 1976.

M. Boyer: And L left at the same time.

Interviewer: But that wasn't because of retirement.

Mme Boyer: Oh no, that was for another job at [*the electric company*]. There were a lot of [*electric company employees*] here.… And the G's went back to Brittany. He was a taxi driver, he kept on working a little bit on the side and after he had a chicken farm. And then Mme G got a shoe store. (*To her husband:*) In what year did the G's leave? (*Thinking*) Thierry wasn't in middle school with Laurent, they left before then, it must be in '74, around then.

Interviewer: And after them?

Mme Boyer: That was M. and Mme N, and after that, well, the Chaldeans.

…

Interviewer: Before '87, you never thought of moving, when you saw people leaving?

M. Boyers: Well, it's that people moved back to their region and they couldn't always adapt to it that well, because some of them came back.

Might the fuzziness of memories and the description of departures, in their chronology as well as the reasons behind them, serve to preserve a positive self-image and justify the fact that they are still there even though they tried (unsuccessfully) to move away? It was not until the end of our third interview that Mme Samson expresses her disappointment that they were never able to have a "real house." Although the Poplars continues to offer forms of sociability—less intense, certainly, but persisting—that these aging couples appreciate, those who still live there were somehow unable to leave, for a variety of reasons not purely limited to economic constraints.

Mme Samson: I sure would've loved a house, a real house, but oh well, I'll die without a real house.

Interviewer: "A real house," you mean a single-story house?

M. Samson: A single-family home.

Mme Samson: Yes, a house, like without shared walls, where you can walk all around it. That, basically, but it's not meant for us. Maybe in another life. We already have a house, y'know. That's what I was saying, we had parents, you and me, who didn't have the means to have a house. My parents got one, but really late.… So buying it made us successful.

As Mme Samson's words suggest, one might think that the departures of neighbors seen as "equals" contributed to the modification of the individual perceptions of the neighborhood and its houses. Their departures exposed the modest aspect of the row house that had been kept in the background the neighborhood's early years as its families grew. It becomes evident that residential mobility became possible for some but not all of them, all the more so when several pioneers bought houses in newer, more upscale developments very close to the Poplars (the Lenormands and Bertaux), in individual homes built on plots apportioned in the 1920s (the Legris and Pageots) or in Arnouville. Bit by bit, the Poplars, home to the invention of a residential group and a local domestic culture, began to manifest individual inequalities and became a place where individual life courses cross paths.

In such a sociable context, people did not sell their homes without justifying their choice to their neighbors, and they still do so to this day in interviews. These justifications (the search for a single-level house after retirement, a "real house" with a big yard, the simple life away from the hassles of metro Paris, a return to their home region) reminded those who remained of the neighborhood's limitations and ultimately devalued them—and this well before the arrival of people summarily labeled as "Turks." The departure of neighbors-become-friends came to challenge the feeling of equality and remind those who remained of their limited resources and the modesty of their houses.

After giving detailed accounts of the fates of many former neighbors, Mme Boyer and her husband explained that they had thought about leaving but ultimately stayed for lack of means. Unable to buy another house, they significantly renovated their home both in anticipation of old age and to adapt to the changed neighborhood. They enlarged their house to be more comfortable and independent from each other (a bathroom for each of them) and more independence when their children visit from elsewhere in France (the third floor is reserved entirely for them). But the improvements also provide some desired security, blocking access to the house from the rear. Doing such significant and costly work on the house appears to be a way to put an end to dreams of leaving and the uncertainty and talk of moving that come with it. The Boyers, like many couples, began renovation as soon as they gave up hope of moving. Cases of row-house ownership by sale or gift from parents to a married child (as with the Lenormands and the Heurtins) also affirm their humble status, making it transitional housing for young couples just starting out more than a permanent home.

Neighbors' departures contributed to the devaluation of the image the remaining owners had of their houses, their neighborhood, and ultimately themselves. The interviewed pioneers sometimes took an ironic tone when showing us their homes and repeatedly joked about the size of the house and yard. Their neighbors' departures have made them sensitive and dealt a blow to their self-esteem and the prestige of the neighborhood, which gradually went from a place of conquest and rootedness to a place of transition.

Aging and Concentration on the House

Like these initial departures, pioneers' aging also obviously contributes to the decomposition of the local domestic culture. We have said that children and child-related activities were the main component of this culture for both men and women, so it follows that the aging of the pioneers and the neighborhood began with their children's departure, or at least their passage into adulthood. Children's and grandchildren's wedding pictures, often poster-size, decorate walls and shelves, materializing aging and the status of grandparent in everyday space. They also suggest a reduction of and disengagement from child-related activities compared with their young neighbors consumed by the care of multiple very young children.

> Mme Samson: Bit by bit the children grew up, they went to middle school, *lycée*, and all.
> M. Samson: They left.
> Mme Samson: Bit by bit the Poplars got old. On top of that, our neighborhood was really quiet. There was a while there when it was really too quiet.
> M. Samson: Too quiet, yes!
> Interviewer: Too quiet?
> Mme Samson: Too quiet.
> M. Samson: Oh, well, too ... too noisy isn't good, but too quiet's no good either.

Children of several couples (the Samsons, Boyers, Sanchezes) initially moved into a row house in the Poplars as they were starting their adult lives. As Mme Samson pointed out in a previously quoted interview, having children nearby is a (more or less retroactive) explanation for the neighborhood's continued existence. But this proximity still does not prevent people from feeling isolated and fragile where aging is concerned, as they still express fear of being a burden, wonder about their children's attitudes in the future, and so on.

Aging also means men's return to the home. It usually happens at retirement, but we should also point out that several of the pioneer men had been laid off or given early retirement (M. Boyer, M. Boucher), which also financially and psychologically weakens them. In parallel, children ask their mothers (Mme Boyer, Mme Samson, Mme Morin) to help with watching their grandchildren. As a result, retirement can lead to a sort of closing in on the domestic and local space. The care M. Samson puts into the yard work and M. Boyer's investment in building the model ships that decorate the walls of his home testify to this masculine reinvestment in the domestic space.

Likewise, the precision with which the interviewed couples (Samson, Boyer) relate the habits and microevents of their neighbors' lives suggest that they spend a lot of time observing what happens in the streets and little squares where they live. This must be taken into account in understanding their relations with their current-day neighbors, whose social lives unfold in part outside the domestic space.

Although home and yard maintenance is a central activity for pioneer couples (more than for their young neighbors burdened with family and with more limited incomes), we should not overlook other activities and forms of sociability that draw them out of the domestic and neighborhood space. Several women take regular aquagym classes, thus perpetuating friendships made when they moved into the Poplars. Mme Boyer is in a painting club in Arnouville. Mme Samson and Mme Legris volunteer at Secours Catholique. And above all, all the couples leave their house and the neighborhood for several weeks a year. The Boyers have a little apartment in Brittany, where they go often, and they also take off for two months a year in a camper. The Samsons take two weeks vacation every year. Taking vacations and traveling are also how they have chosen to age in the neighborhood. Although they do find themselves more present at home and in the neighborhood's common spaces due to their ages and unemployed status, they are not trapped there.

Well before the families of Turkish origin moved into the neighborhood in the 1990s, then, the pioneer group's foundations, strength, and even culture had already been weakened by the transformation of the physical setting (the construction of several housing developments and the disappearance of the free plots that had made the neighborhood feel "green" and open) and the departure of neighbors throughout the 1970s and 1980s in pursuit of residential promotion by access to a free-standing single-family home. Aging also contributed to weakening the group, which was initially a group of young parents. This neighborhood setting with a disintegrating local domestic culture would go on to become a particularly attractive living environment for immigrant families and families with foreign backgrounds moving out of housing projects in the 1990s. Keeping this process in mind will help us understand the relationship that develops between these increasingly isolated pioneers and their new neighbors in all its complexity and ambiguity when we come back to them in chapter 4.

NOTES

1. G Groux and C Lévy, *La possession ouvrière. Du taudis à la propriété (XIXè–XXè siècle*; Paris, 1993).

2. R Castel, *From Manual Workers to Wage Laborers: Transformation of the Social Question*, trans. and ed. R Boyd (New Brunswick, NJ, 2003).

3. Verret, *L'espace ouvrier*. See chapter 1, fn 36 for discussion of French census categories.

4. M Young and P Willmott, *Family and Kinship in East London* (London, 1955), and *Family and Class in a London Suburb* (London, 1960), and Gans, *The Levittowners*.

5. One obvious reference is H Coing, *Rénovation urbaine et changement social* (Paris, 1966).

6. Magri, "Le pavillon stigmatisé," 191. For an example of the thesis that social heterogeneity contributes to intergroup tensions and the dissipation of the community sociability particular to traditional laborers' neighborhoods, see especially Chamboredon and Lemaire, "Proximité spatiale et distance sociale."

7. Magri, "Le pavillon stigmatisé," 196. There were two studies of small homeowners: Haumont, *Les pavillonnaires,* and Raymond, Haumont, Dezès, and Haumont, *L'habitat pavillonnaire.*

8. Magri, "Le pavillon stigmatisé," 197. See also P Bourdieu and M Saint-Martin, "Le sens de la propriété. La genèse sociale des systèmes de préférences," *Actes de la Recherche en Sciences Sociales* 81–82 (1990): 52–63.

9. Faure, *Les premiers banlieusards*. It is also worth indicating J-N Retière's study of Lanester, a small working-class city in western France where the configuration of social and political relations is such that workers' access to single-family home ownership comes with intense sociability; J-N Retière, *Identités ouvrières. Histoire sociale d'un fief ouvrier en Bretagne 1909–1990* (Paris, 1994), 141–42.

10. We use Magri's notion of "ways of living" here, which highlights the need to look at how housing is used, especially practices of arranging living space (the organization of domestic space and the functional specialization of rooms), furnishing (the uses and variety of furniture), and decoration (an abundance or dearth of decorative items, for example): S Magri, "L'intérieur domestique. Pour une analyse du changement dans les manières d'habiter," *Genèses* 28 (1997): 150.

11. On this theme, see Hoggart, *The Uses of Literacy,* and Weber, *Le travail à côté.*

12. P Cuturello and F Godard, *Familles mobilisées. Accession à la propriété du logement et notion d'effort des ménages* (Paris, 1980).

13. See M Avanza, G Laferté, and E Penissat, "O crédito entre as classes populares francesas: o exemplo de uma loja em Lens," *Mana. Estudo de Antropologia Social* 12, no.1 (2006): 7–38. The rate of French households with bank accounts went from 20 percent in the 1960s to 95 percent in the early 1980s.

14. According to Young and Willmott (*Family and Kinship in East London*), this is what happened at Greenleigh, and Chamboredon, "Construction sociale des populations," makes similar observations about French apartment complexes in the 1960s.

15. See Cuturello and Godard, *Familles mobilisées.*

16. The salience of a particular relationship to money acquired in childhood, even when social ascension makes it unnecessary, also appears in R Hoggart, *A Local Habitation: Life and Times, 1918–1940* (London, 1988).

17. For an example from banking, see Y Grafmeyer, *Les gens de la banque* (Paris, 1992), and on the postal service, see M Cartier, *Les facteurs et leurs tournées. Un service public au quotidien* (Paris, 2003).

18. This is how Coing describes it when writing about a Parisian working-class neighborhood in the late 1950s (*Rénovation urbaine et changement social*, 76).

19. See G Noiriel, *Les ouvriers dans la société française XIXe–XXe* (Paris, 1986).

20. See A Chenu, *Les employés* (Paris, 1994).

21. J Goody skillfully points out how deeply simplistic the traditional/modern dichotomy running through all social sciences is, especially when looking at the family, because it makes a caricature of the past as well as the present; J Goody, *The European Family: An Historico-Anthropological Essay* (Oxford, 2000).

22. Although not stated explicitly, these are the social groups that were the subject of major studies of this period; the works of F de Singly, *Le soi, le couple et la famille* (Paris, 1996) are in line with the "modern" theme. See in particular S Gojard's review of de Singly: S Gojard, "François de Singly. *Le soi, le couple et la famille*," *Genèses* 27 (1997): 164–65.

23. Schwartz, *Le monde privé des ouvriers*, 144–45.

24. M Maruani, *Travail et emploi des femmes* (Paris, 2000), 15–16.

25. C Bidou, *Les aventuriers du quotidian* (Paris, 1984), 106ff.

26. The *brevet* is a degree received upon completion of middle school, and the *certificat* (*d'études*) marked completion of primary school at the time.

27. See Schwartz, *Le monde privé des ouvriers*, 97. Among our informants, although some women had pursued studies in secondary school while their husbands had stopped after a *certificat d'études* or a CAP (Certificat d'aptitude professionnelle, a secondary-level vocational degree), others had less education than their husbands.

28. See Coing, *Rénovation urbaine et changement social*, 64.

29. On how domestic constraints may provide resources, see Y Siblot, "'Je suis la secrétaire de la famille!' La prise en charge féminine des tâches administratives en milieu populaire. Entre subordination et ressource," *Genèses* 69 (2006): 46–66.

30. The CFDT (Confédération française démocratique du travail) is a center-left labor union that emerged from Catholic organized labor in the 1960s, which off and on has had ties with the Socialist Party and is currently one of the two largest unions in France.

31. Bidou, *Les aventuriers du quotidien*, 89–136.

2

CHILDREN OF THE PROJECTS
IN QUEST OF RESPECTABILITY

Public housing projects have been in decline since the 1970s economic crisis. The unemployment rate is distinctly higher there than elsewhere, and young people without qualifications bear the full brunt. Living conditions are deteriorating, buildings degrading, and street culture getting tougher. Tensions between young people and the police have regularly erupted in riots since the early 1980s. So the most stable fractions of the working classes fled housing projects and tried to buy their own homes, often new single-family houses that could be quite far from the city center. Meanwhile, housing projects came to specialize in sheltering the most insecure populations, which in the Ile-de-France region predominantly means immigrants. Although immigrants in the 1960s and 1970s came for employment reconstructing the country, this flow slowed dramatically in the 1970s to be replaced with family immigration (through policy to reunite families) and political immigration (refugees).[1] The newer waves of immigrants mostly came from North and sub-Saharan Africa.[2]

Housing policies encouraging broad access to home ownership reinforced the lower middle classes and stable fractions of the working classes' flight from housing projects. In the late 1980s, nearly half of laborers were homeowners (64 percent of which became so between 1969 and 1986, another 28 percent between 1980 and 1986). This movement out of housing projects has continued, although not at the same scale today as in the 1980s. About 66 percent of the inhabitants of public housing in areas designated as at-risk urban zones (zone urbaine sensible; ZUS) in 1990 lived elsewhere in 1999 (compared with 51 percent in other neighborhood types).[3] Of these households that moved, 40 percent became single-family homeowners.[4]

Moving is also about schooling, namely the possibility of sending children to schools with better reputations, sheltered from the antischool culture perpetuated by the students most resistant to the academic order. Indeed, ascension in this kind of social trajectory is supposed to take place through children's academic success, a degree being a precondition for future social status. But France is far from egalitarian in this regard, despite the gradual implementation of policies for "academic democratization" since the 1970s (making a single middle-school system in 1975, opening up *lycée* (high school) access in the 1980s, and setting the goal of 80 percent of each class passing the *baccalauréat*).[5]

So if the row-house pioneers of the 1960s came from rural areas and classic working-class neighborhoods, the next generation, arriving in the late 1970s, was predominantly leaving high-density subsidized public housing complexes in greater Paris to buy single-family homes. The recent residential mobility of former housing project residents takes various forms. Some families in the Poplars's row houses have experienced what could be called horizontal mobility: there is no career mobility, and their single-family homes had been left with a downgraded status by their former (non-migrant) owners. For other Poplars families, mainly living in the more recent New Poplars subdivisions,[6] this mobility is accompanied by a change in occupational status and a near-obligation that both members of the couple be employed, given the generally high cost of real estate. While immigrant families predominate in the row houses, the New Poplars is largely occupied by the adult children of immigrant families (not immigrants themselves), socialized in the housing projects, for whom the new subdivisions represent spaces of upward mobility. This chapter is devoted to the residential movements of these children of the housing projects.

It focuses specifically on those who achieved what Bernard Lahire calls "small social mobilities."[7] These new homeowners are not exactly transfuges, the most frequently studied type of upward mobility that people who grew up in housing projects, especially children of Maghrebian immigrants, may experience.[8] Instead of trajectories spanning a wide social space, theirs have taken modest steps upward. In this sense, they are little-middles just like the pioneers, from different fractions of the working classes but whose trajectories rise at a comparable angle. Instead of becoming teachers, engineers, or artists, these children of Algerian or Moroccan laborers became administrative employees, bus drivers, or accountants. Their scholastic careers were not exceptional, and although they were able to leave the projects, it was to buy a home in a periurban area with very little geographical distance from the world where they began.

But even a modest social move is an opportunity to acquire new dispositions, if only through contact with people who act and think differently from the people who raised them.[9] What opened opportunity to these children of the projects during a period of unfavorable economic conditions? What traces do their little mobilities leave on their behaviors, tastes, values, and lifestyles? How is the distance they took from the world of the projects reflected in their relationships with it and their new neighbors? And how do these families perceive and direct their children's scholastic futures?

To answer these questions, we concentrated on the social and residential trajectories of three households. Our interviewees are all mothers and public employees of Algerian origin. Between 1995 and 2005, all three bought houses in the New Poplars subdivision, where *cadres* and midlevel employees (census category "intermediary occupations") are overrepresented.[10] We conducted repeated lengthy interviews with them, which allowed us to get into the details of their trajectories and practices. They all became first-time homeowners between the ages of thirty-two and thirty-six (thirty-one and forty-five for their husbands), which is a little older than the row-house pioneers (some of whom were under thirty), whose residential mobility was facilitated by rapid access to employment and job security. Their purchase of a home had also been spurred by a dearth of affordable rental housing near workplaces at the time.

The situation was different for members of this younger generation, who turned twenty in the 1980s. The job market was tight due to economic stagnation, but the housing market was more flexible thanks to the increasing supply of subsidized HLM housing in the *banlieue* since the 1960s. This situation partly explains why our informants did not take steps to home ownership earlier, consistent with all first-time homeowners of the period.[11]

If they were relatively older at the time of purchase, it is also because the women we spoke with had to convince themselves that it was truly possible for them to own property. The experience of growing up in the projects in immigrant working-class families left its mark, especially in the form of a persistent assumption of an inferior position. To be able to take the plunge, our interviewees had to gradually acquire new attitudes toward housing and change their perception of their place in French society and the employment market.

THE SOCIAL CONDITIONS OF MODEST UPWARD MOBILITY

Our three informants' fathers all migrated from Algeria in the mid to late 1950s, ahead of the main wave of Algerian immigration to France. Samira Ben M'Rad's father was a trucker, and the father of sisters Nadia and Karima Dhif was a solderer in a metal factory. Like so many immigrants of this generation, these men first migrated alone, then sent for their wives and children. Samira is the eldest of seven children; the first five were born in Algeria and the last two in Aulnay-sous-Bois, where the family settled in an HLM in 1973. Karima and Nadia also come from a family of seven children, all born in France. Their mother joined their father in 1961, after the war in Algeria that forced thousands of women to emigrate. The family lived in a housing project in Bondy until 1993.

All three had already moved out of the projects where they grew up by the time they became homeowners. Their residential trajectories took roughly the same course: they found work when they finished school, met their partners (at work, in two cases), got married quickly, and soon thereafter moved to a new dwelling and started having children. They only began to plan homeownership after renting for several years in Paris's northern *banlieue* (Samira Ben M'Rad and Karima Dhif in an HLM, and Nadia Dhif in a regular apartment building).

All three women are public employees, which protects them from unemployment, and each couple's income level is above the national household average. These characteristics bring our informants and their husbands toward the middle classes. Their trajectories distance them from the working classes and the increasingly insecure conditions of housing project residents. This is especially striking when their situation is compared with those of their siblings, trapped in HLMs, long unemployed, or living off a series of short-term jobs. In fact, our interviewees have difficulty talking about their siblings' situations for fear of giving the impression that they and their group of origin are not succeeding. We probed them to talk about it so we could better understand the singularity of their life courses and trace back the resources they were able to muster to give their trajectories their particular arcs.

Samira Ben M'Rad: A Long-Sacrificed Social Ascension

Samira Ben M'Rad, who has a *bacclauréat* in social and economic sciences and a secretarial degree, cannot really explain how she did better at school than her siblings. Their father manifested the same desire to see all his children do well in school, she said: "He was always behind us, always shook us, pushed us, motivated us for school ..." For an immigrant child who spoke

French poorly when she arrived at age eleven, this encouragement was essential—but it did not have the same effect on all her siblings.

SAMIRA BEN M'RAD'S SIBLINGS

Samira: Born in Algeria in 1962, *bac B* (in social and economic sciences) and a post-*bac* secretarial degree (BTS, brevet de technicien supérieur). Married, three children, employed at a retirement fund since 1984. Reached a personal assistant position in 2004. Owns a house in Gonesse.

Ahmed: Born in Algeria in 1964, abandoned higher studies for a secondary-level vocational degree (BEP) in accounting. Unemployed for four years since being laid off from a store manager position. Lives with a woman of French origin, recently had a child. Still lives in the projects of Aulnay-sous-Bois.

Rachid: Born in Algeria in 1965, has the *bac* in literature, did not finish studies for a post-*bac* degree (BTS) in sales. Worked as a retail department manager for several years until he was laid off. After a long period of unemployment, he ended up finding a job as a baggage handler at Charles de Gaulle Airport, well below his ambitions. He has owned a small apartment for two years.

Zinedine: Born in Algeria in 1967, has a secondary-level vocational degree (BEP). Became a bus driver at Charles de Gaulle Airport after a long period of unemployment. Lives in Aulnay-sous-Bois in an HLM, two children.

Selma: Born in Algeria in 1970, has a vocational secretarial degree (CAP). Quickly found work as a cashier. Married to a man of French origin. They live with their two children in an HLM not far from Aulnay-sous-Bois.

Karima: Born in France in 1977, left school at sixteen. Does rather regular temp work as a receptionist. Lives with her parents.

Mehdi: Born in France in 1983, stopped going to *lycée* but passed his *bac STT* (a technical *bac* in management, marketing, and finance). Works off and on as a temp without steady employment. Lives at home with his parents.

One might think that the children born in Algeria could not pursue higher education because they did not have the support necessary to believe they might succeed. Indeed, immigrants' children of this generation were frequently oriented toward vocational tracks, with no way to contest the decision.[12] This was partly because their grades were too low to hope for another orientation, and partly because they dared not dream of another academic destiny. In middle school, when students around thirteen years old are put on specific tracks, Samira wanted to pursue a low-level secretarial degree (CAP) in a vocational school because the prospect of going to an academic *lycée* seemed so unattainable and intimidating. Her French teacher convinced her to finish her secondary education, daring her to cross the low but still daunting barrier for entry into *lycée* by sitting for the examination for the *brevet de collège* that caps the end of middle school. Samira has no doubt that without her teacher's intervention she would have joined the other neighborhood girls who went to vocational middle schools in tracks preparing them for low-skill occupations typically reserved for women.

Her academic success, which is significant given the chances of laborers' children of her generation and even more so for daughters of Algerian immigrants, was also made possible by new encounters in *lycée*, where she made friends with girls from higher social strata than her own: "I was pulled along in their wake, by their desire to succeed." These contacts had a lasting influence on both her self-image and her faith in a better future. Going to *lycée* also helped her avoid early marriage.

> Samira: Girls couldn't go very far in their studies because the thinking was that they should stop pretty early, that they will get married and then the husbands aren't going to accept them working, so there's no point in longer schooling. But I was lucky to have a father who wanted me to succeed, because he'd suffered every day all his life to feed us. He was always there behind me, "But of course you'll have your *bac*." And alongside, the teachers too. And he was behind me to go at least as far as the *bac*. And he never forced me to get married, he always said "Listen, if you stay serious, if your studies let you continue and I see that you don't go off-track, there's no problem, I'll keep helping you as best I can, to take you as far as possible." And then, I was a little like that, too, since I said, "Well, the husband who doesn't want me to work, it's not worth the trouble." I said that pretty early. "What if I go for higher studies to be free? For me, it's for my personal well-being."
> Interviewer: You said that around what age, more or less?
> Samira: Around *lycée*, as soon as I saw I was on the right ... as soon as I was sure of myself, that I'd be able to do it, to try to do it. Because in *lycée* I thought I'd escaped the BEP, the CAP. So you're there, and, y'know, you go for it.

Once she had opened the door to higher studies, and despite having to repeat a year in middle school, Samira passed the *bac B* on her first try and went on to earn a secretarial BTS. In interviews, she likes to say, "you've got to fight" to succeed, that "nothing comes from nothing." These expressions are rooted in her past as an immigrant laborer's daughter who is much more highly educated than most girls of her background. But she also uses them today to condemn her youngest siblings' attitude, which she finds "defeatist."

> The two that were born here, they've got today's mind-set, it's "Oh no, I don't want to work, there's no point. Anyway, even if we have some training, there aren't any jobs." ... The baby of the family, he's king. He has everything we never had—his little car, his own room, his TV, his stereo. We didn't have any of that at all—I was just telling him that the other day. There were three or four of us in a room with bunk beds. We didn't live the life you see today. He's coddled, fed, housed. He works as a temp, and it's his spending money.

There are twenty years difference between the eldest and the youngest in the family, which means they did not grow up together and, more importantly, were not socialized in the same conditions. They belong to two generations that are socially constituted in very different ways.[13] Samira and her siblings who turned twenty in the 1980s could find work easily (Samira, for example, was hired by a retirement fund in the year following her BTS internship, in 1984). This generation did not come of age amid unemployment and job insecurity like the generation that followed.[14]

Samira, who dreamed of becoming a teacher when she was in *lycée*, decided to prepare for a secretarial BTS. She seemed to have been afraid of the uncertainty of higher education, which was still socially selective in the early 1980s. She did not really try to make the most of her BTS on the employment market, either, staying in the same secretarial job for nearly twenty years despite the fact that her degree qualified her to aspire to a higher position. Samira Ben M'Rad got married soon after finishing school, as if making up for lost time in relation to the norms of her peers.[15] She met her future husband, an office worker at a retirement fund, when she was in the second year of her studies for the BTS. An Algerian who migrated to France when he was twenty, he is ten years her senior and has no French degrees. Divorced with a child, he was living in Gonesse, in the Cité du Nord. His intervention got her the internship that led to her being hired as secretary in the retirement fund where she still worked at the time of our study. Upon marriage at age twenty-three (in 1985), Samira moved into his housing project. The contradictions in her trajectory are significant given the resources she mustered to get what was a rather exceptional education for a girl of her generation compared with the modesty of her job. Her social mobility stagnated for several years, and she devoted herself to raising their three children, born in 1988, 1989, and 1994, without trying to improve the returns on her degrees or change neighborhoods, but eventually the direct and indirect influences of some neighbors and coworkers prompted her back into action.

The Cité du Nord school parents' association (FCPE) played a key role in her developing a plan to leave the projects. The association's social activity was a springboard that expanded her options for meeting people, which had previously been limited to family and coworkers. It introduced her to teachers, social workers, and a doctor with whom she spent time in meetings and other settings (children's sports, school outings, etc.), and she befriended some. These middle- and upper-class parents formed a sort of neighborhood elite, which she quickly joined. As she came to identify with other members of this little elite, their influence changed how she subjectively classified herself and made her inclined to reproduce some of their values and practices.

She thus developed a plan to buy a house while several members of the parents' association were doing the same, although she had never really considered it before. Discussions with other parents convinced her that she, too, could be a property owner, and that it was possible "at the same cost as rent."

> Defending the right to an education, the right to equality for everyone, well, they bring up other things next. I don't know, it opens the mind to other things. And then we said, "We're not going to spend the rest of our days in the projects, why not us?" All the more so because we had the basics to be able to do it. I mean, we both work, like the others. And then, well, among the people I know there were teachers, who naturally saw things differently than laborers or people from the most disadvantaged classes who live in HLMs.

Ultimately, little time passed between Samira Ben M'Rad joining her HLM neighborhood school's parents' association in 1994 and her making plans to leave. In 1995, she began visiting houses and collecting all the relevant information to get one at the best price. In 1997, the family left the projects to become homeowners in the Poplars's new subdivisions.

Leaving the HLM and moving into a housing development with a strong middle class presence changed her relationship with her job by raising her aspirations: "It's clear that in a house, you see things differently than when you stay in a setting where there's only laborers and disadvantaged people. You're much more open-minded, maybe that makes you to go farther ..." Her level of educational attainment was far from low, and it genuinely appears that buying a home in a development led Samira Ben M'Rad to realize it. She was in contact with the generally well-educated mothers in the subdivision who run the FCPE, including the doctor she had met in the Cité du Nord, and it is obvious from how she talks about them that she identifies with these women with high educational capital and/or *cadre* status. In 2002, she requested a job skill assessment and applied for a personal assistant position, which she obtained two years later.

Samira Ben M'Rad's trajectory reveals the bundle of incentives that made it possible for her break away from the traditional feminine model that was still very strong for immigrants' daughters of her generation,[16] a model that was overwhelmingly characteristic of the expectations for working-class women of all backgrounds in the 1980s.[17] The first strand is her father's position when she was in school, always leaving his eldest daughter a chance at a future other than early marriage and motherhood. His desire to see his daughter socially succeed indicates that immigration may in some cases be a decisive factor in changing working-class women's futures. Faced with the "dirty work"[18] delegated to them by French society, some immigrant fathers hoping to improve their families' situations may instill their thirst to overcome such adversity in their children, planting the seeds of social attitudes such as a drive for success and occupational affirmation.

Next came the influence and support of teachers, reinforcing the sense of greater possibilities. Samira Ben M'Rad would never have pursued her studies this far without the encouragement of teachers like the French teacher who challenged her to take the leap into *lycée*. The school system she experienced was not yet that of "80 percent with the *bac*"[19]: Samira says that deserving working-class children stood out and were particularly encouraged.

Last, work was an essential element in representations of her future because women's employment already existed. Women's employment rates in the Ile-de-France region are higher than nationwide,[20] and the outskirts of Paris no exception: the fact that employed women are part of the social landscape helps their activity be accepted as necessary. Residential mobility and encountering other norms (in this case, a neighborhood dominated by middle- and upper-class households and the model of well-educated women) also reinforced aspirations to higher occupational and social ascension for oneself and one's children, and made them attainable.

Nadia and Karima Dhif: When One Sister Pulls Another Along

Elements in Samira Ben M'Rad's occupational mobility are also found in the social trajectories of our other two interviewees. Nadia and Karima Dhif are sisters from an Algerian family who both bought houses in the same new subdivision and are administrative assistants in the national educational system. Nadia, born in 1963, works at a university institute of technology (IUT), and Karima, born in 1969, works at a university in the northern periphery of Paris.

Nadia Dhif got a secondary-level secretarial degree (BEP) and unsuccessfully tried to get back on a nonvocational track to be able to take the *bac*. In the year after leaving school in 1984, she applied for a number of positions in a variety of public administrations. She followed the advice of a teacher who strongly believed that work in public administration offered a solution to the employment problem at a time when the effects of the economic recession were felt severely. This advice paid off: thanks to the teacher's leads, Nadia got a job as an administrative employee in a local educational authority. The teacher thus made it possible for her to start working soon after *lycée* by guiding her toward the public sector, although she had no relatives working in the public or semi-public sector at the time. Immigrants' children of her generation were less psychologically prepared to occupy these public jobs, and she remembers being one of the "first Maghrebians" to work in the institute.

And yet she would wait nine years before taking the civil service exam that would finally assure her a permanent position in 1994. She had long dreaded the competitive exam for fear of failing and seeming less competent to her colleagues. Because the public sector still offered many guarantees for employees on short-term contract, she had been relatively sure her job would be renewed every year. But the increasing insecurity of public contractual employees motivated her to solidify her occupational status. Karima, who began working for the national educational system on short-term contract in 2001 when the situation was getting harder for contract workers, would not wait so long to take the exam, spurred by a desire to escape insecurity (and by her big sister).

Indeed Karima Dhif's trajectory shows her greater difficulty in reaching occupational stability. Her studies went as far as the exam for the *bac G* (administrative-secretarial), which she failed twice, and she tried in vain to earn a degree in a work-based learning program. She gave up on it partly because she could not find a job for the program's work requirement, but mainly because she "didn't have the head for studies anymore" and wanted to start working.

That Karima Dhif gave up on her studies, and her elder sister had such a limited academic career might seem to contradict the earlier observation that immigrant fathers' scholastic ambitions have a positive influence on their daughters' success. In fact, a father's desire to see his children succeed may coexist with cultural impoverishment and a poor mastery of institutions and the conditions for real success. Although he urged his children to get job qualifications and degrees, he himself did not go to school and seemed to lack everything that contributes to children's scholastic success: familiarity with the institution, confidence in his children's capacities, providing constant active learning support, and so on. His encouragement was so effective that his desires might have had a contradictory effect on his children, stimulating some and weakening others, depending on their abilities to satisfy paternal expectations. Karima went up to the *bac* but was unable to pass it. Two brothers have the *bac*, one the *bac* S (sciences) and the other the *bac pro* (vocational). A third brother had no degrees and died of an overdose at twenty.

NADIA AND KARIMA DHIF'S SIBLINGS

Mustapha: Born in 1962, *bac* G3 (commercial studies), narrowly failed a post-*bac* vocational degree (BTS). Married, two children, he is no longer in close contact with his family of origin.

Nadia: Born in 1963, has a secondary-level secretarial degree (BEP), administrative assistant in the national educational system. Married, three children. Had a house built in 1995 in a recent subdivision of the Poplars in Gonesse.

Samir: Born in 1964, died of an overdose in 1984.

Fouad: Born in 1966, *bac S* (science), failed in first year of medical school, now a mechanic for the RATP (metro Paris train network). Father of two, he is thinking about buying an apartment around Bondy.

Azzedine: Born in 1968, *bac pro* (vocational). No longer wants to work in construction, would like to work in computing. Started drinking after his girlfriend's suicide. Lives with his parents. His alcoholism prevents him from holding a regular job.

Karima: Born in 1969, married, two children, administrative assistant in the national educational system. Her husband is mechanic at the RATP. They own a house in Gonesse since 2003.

Sabri: Born in 1987. Adopted at birth. No educational qualifications, unemployed, seems at risk for delinquency. Lives with his parents.

Karima Dhif, who was starting *lycée* when this tragedy struck, gave up on her studies after failing the *bac* a second time. She lived with her parents, who, wanting to flee the projects, bought a little house in the distant suburbs of the Seine-et-Marne east of Paris. She temped a variety of secretarial jobs, then worked for nearly a year in a Mission Locale, a youth training and employment center, in a city adjacent to her hometown. She was put at the welcome desk where she often had to handle people in serious difficulties. The center was in a rough area, and the working conditions were often very difficult.

While working there, at age twenty-three, she befriended her future husband, a former *lycée* classmate. Aziz Abib is of Moroccan descent and had left middle school to study for a secondary-level vocational degree (BEP) to be an electrical technician. After working several years in a chemical company, a job-related health problem put him on reclassification leave. At the time he and Karima got back in touch, he was an activities coordinator at the recreation center of the housing project he grew up in and was looking for a more steady job making use of his qualifications. Karima Dhif helped him find steady work through her connections at the Mission Locale: her small social capital proved to be decisive in her partner's vocational rehabilitation, allowing him to find a job as stock controller with a long-term employment contract. They got married a year later, in 1994, caving to their families' norm that marriage is a precondition for living together, and moved to an HLM in Aziz Abib's hometown of Saint-Denis. Their first child was born a year later.

Before their son was born, Karima found another job in telemarketing, with, as she put it, "a lotta lotta Maghrebians. Why? Because no-one can see us." In spite of everything, she does not dislike the job. She found the working conditions acceptable, and the short-term contract bonus plumped her pay stub a bit. But the company moved to England, and Karima Dhif had to enroll for unemployment: "I took advantage of it to raise my kid." Eight months after giving birth, she found a new job in telemarketing, but the working conditions were very different. She had to sell a maximum of life insurance contracts in as little time as possible, and the pace was exhausting. Worse of all, she became disgusted with the job, which made her feel like she was supposed to "steal from people." With the birth of her second child in 1999, she decided to leave this insecure job she found immoral to take parental leave. Because paid work held an important place in how she constructed her social identity, her retreat into maternity was far from a forgone conclusion.

The couple lived in a HLM and was not in a position to imagine home-ownership. M. Abib's income, around 7,000 francs (1,100 euros) a month, became their sole revenue source. The young couple spent a big chunk of their budget on the purchase of a "beautiful dining room set" on credit and a used midsize car. Their debt made it impossible for them to think of leaving the housing project.

The neighborhood's degradation would finally press them to get out of this situation. Karima began to fear for herself and the children when the practice of setting fires began to spread as a form of youthful rebellion.

> Honestly, what forced us, what really really scared me at Blanc-Mesnil is that they started to burn cars, burn the dumpsters. When I saw that, I said to myself "What on earth is that? And my sons?" You'd think we were in the Bronx. It really scared me. If I didn't have kids, honestly, I'd have stayed, because when you haven't got kids you don't care. I told myself "I'll work night and day, but my kids, they are not going to grow up in all that, in fear." Really, it's awful, awful. I found myself getting up at night because … My neighbor was knocking at the door, in the middle of the night, and she says "your car, your car!" I was afraid, my husband got up and everything, and she says, "they've trashed your car." Actually, they'd set fire to the trash cans and it spread toward the cars, but it didn't get burned. And that's what alerted me, actually. I said, "Argh, I'm not living here anymore, it's over!" Then I told my husband, "I don't care, I don't have the money to buy a house, I don't care, I'm buying an apartment, but someplace nice, not in a neighborhood like this—it's over!" I said, "Imagine the building catches fire!" I said to my husband, "Imagine you've gone to work," I say, "what do I do with my kids, on the fifth floor?" I say, "I jump from the fifth with my kids?" Me, all alone, what do I do? I felt, not imprisoned, I dunno how to explain it.
> Interviewer: Like, trapped?
> Yes, trapped, that's it exactly.

The family, under pressure from Karima who declared she was ready to work "night and day," started looking for housing in a "good neighborhood." Her plan was to leave the housing projects, not to buy, but her sister Nadia's influence convinced Karima and Aziz to raise their ambitions.

In the late 1990s, when stuck in the projects, Nadia had had a house built in the New Poplars. Her marriage had allowed her to make such plans, which she had long thought impossible given her modest income. She got married at age twenty-seven, which was rather late for a woman from a working-class Maghrebian background. She says she was waiting for her "soulmate": a husband she really chose for herself, not one imposed by the traditional community order. It turned out that her choice would nonetheless fall within the range of options acceptable to her parents. She met her husband, Sélim Ghessoum, at work at the institute of technology, where he had been a contractual accounting assistant since 1987. It was his first fairly steady job after having temped since finishing *lycée*. He had grown up in the housing projects of La Courneuve in an Algerian family with ten children, and was the only one to complete secondary education. He was a year younger than she and had a vocational *bac G* in accounting management, making his educational level slightly higher than hers. Nadia describes him readily as a "brilliant student." She clearly admires this man with such high career ambitions who is "always [*trying to*] grow."

He left his first job after two years to take a higher position as accountant in a large company. The couple got married in 1990 and first moved to downtown Bondy (where Nadia was born and her parents still lived in the projects) before moving to a apartment building in the heart of Saint-Denis. Sélim Ghessoum soon began thinking about buying a house. Knowledgeable about public subsidies and tax advantages associated with property accession, he convinced his more reticent wife that building would be their best plan. His accounting skills led him to figure that the cost of buying would be barely higher than their rent (nearly 5,000 francs, 760 euros, a month). This is when Nadia finally decided to take the civil service exam that would give her a secure job. Other than the fact that banks see civil servant status as a strong guarantee, passing the exam also signified that she subscribed to her husband's plans for social mobility and that she shared his desire to improve the family's position. In 1995, the couple moved into the house they had built in the new "golf-course" subdivision, with the two children they had had in the meantime.

Sélim Ghessoum's career trajectory continued to rise. In 1998, he enrolled in an adult education program at an institute of technology to which he devoted two years of weekends until he completed his management degree. Through a recruitment agency, he landed the job of paymaster in a new business in December 2005, finally becoming a *cadre*.

Nadia Dhif spoke of him in detail in interviews, making it possible to appreciate what makes his trajectory distinctive. His father came to France in 1954, and brought his wife over in 1960; half of their children were born in Algeria. The older children quickly cut their studies short, especially the girls, who did not have much choice. The girls born in France, however, all got secondary-level vocation degrees (BEPs), and were all employed at the time of our fieldwork. Their situation seems partly connected to their father's violent death in a work-related accident in 1973. His death shook how the family calculated its future. The eldest sister Zoubida, who was relatively young (six) when she immigrated and thus largely socialized in France, pushed her siblings to pursue an education. Nadia also told us that Sélim belonged to his housing project's youth club and stayed in touch with its director long afterward. This youth counselor had a great influence on Sélim by urging him to work hard in school and offering the possibility of activities and outings outside the neighborhood. Sélim Ghessoum's career success owes much to his encouragement, especially since his background in a large immigrant family weakened by the father's death considerably reduced the probability that he would "get out."

His career aspirations in turn make him coax friends and family to "grow," or as Schwartz put it, "to pull [him]self out of a fate of powerlessness and failure."[21] As we have seen, he played a guiding role in his household, and for Karima and her husband as well. This is how she describes his influence on their lives:

> Interviewer: And your husband, what made him decide to take the bus driver exam— you're the one who pressed him to take it?
>
> Karima: No, it's my sister's husband, Sélim. Because he was beginning to get in a rut in a company where he'd never have had the chance to grow.
>
> Interviewer: What was his salary there, approximately?
>
> Karima: Dunno, 7,000? Its pathetic, 7,000 [*francs*]! So, then, he passed the exam.
>
> Interviewer: And your brother-in-law, he knows the RATP?
>
> Karima: No, but he motivated him. "Yeah, you've got to buy, if you want to buy you've got to do this, that." He could really see that he was off to a bad start in his company. He's not afraid to move, to change companies, he sees far into the future. And it's true that he's more mature, so he gave us advice, and plus he was fed up seeing us like that in an HLM, it was painful for him. So he told us, "I don't get it, you really are capable of getting ahead! I'm sure that you're capable of getting yourselves out of here, you can improve how you live, your living conditions." And he was entirely right, my husband, he slogged along, I let him be.

From this bit of interview, one guesses that Karima admires her brother-in-law, who "knows what he wants" and is "more mature." He gave the couple a model for action that would influence and inspire Karima's husband, who we observe did not entrust his future to private business: his experience in his company convinced him beyond a doubt that his chances of growing there were quite limited. Like other members of his family (who moreover set an example), he believes that public sector employment is the path to improving your situation.

Hired as a machinist at the RATP in 2000, his income went from 7,000 to nearly 11,000 francs (1,600 euros, partly due to bonuses for working the swing shift), which made it possible for the couple "to begin looking around" for a new neighborhood. When her husband landed a stable job with benefits, their new financial security and his higher salary fed Karima's residential aspirations. While previously she would have been happy with a rental in a "good neighborhood," she came to nurture hopes of becoming a homeowner, a sign of success and distance from the world of the projects, but her hopes ran up against the cost. On parental leave, Karima decided to go back to work, spurred by the fact that she was fed up with staying at home. Her sister Nadia urged her to apply for a position that had just opened at a university in the northern Parisian periphery, and thanks to her and one of her husband's sisters who agreed to provide child care, Karima reentered employment. Hired as a contractual worker in 2002, she got a permanent position three years later. In fact, she had learned of her promotion just before one of our visits, and still could not get over it: "That's it! The struggle is over, insecurity over, both of us are civil servants!" Her success made her very optimistic about her career in the future, and she envisaged taking another internal exam to improve her salary and further relieve their financial constraints.

This detailed account of Nadia and Karima Dhif's trajectories reveals how modest and contingent their social mobility is. Given the limitations of their academic resources and the degradation of the employment market, they could just have well have experienced the persistent insecurity that has spread across the working classes, hitting the fractions with low-level (or no) diplomas the hardest. The sisters were able to stabilize their employment and rise above their parents' social position thanks to the sum of their personal networks: for Nadia, the wise advice of a teacher who urged her to work in the public sector and her marriage to a man with the will to "grow," and in Karima's case, the support of her family, since she and her husband were pulled along by Nadia and Sélim's plans for mobility.

Their examples prompt us to draw particular attention to another factor in their social mobility: the variety of public institutions we observe throughout their lives. Whether through the Mission Locale, the employment center, the youth club, the recreation center, or the university, such public institutions are fundamental to small social promotions. Without them, our interviewees and their spouses could not have gotten out of the housing projects, or even dream of doing so. Precisely because of the contingent nature of modest social mobilities, public institutions are of capital importance. The same holds true for public employment, which now more than ever is a stepping stone toward middling social positions, as the employment market degrades and employees from working-class backgrounds struggle to make a career in the private sector.[22]

SEEKING RESPECTABILITY AND FAMILY WELL-BEING

Although their trajectories differ on many points, it is clear that buying a home was the result of a shift in the occupational space as well as a desire for respectability—getting away from the world of the housing projects and the stigmatization and degradation associated with them.

This desire for respectability structures how they relate to the subdivision and makes the financial constraints of home buying considerably easier to accept. Our interviewees pay dearly, though unequally, for their transitions to homeownership, but its sacrifices are attenuated by their HLM histories and the image they have of housing projects today. In addition, our informants' lifestyle means they are not frustrated by their budgetary constraints and do not see them as an indication of want. Indeed, they seem more attached to the family's well-being and their children's success than to the house itself.

"Fleeing the Zone"

Acquiring a single-family home was unquestionably these households' main opportunity to get away from the housing projects. All three were adamant in interviews that they would not want their children to grow up where they were raised, in Bondy or La Courneuve.[23] In addition to their own unhappy experiences, their repeated remarks on how the projects were plunging into crisis highlight their happiness to have gotten out. Nadia Dhif mentioned the mediocre academic level of her nieces attending the school at the Cité des 4000 in La Courneuve. She compares their homework and course plans to those of her own children and laments the chasm between them. Samira Ben M'Rad spoke of her youngest brother, who was being pulled into the projects' grips: he stopped attending *lycée* and was not looking for work. Karima rejects her youngest siblings' fatalism: "whenever you say anything to them, it's 'yeah, no one likes us, we're Arabs.' Now that's quitter talk."

These views on housing projects reinforce their conviction that they made the right choice in distancing themselves from what all three now call "the zone." One could say that they look down on the housing projects, sometimes with a hardness that is a sign of recent and still-uncertain membership in the world of the middle classes, the world of those on the right side of the tracks. For example, they sometimes contrast their household's deservingness with the lack of will of "people from the projects" that supposedly explains why so many of them are in insecure positions. But generally speaking, their words oscillate between two contradictory representations of "people from the projects": fear or contempt on one hand and an evident loyalty to their near and dear who cannot leave on the other. Teenagers depress them the most, especially those they think lack "courage."

For our informants, becoming a homeowner is automatically tied to a quest for social advancement and a rejection of the marginal city zones that society assigns to foreigners and the impoverished. They have succeeded in achieving their ideal distance to varying degrees (see Table 2.1). Their trajectories echo the observations of Chicago-School sociologists who revealed the gradual shift of immigrants' children between the two world wars from the poorest parts of the city toward more heterogeneous middle-class neighborhoods, at least in terms of their residents' social and ethnic origins.[24] In purchasing a single-family home, our informants tried to make a place for themselves in the socially mixed neighborhoods, where "all the categories are represented" (Samira Ben M'Rad), where "there aren't only people with the same origins" (Karima Dhif). "It's awful, to put people of the same origin in the same neighborhoods. I didn't want that, I wanted to live in a normal neighborhood," Nadia Dhif told us. All also express their desire to live in a "quiet place."

Karima Dhif "fell for" a housing development located in Deuil-la-Barre, a small town in the Val-d'Oise department that she describes as a "calm" and "well inhabited" town with schools "at a good level." Her sister Nadia would like to have moved to Villeparisis for the same reasons. Samira Ben M'Rad would like to have settled in Livry-Gargan, a "nice town, with no problems." The contrast between the towns where they would have preferred to buy and the towns they came from is striking: census data confirms that the middle and upper classes are heavily represented in the former and that the unemployment rate and the percentage of foreigners are much lower there than in the housing projects of Saint-Denis where they spent most of their lives. After visiting numerous houses in these towns and all over the northern and northeastern periphery, they ultimately chose the Poplars's newer subdivisions. It is evident that if they had been entirely free to chose the location, they would have preferred a town other than Gonesse, midway on the spectrum between places where the middle classes set the tone and places that seem given over to the poor and immigrants.

But they were also unable to move to the towns that appealed to them because their aspirations did not entirely match those of their husbands, who were more reluctant to move too far from their home neighborhoods.[25] Being female may indeed have predisposed them more than males to reach for more socially elite towns, to truly distance themselves from the world they grew up in. As teenagers, they barely spent any time in public in their neighborhoods, due to their upbringing and its limitations on their freedom of movement. As girls, they quickly came to see the projects as a world of boys, especially those loitering in the streets; it was a degraded environment that they came to treat with caution. Nadia's explanation for not noticing her brother's gradual drift leading to his death by overdose is telling in this

TABLE 2.1. Towns from which people moved, towns where they had hoped to live, towns to which they actually moved.

In percentage	Town of origin				Ideal town			Town where they live
	Bondy	La Courneuve	Aulnay-sous-Bois	Villeparisis	Livry-Gargan	Deuil-la-Barre	Gonesse
*Cadres** and intellectual professions (in percentage of the population over 15 years)	16.7	11.7	5.7	22.7	23.9	28.2	18.8
Basic employees (idem)	21.5	21.4	19.8	21.9	19.5	21.5	24.1
Laborers (idem)	16.7	20.1	17.4	16	12.5	16.7	16.9
Unemployed (in percentage of active population)	17.1	24.3	16.8	10.7	10.4	9.4	14.7
Without educational qualifications (in percentage of population over 15 years having left education system)	24.2	34.2	24.4	20	18.6	13.8	25.6
Foreigners (in percentage of total population)	18.5	26.9	19.7	10.5	9.4	9.8	14.7
Individual housing (in percentage of housing)	29.4	11.4	42.8	52.7	45.3	40.6	36

Source: Data from the 1999 census, INSEE.
*For a discussion of French census categories "*cadre*" and "basic employee", see the introduction, fn 36.

regard: "I didn't hang out in the street," she explained, unlike him and his male friends who had greater autonomy (which could turn against them, as her brother's story demonstrates). Their gendered socialization, along with their academic socialization, made them mentally break away from their neighborhoods early, and to see it, if not negatively, at least quite differently than their spouses.

Sélim Ghessoum's example is very enlightening on this point. He first tried to buy a piece of land near the Cité des 4000 in La Courneuve, to stay close to the neighborhood where he had still had many ties: his mother, some of his siblings, and two friends he regularly played soccer with on Sundays. Although he did not want to live in the projects any more, he remained faithful to them. His ideal was to build a house adjacent to the project, far enough from its problems but very close to his main social circles. Karima Dhif's husband also wanted to live near his family, and consequently did not want to go too far from the HLM neighborhood where he and Samira first lived together, in Gonesse's Cité du Nord (where his mother and a son from a previous marriage still live). He only agreed to start the home-buying process on the condition that they stay close to his family.

In addition, the three women we interviewed moved closer to their husbands' families when they got married, which happens to conform to tradition. This is a major reason for the fact that they lost contact with the friends of their youth. Early withdrawal from the projects, at least in psychological terms, leads friendships to fade. Neither Nadia's nor Karima's husbands had broken with their youthful friendships.

The Cost of Leaving the Projects

Gonesse was not really our interviewees' first choice; they moved there for lack of anything better. Of course there were financial reasons for this: they had to aim lower and smaller. As Karima Dhif said, "there is a moment when you've got to make concessions. You can't have everything."

Nadia Dhif and her husband looked for a plot of land to build on for a long time. The ones the contractors suggested were either out of their budget or located too far from La Courneuve and Nadia's workplace. Sélim Ghessoum combed the northern suburbs over a year looking for a satisfactory plot; he ended up finding it in Gonesse.

Initially, neither Samira Ben M'Rad nor Karima Dhif wanted to move to Gonesse. Karima knew the town a little already from visiting her sister. She liked the subdivision, but not enough to think of buying there right away. She hoped for better—Gonesse seemed "a little too *banlieue*," which is to say that its social composition was not far enough from the housing projects— but the force of circumstances made them chose the Poplars. Her sister told her about a house for sale: the owners were divorcing and were in a hurry to unload their property. Karima Dhif and her husband were able to buy it for 1 million francs (150,000 euros) in 1997, when prices were low. As for Samira Ben M'Rad, she and her husband were renting in Gonesse, and she had hoped to be able to move on to a "calmer" town (to use one of their favorite terms), but the houses she liked were beyond their means. In addition, her husband was fearful of taking on a significant debt. Gonesse, then, was a compromise for the couple. They, too, benefited from a quick sale due to a divorce: without this chance, they might not have been able to buy in the neighborhood.

Even in Gonesse, where the prices are lower than in the towns they initially targeted, these couples faced new expenses that strained their budgets, at very least obliging them to make some additional concessions. The Ben M'Rads had paid 3,300 francs (470 euros) rent in an HLM; at the time of our interviews, she estimated that the equivalent of one person's salary "went into the house." In addition to monthly payments of nearly 5,200 francs (780 euros), there are utilities and taxes, which are higher than in HLMs. Karima Dhif, whose household also devotes one salary to their housing (the equivalent of 1,000 euros), explained that these expenses came as a surprise: water, heating, local and property taxes add up to over 4,000 euros a year on top of loan payments.

They say they "accept a lot of sacrifices" to stay in budget. Samira Ben M'Rad gave up going away for vacation, although she used to leave every year. When she lived in an HLM, Karima Dhif skied nearly every winter and went away three weeks in the summer—pleasures the household had to give up when they started repaying the loan and their budget was indeed stressed to the limit. She knows that "it'll be very difficult" for twelve years, but once they have paid off their first loan, from her husband's employer, "it'll be better."

For these homeowners with modest incomes, further investment in home improvement is out of the question. None undertook significant work to enlarge the house or customize it to their tastes. For example, Samira Ben M'Rad would like to have renovated the attic, which would have allowed the children their own rooms (the two daughters share). But it would have been expensive, even without the additional heating costs. The interior of Karima Dhif's house also reveals her budgetary constraints. The couple literally moved into the previous owners' décor, the wallpaper and paint unchanged. For the two years Karima has lived there, she has dreamed of changing the decoration "a little." She showed us "the old stuff" she is "fed up with" and would like to replace: a large mirror she bought on sale when she worked in telemarketing, the chandelier from her HLM dining room, the old oven her parents gave them when they moved in. Their finances do not allow much in the way of purchases; the couple had not bought any new furniture, and the main room contains the dining room set they bought when they got married. Despite the fact that the cost of home buying burdens their budgets, these women in no way feel they made a bad choice. For example, unlike some of the new homeowners interviewed by P Cuturello who were surprised by the high cost of home buying relative to their actual means, none say that they "would never have gone into property ownership if [*they*] had known."[26] They have no doubt that they made "the right calculation" in becoming owners. Even after having detailed the constraints associated with home buying for us, they still think that "renting is a loss of money."

This point of view reflects the internalization of housing norms overvaluing property ownership. Heavily reinforced by ubiquitous advertisements found everywhere from bus shelters to magazines, the primacy of property has become established in families' minds as the obvious pinnacle of their residential trajectories. It considerably devalues all other housing statuses, above all rental in an HLM, which is synonymous with low social status. Moreover, the house has an essential symbolic dimension, embodying the desire to bring the family together and pass it along to the next generation. This urge is tied to the positive depictions that builders and their financial intermediaries know how to manipulate so well.[27] But there are yet other factors that explain why they consent to pay more than expected to own a home.

First of all, as we have seen, their HLM pasts have given them a sort of social distaste for housing projects, which to them symbolize a degraded and degrading world for those living there today. Buying a home is the price of escaping the delinquency and minor everyday chaos of HLM life and the more fundament disdain to which their residents are doomed today. Becoming a homeowner is a prerequisite for becoming a "respectable" family, "normal" and "like the others": this simple goal alone helps make the sacrifices of property ownership tolerable.

Second, to become homeowners, these couples had to convert themselves to borrowing and understand the credit system. They did not stumble along blindly, but proceeded with precise knowledge of the sums to be paid and how they would be spaced out.[28] In addition, real estate prices have not stopped climbing since 1997. Like many neighborhood residents, our interviewees had their houses appraised to know what they were worth, even though they have no intention of moving soon. This rising real estate value may be perceived as a compensation or reward for their willing sacrifice.

Last, although the financial challenge in keeping the budget balanced is very real, the neighborhood's shared economic morality—the same as the row-house pioneers'—makes it more mundane. Keeping a close eye on expenses seems normal. Our interviewees' households' social prospects are not limited to the present, as may be the case for more impoverished or socially vulnerable working-class households. Thanks to their social trajectories and the confidence in the future they have acquired, their current concessions are more tolerable because a good outcome is in sight.

Choosing Family Well-Being over Renovating the House

As we mentioned earlier, our interviewees did not start any major renovations. This is partly explained by lack of funds, and also by the fact that our interviewees' husbands had little inclination to do work on the houses themselves. Karima Dhif's husband and father-in-law only redid the bathroom tile and the wallpaper in the children's rooms. Samira Ben M'Rad and Nadia Dhif's husbands preferred hiring people to do small home improvement jobs like pouring a concrete slab for a garden terrace. It seems these men never learned to work with tools, and their homes are less "personalized" than homes where the husbands are handy and may devote themselves to partially renovating the house themselves. This trait clearly sets them apart from the row-house pioneers, who as we saw in chapter 1 also experienced upward social mobility through their employment and housing, but remain closer to classic working-class culture. From working-class families but not having experienced manual work themselves, Samira Ben M'Rad's and Nadia and Karima Dhif's husbands assimilated other cultural references that led them to develop another relationship with time and the house that do not tap all their free time or their entire income.

Thus, Nadia's household, which has been paying its mortgage for ten years now, indulges in many relaxing activities, like going to restaurants or the movies with the children. The family has already visited Algeria twice to learn about their parents' country. These are moments of discovery and celebration of the family history that Nadia and her husband would not miss out on "for anything in the world." "Too bad for the house," she went on to add, "we do it gradually, it's not our priority."

Karima Dhif's household cannot take trips like this for now, but the lack of money does not entirely deprive them of pleasure. Sundays the family often goes to the forest, visiting grandparents living in the Seine-et-Marne department to the east of Paris. They are on very good terms with some of Aziz Abib's siblings' families, and they get together often. All these activities take place away from home, are unrelated to the house, and are more focused on seeing family and spending time together.

These adults come from large families, and their siblings are now parents and even grandparents, making a lot of people to see and occasions to get together. This attachment to the family is typical of working-class culture, which has more developed sociability with extended family than other social classes and a greater variety of occasions for meeting people. Moreover, and perhaps even more so for these children of immigrants, family is a "safe" relational space, protected from the ever-dreaded assumptions about "origins." Our interviewees and their spouses sometimes see coworkers outside of work, but much less than they see family. As Karima Dhif says, "I feel natural with my sisters-in-law," which is less the case with her colleagues and their spouses whose tastes, conversational topics, and dietary practices (such as consuming alcohol) are not entirely the same as theirs. The social distance our informants and their husbands took from their families is not so great they would entertain thoughts of severing such close relations.

At the same time, their little climb in the social space has very real consequences on their family sociability: they are closer to siblings whose life courses resemble their own. They go on vacation and spend weekends with siblings who became white-collar workers like themselves. They are not equally close to everyone in their family of origin: there is the family they inherit, and the family they choose to be closer to, where relations are built on social proximity. They do not use the family as a means to stay within their group or take refuge, as may happen in laborers' households more fearful of the outside world. Instead, family supports and reinforces their mobility thanks to its numbers and social diversity.

Furthermore, these family relations are far from being defined by tradition. Time spent with family comes with a desire to imprint these relations with modernity. The pleasure of being together is backed by a desire for equality, or at least closeness, between parents and children and thus of practices bringing them together, even if it is only to watch a video together on Sunday afternoon.

These couples do not raise their children as their parents raised them, or like working-class families in general. Their parenting style is much closer to that of the fractions of the middle class with a certain degree of cultural capital. As Karima Dhif put it, "we talk with our children," whereas in the family where she grew up, this was not the case: it was difficult to really talk with her parents because conversation was subject to many taboos and forbidden topics. To the contrary, she affirms the importance of talking and the development of each person, which are commonly held values in social worlds exposed to psychological talk, such as women working in the public sector like herself. We must not forget that she also worked in a Mission Locale in regular contact with social workers accustomed to interpreting the world through the lens of psychology.

Our interviewees' husbands are not absent from these exchanges, unlike their fathers who would keep their distance. They are also much more involved in domestic work. Nadia Dhif's and Samira Ben M'Rad's husbands handle the children's athletic activities. Karima Dhif's husband, who works the swing shift, also takes charge of feeding the children lunch. He told her, "I didn't have kids to send them to the cafeteria," and Karima explains that he not only knows how to care for children, he loves doing it. Aziz Abib seems to have no reservations about treading on what was traditionally maternal territory. The distance between the generations was great in the household where he grew up, but for many years, he worked in a recreation center where he got used to contact with children and, perhaps more significantly, was exposed to a relationship to domestic practices that is usually found in the well-educated middle classes. This RATP bus driver thus cannot be defined exclusively by the social position of his family of origin, nor can he be entirely classified with working-class men: his practices are testimony to the profound effects that protracted socialization in scholastic and sociocultural institutions may bring about. In many ways, he seems closer to the social milieu of youth counselors than the world of laborers.[29]

FEAR OF LOSING SOCIAL STANDING
AND THE STAKES OF EDUCATION

These households became property owners with an overwhelming desire to escape housing projects and no longer be seen as inferior, poor, or immigrants. At the same time, their subdivisions are not far from public housing areas like the Cité du Nord, and they are adjacent to the Poplars's row houses, where there are quite a few immigrant families. This proximity feeds a real anxiety in some of our interviewees, who fear the effects of contamination "from below."

Fear of Being Lumped Together

This physical proximity to lower social categories is visible in many ways. The presence of the children and teenagers from the row houses who come to play in the subdivisions is one example, as are some acts of delinquency that the individual homeowners of the neighborhood attribute to them.

Samira Ben M'Rad claims "You can feel it's going downhill." She complains about the youths who park under her entryway shelter on rainy days. The street where she lives is "American-style," as she puts it, with a strip of grass between the houses and the street, in contrast to the more common French style of the house abutting the sidewalk or a wall enclosing a paved or terraced space between the house and street. Unlike other homeowners who decided to build such walls to clearly mark their property boundaries, she chose to plant a hedge, but it is not enough to protect their private space. She does not want to break the homeowners' association rules against walls, but with the way she thinks the neighborhood is going, she is inclined to follow in her neighbors' footsteps.

Samira Ben M'Rad's trajectory makes her susceptible to judge some of her neighbors harshly, particularly the heavily stigmatized minority of Chaldean families living in the row houses and in some of individual houses dating to the 1980s and 1990s. Commenting on how the neighborhood's social composition has evolved, she said "As time goes on we notice that, when people leave, the more there's ... You get the feeling that the [old] Poplars is going to spread again, to here, gradually as people leave." This reference to a "spreading" of the "old" Poplars designates the slow penetration of households of immigrants or people seen as such based on their physical appearances or lifestyles (especially "the Turks" in the row houses). She points out that she herself is Algerian and what she says is not racist, but at the same time, she is at pains to distance herself from these newcomers who she does not dare name more explicitly.

In buying a house, Samira Ben M'Rad had hoped to melt into the middle classes and escape being labeled by her origins. When she moved to the new subdivision in 1997, it was still very white and middle class. This is less true today, and the middle-class households are more tempted to leave.[30] This development runs against her efforts to climb socially and escape stigmatization. In the following quote, she tells how her family was initially seen as Arab, bringing degradation in its wake. She was gradually able to get the family recognized as "the same as" the others. Now that the neighborhood population is changing color, she fears that she will no longer be able to escape being lumped together with the others. She expressed genuine anguish at the idea of being "poorly thought of" or seen in a negative light.

> The day they saw me arrive, people later told me: "You know, when we saw you arrive, we said 'There it is, the neighborhood's going downhill, there's foreigners coming in, it's going to go badly, we're going to see more headscarves, and this and that,' when actually, nothing happened."
> Interviewer: You had to work to get accepted?
> That was later, when they saw how we live, saw us working, our children and how we behaved with them and who we really were, that they said "Oh, but you're different." But I don't like that way of talking, "But you're different."

Less than seven years after buying in the neighborhood, Samira Ben M'Rad is thinking about leaving it herself, perhaps to move closer to her parents by buying a house in the better-off section of Aulnay-sous-Bois. When we met, she had just renegotiated her mortgage to be able to pay it off more quickly in order to take out a new loan. Because she anticipated a "decline in the neighborhood," she thought it best to keep tightening the belt, when she might otherwise have been able to take advantage of a little more economic freedom.

The other two informants do not share this feeling of a "return to stigma." Most likely because they and their husbands were born in France, they feel more legitimately French than Samira Ben M'Rad. In an interview, Karima Dhif described having felt "the rather fearful looks" of her "French" neighbors, but she does not think it was prompted by her family's Arab origins. She claims that her neighbors, retirees, were instead worried about the kind of family that was moving in nearby, how the children behaved and the like, and actually broke the ice their first days there by dropping by to wish them welcome. At least, this is how Karima Dhif interpreted their visit, and today she shows no hint of suspicion about their intentions. She has a good relationship with this neighboring family, even if they have never invited each other over. The wives offer each other little gifts at ritual moments: in the spring the neighbor gives Karima a basket of cherries, and every Ramadan Karima gives her homemade pastries.

When questioned about her relations with families in the area, Nadia Dhif has no disparaging attitudes to report either. But either way, she seems disposed to ignore them. "People will think what they want, there will always be racists, can't live with that in your head. I have good relationships with my neighbors, I don't think they see me like an outsider.... We get along well, we raise our kids more or less the same way—I mean, we do everything for them, and that's what counts."

In the area of single-family homes where she lives, in addition to their high cost making them less accessible to "foreigners," some homeowners with a house on the market select among potential buyers. We were able to identify two cases where owners avoided selling to foreigners because of their neighbors' implicit desire that they "not sell to just anyone." An interviewee who was preparing to move explained that he had declined to sell his house to a "black" family with several children. His neighbors would have taken it badly, he said, and he did not want to run the risk of inflicting a problem family on them.

Nadia Dhif said she was not aware of this kind of practice blocking foreign households' access to the better parts of the neighborhood. She doubts that they even exist, or that they could be interpreted as racist. Whatever the case, she is not opposed to the idea of controlling the entry of new families into the neighborhood: "We see so many truly strange things now, it's true that we've got to watch out. Sometimes all it takes is one problem family to give the whole neighborhood a bad ambiance." She thus shares the common homeowner concern of preserving the level of the neighborhood, all the more so because she probably sees it as necessary for maintaining her own respectability.

Her neighbors are still *cadres* and professionals who built their homes at the same time. She gets along with them well because of the children, who go to the same schools. Indeed, unlike Karima Dhif's and Samira Ben M'Rad's children, hers are enrolled in the neighborhoods' best schools, which also explains why she does not feel a drop in status like Samira.

The Appeal of Private (Catholic) School

Peoples' relationship to the neighborhood largely depends on the question of schools: which school the children attend, its reputation, its level. After nursery school (located in the new part of the development), children are assigned to one of two schools according to their street. Half go to Victor Hugo primary school followed by Gérard Philippe Middle School, and the others to Emile Zola primary then Willy Ronis Middle School.

The way their student bodies are assigned means that the schools' reputations are far from the same. Victor Hugo is in the row-house part of the neighborhood, and the Gérard Philippe Middle School, Gonesse's only school designated as an Education Action Zone (zone d'éducation prioritaire, ZEP), is in the Cité du Nord. From subdivision parents' perspective, this makes them the schools to avoid. In contrast, the Emile Zola school, which dates to the 1930s, is between the older single-family homes and the subdivisions from the 1980s, and Willy Ronis Middle School is in a neighboring residential development with a reputation for being calm.

LITTLE SOCIAL MIXING IN SCHOOL

The student body of Victor Hugo Primary School is predominantly composed of the children of working-class and immigrant families. The school principal estimates that in 2004, 40 to 50 percent of her students were of foreign origin, mostly Chaldean, while they were only around 20 percent of Emile Zola's student population. This distribution seems much more balanced when compared with a few years earlier, when Victor Hugo was almost exclusively children from the row houses. Given its concentration of large "foreign" families, the neighborhood's nursery and primary school became "ghettos," according to the principal.

When city hall went left in 1995, the new socialist municipal government changed the school districting to balance the student populations. It tried to mix the populations more by bringing more advantaged children to Victor Hugo. Children from some streets of the 1990s and 2000s subdivisions were assigned there, and city hall refused most of the ensuing influx of requests for exemptions.

The streets concerned by this measure are those closest to the row houses, where the most modest new houses are found. The more distant streets, bordering the golf course and populated by better-off households, are still in the Emile Zola district.

Emile Zola and Willy Ronis schools take in a public more endowed with economic and cultural capital. In addition to children from the new subdivisions, Emile Zola primary also takes children from the old single-family homes (today largely inhabited by middle- and upper-class households), apartment buildings occupied by lower-level civil servants, part of the village-style subdivision of the 1970s and 1980s, and another nearby development. Although the Willy Ronis Middle School also has some students from the housing projects, they are fewer since the Gérard Philippe Middle School was built closer to the Cité du Nord. While Willy Ronis seems to be calmer and to perform well, Gérard Philippe is a designated ZEP and has problems typical of a housing-project middle school.[31]

─── ⁊

Karima Dhif and Samira Ben M'Rad's streets are in the Victor Hugo/ Gérard Philippe district, and that is where they enrolled their children. Karima Dhif's eldest is starting primary school, and Samira Ben M'Rad's third child is finishing primary and preparing for middle school. Her two older daughters attended this school before going to Gérard Philippe. They were in *lycée* at the time of our study, one in her first year (on the sciences track) and the other in her last year (on a technical track) after having been held back. These mothers chose public schools aware of the bad reputation of their school district: all the subdivision parents talk about it, and a growing number of children have transferred to private schools since the redistricting. Parents opting out of the imposed educational progression place considerable pressure on parents who do not have a choice or who still want to have faith in public schools. Karima Dhif and Samira Ben M'Rad joined the FCPE, the main nationwide association of school children's parents defending one school for all, "open and free to all." For all that, they are not hard-liners and can sympathize with public school detractors, at least when it comes to their school, because they became homeowners in hopes of escaping the ZEP and are naturally somewhat anxious about their children's schools. Karima Dhif tries to convince herself that Victor Hugo is a good school, but Samira Ben M'Rad is considering putting her son in private school because his entry into middle school amplifies fears that he might fail.

Karima Dhif explained that she would not have hesitated to put her children in private school if she had stayed in the housing projects. She would have done like most parents with a steady income—flee schools that were at least perceived as low-level. Given the high mortgage payments this was no longer an option, so she was resigned to enrolling them at Victor Hugo. She confessed her surprise at discovering the number of immigrants' children there, reminding her of the school in the projects. Like most parents in the school district, it initially scared Karima Dhif because it seemed so unlike the school she wanted for her children. Not being able to run away, she decided to get involved in its FCPE.

> The first time my husband said "But where are the whites? Are we in Blanc-Mesnil or what?!" But seriously, [*laughing*] this can't be possible, in the schoolyard s'all there is! Sixty percent Turks, twenty percent Maghrebians, after that ... But the schoolyard in Blanc-Mesnil [*lowers voice*], there were only blacks. They are nice, the moms too, they are super-nice [*laughs*]. That's where we are—no way, but where are the whites?! [*laughing*] It's Turkish! But they buy everything, all the houses. And it's really the old tradition with them. I saw a report on TV—it's like we were before, girls are put down....
>
> Interviewer: And what did you think when you found out you were going to Victor Hugo? ...
>
> I was afraid! Yes, honestly, I was afraid. What I did was easy. I remember, it was June 30th, I called and asked, "Can you see me, please?"
>
> Interviewer: The principal?
>
> Yeah. I brought my son's school report book, I met his teacher for his supplies, I talked with her, and I was really afraid, I hear bad things about that school. A lot of people asked for exemptions so they could go to the other school, Emile Zola, where there aren't as many Turks, that's why. But me, since I'm there, I tell them, "Listen, I come truly from outside. I was afraid too, but I'm not asking for exceptions and I want to tell you that you aren't going to find a teaching team like that everywhere! I tell 'em, "It's a great team." And then the other children, the Turks, it's not their fault they're like that. But what I said to the teacher, what we, the parents who are really backing their children, are really afraid of is that they abandon our children who still have, well, I'm not going to say they're excellent, but still, there are some really good ones—he works at home to get his "very goods"—that's what I tell them. I told her, "I hope that you don't abandon our kids like that, when you help the ones that are having trouble. Of course you've got to help them, but you can't forget the plan, because you also have to move forward in the teaching plan." ...
> But actually in this school, they don't do that [*neglect the course plan*]. And so when I was on the school board, I asked that for the older children in nursery school who will be going to primary school the following year, that the principal and future teacher see the parents, to reassure them.... There are some parents who don't give a damn, but at least for the parents who care, to reassure them that they can spend their vacations in peace because of the anxieties about it all, then you pass it on to your kids, it's hard.

Her discourse exemplifies a tactic used by some parents who, unable to flee poorly reputed schools, develop what Agnès Van Zanten calls a school "colonization strategy" based on an intensive and vigilant presence.[32] She is part of a small core of parents from the new subdivisions that is very involved in Victor Hugo primary. Affirming their loyalty to public schooling, they are not only the first to lend a hand for school outings and organizing the school fair, but they also attend meetings and represent other parents. Given that most of the families in the row houses remain withdrawn from the school, lacking the codes for understanding and participating, these active parents are even more precious.

At the same time, they monitor the scholastic situation as best they can by maintaining constant vigilance over the course plan and school life. Karima Dhif bought a copy of her son's course plan and follows his progress step by step. She has no compunctions about asking the teacher to explain her methods or why they might be running behind; these are ways of pressuring the teacher so she will not neglect her son and the other children from the recent subdivisions. She also plans on making what she calls "surprise cafeteria visits" to ensure that mealtimes go smoothly and check up on the behavior of staff and children alike.

This strategy for appropriating the school is a way to ensure the quality of the school where she is obliged to send her son. The strategy undeniably runs up against the lack of parental forces, though, because few subdivision parents are active or as invested in the FCPE as Karima Dhif, and even fewer from the district with the lesser-reputed schools. Some modest homeowners have rather limited educational backgrounds and may be intimidated by schools. The rise of Karima's social trajectory favors her engagement, and the fact that she works in the national education system might have an even greater influence. Although she only reached the lowest tier of the educational system herself, she does not feel entirely illegitimate facing primary school teachers because she also works in the educational system. Last, many parents are less prepared to get involved in the primary school parents' association because they have already decided to "exit" to private schools in the future. They wait until their children start middle school to change educational paths, either by exploiting the system of "options"[33] or by switching to private schools.

Samira Ben M'Rad was thinking of enrolling her young son in private school at the time of our study, which diverted her from involvement in the parents' association. She used to be a parents' representative at Victor Hugo and Gérard Philippe Middle School, where her daughters went to school. At the time of our first interview, when her son was in his last year of primary school, she seemed a lot less loyal to public schools. She had stopped going to parents' association meetings and seemed to want to break away from the school. Although she had shown herself to be rather tolerant of the academic, social, and ethnic mix in primary school, her son's move on to middle school worried her greatly.

She believed that the middle school's environment had changed since her daughters were there. The principal had changed, there was supposedly less discipline, and the school's graduation exam (BEPC) results had dropped considerably. She also said that her son was "easily influenced," and she was worried he might get caught up in the "wrong crowd." Her son had more friends from the Turkish and Maghrebian families in the row houses (his classmates at Victor Hugo) than from the subdivision. Although they are "nice children," they were far from the model of serious and academically motivated friends Samira wanted for her son.

She was afraid of losing control of her son when he started middle school, and that he might go astray. This fear was not as strong with her daughters, who were more reserved and whose friends were less present than her son's—all consequences of gender-differentiated socialization that made her worry much more about her son. Her experience as parents' representative at Gérard Philippe Middle School had convinced her that boys are at greater risk of academic decline than girls. She spoke of disciplinary meetings where she had become aware of how susceptible boys are when exposed to gang thinking. Terrified of being taken for "clowns," some students take the worst extreme as role model and end up failing middle school, although their grades had been perfectly good when they started.

The decision had not been made at the time of our first interview. Private school (meaning Roman Catholic, which dominates private education in France) is not part of the value system of this mother from an Algerian immigrant family, who has great respect for the public school system she herself attended. But private school seemed nearly unavoidable given the local middle school—she did not want to sacrifice her son on the altar of her values. Her hesitation stemmed from her son's refusal to go to private school, which he saw as "a punishment" because private school was "a school for the bourgeois" that would cut him off from his friends. His mother did not want to run the risk of forcing him to go, thus pushing him to failure. People she knew who had sent their children to private school against their will came to bitterly regret their decisions, because their children stopped studying and their grades became worse than when they were in the public school. So before he started his last year of primary school, she had considered several alternatives, such as exploiting the options system to get a dispensation allowing him to attend one of the other two middle schools in town. She tried to warm him up to the idea of taking the option of German as a foreign language, but once again he refused.

When we met again in June 2005, they had come to a compromise. Her son had applied to a sports-focused program (with a basketball option) in another middle school in Gonesse. If accepted, he would avoid going to Gérard Philippe while remaining in public school (recalling a strategy seen again in chapter 4, where parents enroll their children in the sports option). He seemed to have looked into this option himself, a possibility that would protect him from private schools and the accompanying immersion in a world he sees as superior, different, or downright hostile to his own. Although he had not previously been particularly into basketball (he was in the judo club), he quickly joined a basketball club to make his request more credible. This development was a comfort to his mother, even though it was not a done deal. As she put it, he still had "to get several visas" before getting into this option and a new middle school. Her expression eloquently expresses the challenge of going from one middle school to another, as if making a difficult border crossing subject to many controls.

Other than her desire to avoid her district's middle school, Samira Ben M'Rad expressed other feelings that help us understand the attraction of private schools for some subdivision homeowners. She offered an array of complaints with the public school: delays in finding substitute teachers, re-placements not up to the job, classes with many discipline problems where lessons do not start until it settles down, the fatalism that ended up reaching the teachers themselves, who seem to have lost faith in the students and given up on motivating them. Whether these grievances were founded or not, the important thing is understanding that for her (like many other subdivision homeowners), the public school was not up to the level she ex-pected from a good school: high-quality teaching, discipline, stimulation to succeed. The chances of success were lower here than elsewhere, and were more dependent on the students' academic strength, their powers of con-centration, their capacities to resist the street culture infiltrating the school, and their parents' abilities to help and support them daily in their home-work. Private school seemed to offer a way to reduce the risks. In addition, Samira Ben M'Rad felt that schools today "no longer distinguish" between the students who are willing to work and the rest, or between the parents who support and help their children and those who are utterly helpless or seem not to care: everyone is put "in the same basket." In her district's public schools, it seemed to her that the "deserving" families were lumped in with the rest and treated the same way, which is to say, often handled without any particular concern for everything they do to raise their children well, the ef-fort put into escaping the projects and improving their living conditions, or their academic goodwill. At least in private schools, Samira Ben M'Rad told us, "you aren't treated any old way."

It matters little if this glowing representation of private education is illu-sory or not; understanding what is behind this assessment is the important thing. Samira offered several anecdotes that help us grasp the perspective of a mother of Arab descent in upward mobility who constantly feels negatively judged by the school, reduced to her working-class and immigrant origins.

> At least being a lawyer, doctor—because of your status, maybe they'll think a little
> more of you. But in today's society, when you come from a working class or other
> background the parents aren't really listened to.
> Interviewer: Listened to by the school? The teachers in particular?

Yes, by the school, teachers, the principal. I remember a story, I don't know if I've already told it to you. My daughter had just started middle school. The principal, who was very strict and rather military in his style but was good, too, had attitudes that were a little ... he was brusque with the students. Mostly you couldn't ever say he was wrong, teachers and parents alike had trouble being able to discuss anything with him because he was always right, that was how he had to manage his school. And he had attitudes that were a little too violent with the children, like if a child wasn't lined up, he'd grab him and throw him against a wall. He'd be really rough, it happened to several students, and we heard about it.... And one day he did the same thing to my daughter, and I asked her, "Did you do something serious that made him do that?" She says, "No, I wasn't lined up when the bell rang. He was going by and another student bumped into me." And so she ended up out of line. He grabbed her and threw her like that. Well it was pretty intimidating for a sweet little thing just starting middle school.... So my husband called saying that he shouldn't do that, that he was unhappy about what he did. Even if she wasn't in line, that's no reason to grab her and throw her like that against a wall like he was used to doing. He didn't want to listen to him, he sent him packing, he hung up on him, et cetera.

That same week the FPCE had a meeting with the middle school, the teachers and principal. So when the principal got there, he knew some but not everyone. I'd only just arrived, as a parent of an [*incoming*] student, so I was new to him. And when I introduced myself I said, "I'm Mme Ben M'Rad and it's my husband who called you earlier this week." And immediately "Oh, well, excuse me, the other day I got carried away because I was so overwhelmed and everything. It's not your child's fault, but you know what it's like in a school with 600 unruly children." When two days earlier he'd sent my husband packing telling him he was entirely wrong, that if he'd done that it was his school, that he did what he wanted, as he wanted. And there, immediately, he changes his attitude and practically excuses himself, when if I'd gone to talk with him he'd have thrown me out too, because that's what he'd done with the other parents.

Interviewer: It's the status of parent?

That's why I was telling you we aren't taken seriously when we go as a simple parent. Even if what we say or do is good or bad, they won't judge us by our words, or our attitude, or what happened. They will judge us because we come from a housing project and we're at the bottom of the ladder and we finally got what we deserve. And that we should be happy that our children go to school and are being looked after.

Interviewer: You really felt that, this kind of contempt.

Oh yeah, yeah, yeah absolutely, and all the more so when you have foreign origins, uh, yeah origins. That does nothing to help.

This conflict with the middle school principal, which was not very serious in the greater scheme of things and could just as well have been forgotten (it happened six years before the interview), to the contrary holds particular meaning for our interviewee. She saw it as proof that the public school does not recognize parents like her as full-fledged parents, sees them as illegitimate parents from the projects, and that it manifests little concern with demonstrating the respect such parents expect.

Families experiencing a small social mobility hold a fragile position in the educational system, and this weakness is at the heart of tensions between them and the institution, feeding their feeling of being "mistreated" by the public school system. On one hand, Samira Ben M'Rad has a great deal of respect for discipline and the principal whose authority she appreciates: she sees him incarnating professionalism and concern for child safety, necessary conditions for school to go well. But she also suffers from the principal's hostility to the projects. He is a classic example of the ZEP middle school principal who is constantly struggling to hold off the housing projects and their pressures (from juvenile misbehavior to parents' sometimes violent reactions) to preserve the scholastic setting and its rules.[34] We imagine him caught up in his work when Samira's husband interrupts him to challenge his rough methods. He shuts him down, as he probably has to do often with parents from the projects protesting the institution, thus affirming "his" middle school's independence.

Samira Ben M'Rad shows a need to unburden herself to us, ourselves teachers. The interview situation prompts her to become a spontaneous spokesperson for subdivision inhabitants, who complain frequently about the school. The complaint goes hand in hand with a frustration and disenchantment common to parents who rose a bit socially and have high expectations of the institution. Those like Samira Ben M'Rad who are condemned to degraded school districts feel like they are victims of a school that does not acknowledge their position and makes them pay dearly with school segregation.

One Mother in the Thick of Scholastic and Cultural Competition

Now more than ever, schooling is a site of strong investment by households experiencing a small upward mobility. It is no coincidence that our three informants are involved in the school parents' association. For these women from an eminently stigmatized group, school is the place to build social excellence. Nadia Dhif illustrates this well: She is assiduously working to convert to legitimate norms and trying to get her children as far as she can from the projects' youth culture. She stakes her honor as a mother in her children's scholastic success, and her whole environment works in this direction, since subdivision families' reputations are largely evaluated according to the children's educational attainments and activities.

Unlike Karima Dhif and Samira Ben M'Rad, Nadia Dhif arranged for her children to avoid the devalued schools. She got a dispensation for her eldest son to enroll in Emile Zola by arguing that she needed him to attend the more readily accessible school so she could look after his food allergies, but she avoids putting down Victor Hugo where her sister's children go. Both of

Nadia's other sons were able to benefit from the dispensation, since the regulations allow siblings to stay together in the same school, and she became active in its FCPE. At the time of our first interview (in June 2005), the eldest was starting *lycée,* the second was going into the last year of middle school, and the youngest finishing primary. She described them as "very good students" and is very proud of their education. She knows that we are university faculty and seems to use the interview setting to vaunt her parenting work and demonstrate how well she meets the neighborhood's cultural and scholastic norms. She is not helpless in dealing with the school; as a university administrative employee, she knows at least part of the educational system from the inside. At the same time, neither she nor her husband went to a generalist *lycée,* and it is important to understand that this woman with a lowly BEP degree does not have an easy or natural relationship to scholastic institutions. Although she was not ignorant of how the educational system generally works when her children started middle school, she is far from mastering its codes with the same ease as parents who spent longer in school.

It seems conversation with other neighborhood mothers in the FCPE and commuter train is an important occasion for learning about parenting work and strategizing her children away from the allegedly bad classes. Nadia Dhif also buys guides to find her way through the maze of orientations and specializations. Before her son went to *lycée,* she referred to this kind of guide to see what his options were. These conversations and guides shape how Nadia Dhif makes the decisions that she transmits one way or another to her children. She thus wanted her two sons to take the German option in middle school. The eldest followed his mothers' wishes without much complaint, but the second one preferred Spanish. She did not oppose him ("There's no point in forcing children"), but she insisted they both take Latin as a way of getting them in with the school's best students, whichever language they chose.

These examples show the skills she acquired to maximize the return of her children's education and how she combines freedom and constraint in guiding their way. At the time, they seemed to accept their mother's choices, and even to anticipate them. The eldest son was aiming to study medicine and wanted to take a very selective specialization (life sciences) in his first year of *lycée* in preparation for the *bac S* (sciences). His younger brother aspires to become a lawyer. These choices are for a future that of course remains quite uncertain, but which reflect the children's socialization in their parents' social ambitions.

Nadia Dhif closely watches how her children use their time.[35] Her past as a child of immigrants in the projects led her to dread the futurelessness and carelessness she thinks characterize youth of her background. Her own past and family lead her to think that they need to be watched closely (she says boys "seek their freedom fast"). Her everyday vigilance demonstrates that she subscribes to the middle class scholastic morality that associates academic success with constant parental attention. As Nadia Dhif puts it, "it's no secret, if you want your children to succeed, you've got to be behind them." Her sons have to do their homework as soon as they come home from school, and their mother goes over it when she comes home from work. They are not allowed to watch television in the evening, not even the eldest, who has no favorable treatment. The family has a television in the kitchen and another in the living room, but none in the children's rooms. They can only watch it Sunday mornings before doing their homework. On this as so many other points, Nadia Dhif has adopted monitoring practices close to those of neighbors in the upper classes like her friend the doctor (married to a computing specialist). She tries to subtly direct her children toward lei-sure-time activities she regards the most highly, such as reading and music.

Her husband is a regular reader, and his books fill a bookcase in the living room. She does not read much herself for lack of time, but also probably for lack of having developed the habit. She explains that no one read in her childhood household, and she did not want to pass that on to her children, so she tried to give her children the taste for reading very young by reading them stories when they were little, then getting them to read every night. She lets them chose what they read, but goes to their rooms to confirm that they are indeed spending the allotted time on it (at least fifteen minutes for the youngest two). Nadia Dhif says that it is not a burden for her children, who say they love to read and regularly buy new books. It is usually escapist reading, often fantasy, written specifically for teenagers.

In addition to reading, the children do sports and play musical instru-ments. And here again, they were oriented toward the most socially selec-tive activities. The eldest plays tennis and piano. The middle one swims and is learning the cello. These musical and athletic choices reflect their moth-er's hope of seeing her children slip socially into the upper classes, but she arranges it so that they choose the activities on their own so that nothing is imposed.

Compared with Samira Ben M'Rad, she was quicker to demarcate a dis-tance from the children of nearby working-class families, especially those in the row houses, but without completely breaking with them. During school vacations Nadia Dhif's children went to a recreation center with many chil-dren from the row houses as well as the children of her doctor neighbor Mme Fayard (who also happens to be a neighborhood councilperson elected from the Socialist Party). Policemen run the center's activities, which reassures subdivision parents. And although Nadia's sons have more freedom during vacations, they cannot escape homework, because she buys them vacation workbooks and makes them work an hour every morning.

During the school year, Sunday morning is devoted to review work, which her children accept with more or less enthusiasm. At the time of one interview, which took place during the last week of school, she and her eldest son were at odds because the preceding Sunday he had not wanted to study because he was impatient to play soccer with his father in La Courneuve. In punishment, she forbade him from going, which was severe given how much he enjoys these outings. This episode deserves attention because it is telling of the tensions in the couple and family relations arising from the adoption of new parenting practices. Nadia readily accepts her husband taking the children to play soccer in her old neighborhood, and entirely understands how much he enjoys seeing his two best childhood friends, his brothers, and his nephews. At the same time, Sunday morning activities are subject to competition between them, the father-children pickup game versus the hours their mother spends spurring them on in their studies.

Nadia Dhif has the reputation of being "too strict" in her husband's family. Although she gets along well with her sisters-in-law in La Courneuve, she avoids controversial subjects (especially school and child-rearing) when they talk. Their children have had very irregular educations, and several of them (mostly boys) left school early at the secondary (BEP) level. Nadia's sisters-in-law are much more flexible when it comes to television, going out, and who their children hang out with. Visits to La Courneuve are tense for Nadia, who is torn between genuine pleasure in seeing people she likes and a wariness of who they are socially. She has trouble understanding her sons' fascination for project life.

This detailed analysis of the social trajectories of Samira Ben M'Rad and Nadia and Karima Dhif highlights three points. One is that social mobility is still possible for households that come from the disadvantaged fractions of the working classes living in big public housing projects today. These three interviewees found in themselves and their surroundings the resources needed to socially pull themselves up a little. The analysis especially showed that public employment had allowed them to find steady jobs and think about the future more optimistically. But the social and economic conditions were less favorable for them than for the row-house pioneers, and the rise of their trajectories seems slower and will probably end up being less steep: the social horizon is not as open as it was in the 1960s, and career possibilities are less present in their thoughts than they may have been for households in the prosperous postwar decades. In addition, this chapter only featured women's accounts, and women with children at that: their occupational mobility remains lower than other categories of the working population.

Second, when children of the projects buy a house, it clearly signifies a break with the deteriorated living conditions of housing projects and perhaps even a rejection of the negative image of their group of origin. They felt that moving into a housing development made them "like everyone else" and gave them the resources of respectability. The considerable attention devoted to their children's educations is the corollary: they now pursue their household's promotion through them, and part of their social honor also depends on them.

But the satisfaction they feel in having successfully left the housing projects and the hopes they have for their offspring are counterbalanced by changes in the neighborhood's population—the possibility that it might become another neighborhood of downward mobility and the risk that their children might be pulled down. These threats, real or feared, make them to want to withdraw from their immediate environments, especially by pulling their children from schools with poor reputations. In interviews, they express anxieties unknown to the row-house pioneers, or at least not to the same extent. Beyond transformations in the neighborhood's social composition, the increasingly challenging conditions for access to steady skilled jobs increase young parents' anxiety. The social and occupational promotion these women experienced opened new possibilities, but their ascendant paths are not enough for them to feel safe from a social fall. To the contrary, their social trajectories' modesty sometimes seems to predispose them to reject lower social categories whose hierarchical proximity intensifies their feelings of having a weak hold on their social status. Yet by and large, the women in this chapter are not very different from other neighborhood parents: their parenting practices and attitudes about the neighborhood are found in other little-middles. Children of the preceding generation of arrivals, the "suburban youth" of our study, are socialized under particular tensions that are probably unique to this social stratum, which the following chapter explores in detail.

NOTES

1. In 2003, 79 percent of long-term entries were granted for family reasons, as opposed to only 5 percent for employment, see INSEE, *Les immigrés en France* (Paris, 2005).
2. In 1968, three quarters of immigrants in France were from elsewhere in Europe, and 20 percent were from North Africa. In 1990, 50 percent were from Europe, and 36 percent from Africa (30 percent from North Africa and 6 percent from elsewhere on the continent). In 2008, 42 percent were from Africa, 38 percent from Europe, and the percentage from elsewhere (Asia, the Americas) rising, see INSEE, *Immigrés et descendants d'immigrés en France* (Paris, 2012). The proportion of foreign-born residents in the region Ile-de-France was 12.4 percent in 2006, double the national average, and by 2008, it was 17 percent with concentrations in areas like Seine-St-Denis, the department bordering Gonesse, one quarter immigrant.
3. Although this concerned 38 percent of such households from 1979 to 1984, it only concerned 28 percent in 1997–2002, despite the introduction of a new home acquisition policy with interest-free loans in October 1995. See T Debrand and C Taffin,

"Les facteurs structurels et conjoncturels de la mobilité résidentielle depuis 20 ans," *Économie et statistiques* 381-82 (2005): 125-46.

4. This breaks down into 13 percent in new neighborhoods and 29 percent in rural or periurban areas. See the 2005 ONZUS (National ZUS Observatory) annual report (ONZUS, *Rapport de l'Observatoire des zones urbaines sensibles* [Paris, 2005]), especially pages 116-53.

5. The Organisation for Economic Co-operation and Development (OCDE) studies evaluating educational systems in sixty countries (PISA studies) indicate that France is one of the most sensitive to sociocultural differences and has an especially significant gap between very good and very poor students that has been worsening since 2000; see "France. PISA 2012: Faits Marquants," (Paris, 2013, http://www.oecd.org/france/PISA-2012-results-france.pdf).

6. On the construction of these new subdivisions since the early 1990s, see the introduction. About 200 houses were built by various developers or owners who bought land and had a house built for themselves.

7. Lahire, *La Culture des individus*; B Lahire, "The Individual and the Mixing of Genres: Cultural Dissonance and Self-Distinction," *Poetics* 36 (2008): 166-88.

8. For examples from France, see E Santelli, *La mobilité sociale dans l'immigration, itinéraires de réussite des enfants d'origine algérienne* (Toulouse, 2001), and S Laacher, *L'institution scolaire et ses miracles* (Paris, 2005).

9. Lahire, *La Culture des individus*, 417.

10. In 1999, the active population of the New Poplars counted 12.1 percent *cadres* and 24.8 percent midlevel employees, in contrast with 7.6 percent and 22.6 percent in all of Gonesse.

11. In 1996 and 2000, only 12 and 13 percent of those buying their first home were under age thirty. See M Daubresse, "La reprise de l'accession à la propriété," *INSEE Première* 913 (2003): 1-4.

12. Moreover, in the early 1980s, children of Algerian immigrants were unambiguously overrepresented in what was then called "special education," in both primary and middle school. See the LeBon-Marangé report for the Ministry of Labor (J Marangé and A Lebon, *L'insertion professionnelle des enfants d'immigrés* (Paris, 1982).

13. On the generations of immigrants' children, see S Beaud and O Masclet, "Des 'marcheurs' de 1983 aux 'émeutiers' de 2005. Deux générations sociales d'enfants d'immigrés," *Annales* 4 (2006).

14. As seen later, Karima Dhif, born in 1969, has an intermediate position between this generation and the "housing project generation," as unemployment was already high by the time she entered the job market.

15. For an analysis of the tensions between studies and marriage, see M Gouirir, "Ouled el kharij: les enfants de l'étranger. Socialisation et trajectoires familiales d'enfants d'ouvriers marocains immigrés en France" (PhD diss., Université Paris-X Nanterre, 1997).

16. N Guenif-Souilamas, *Des beurettes aux descendantes d'immigrants nord-africains* (Paris, 1999).

17. Schwartz, *Le monde privé des ouviers*, especially chapter 3.

18. G Noiriel, *The French Melting Pot: Immigration, Citizenship, and National Identity*, trans. G De Laforcade (Minneapolis, MN, 1996).

19. A public policy announced in 1985 pressed for a dramatic increase in students passing the *baccalauréat*, aiming for 80 percent. Stéphane Beaud analyzed the resulting

flooding of the school system and its social consequences in his book *80 % au bac...
et après? Les enfants de la démocratisation scolaire* (Paris, 2003).

20. The French employment rate for women (the percentage of women twenty-five to
forty-nine who are employed or seeking work) is around 85 percent. One reason
for this relatively high rate is that child care is provided for free by the public school
system from age three (or two in some towns).

21. O Schwartz, *Le monde privé des ouvriers*, 225.

22. S Gollac, "La fonction publique: une voie de promotion sociale pour les enfants des
classes populaires?" *Sociétés contemporaines* 58 (2005): 41–64.

23. For an overview of one of these neighborhoods and the challenges facing its residents, see D Garbin and G Millington, "Territorial Stigma and the Politics of Resistance in a Parisian Banlieue: La Courneuve and Beyond," *Urban Studies* 49, no. 10
(2012): 2067–83.

24. See L Wirth, *The Ghetto* (Chicago, 1928), and R Park, *Race and Culture* (Glencoe,
IL, 1950).

25. On boys' attachment to the neighborhood in France, see S Beaud and Y Amrani,
Pays de malheur! Un jeune de cité écrit à un sociologue (Paris, 2005), and for a comparable example from the United States, Pattillo-McCoy, *Black Picket Fences*.

26. P Cuturello, *Dialogues de propriétaires. De comment le devenir à comment le rester,
deux décennies de stratégies d'accession à la propriété du logement (1978–1995)*, report
funded by the Ministry of Equipment (Paris, 1997), 84.

27. P Bourdieu et al., "Un placement de père de famille. La maison individuelle: spécificité du produit et logique du champ de reproduction," *Actes de la recherche en sciences sociales* 81–82 (1990): 6–33; for a comparable analysis from the United States
see Townsend, *The Package Deal*.

28. O Schwartz has observed that homeownership has given the secure fractions of
modest wage-earners "skilled social forms" that distance them a little further from
the classic working classes; "*La notion de 'classes populaires'*" (HDR thesis, Université de Versailles-Saint-Quentin-en-Yvelines, 1998).

29. On these institutions' influence on the habitus of working-class youth, see Schwartz,
"La notion de classes populaires," 147–53.

30. In her book *Black Picket Fences*, Pattillo-McCoy noted a comparable phenomenon
in the Chicago suburb of Groveland.

31. Social and ethnic segregation in middle school leads to significant differences in scholastic results; G Felouzis, "La ségrégation ethnique au collège et ses conséquences,"
Revue française de sociologie 44 (2003): 413–47.

32. A Van Zanten, *L'école de la périphérie. Scolarité et ségrégation en banlieue* (Paris,
2001), 101.

33. In French middle schools, students remain in the same classroom with the same
classmates, as in primary school; these groups are sometimes formed around a slight
specialization, called an "option," meaning they will spend a little more time on that
subject than children in other class groups. As we see in this chapter and elsewhere
in the book, parents use the options system in various ways to guide their children's
social and scholastic lives. One classic tactic is getting a child into the Latin or Ger-
man-language option as a stepping-stone on the path to generalist *lycée* and university; see A van Zanten, *Choisir son école. Stratégies familiales et médiations locales*
(Paris, 2009).

34. For testimony from a ZEP principal, see G Balazs and A Sayad, "Institutional Violence," in *The Weight of the World*, ed. P Bourdieu et al., trans. P Ferguson et al. (Stanford, CA, 1999), 492–506.
35. Nadia Dhif's practices controlling her children's studies and extracurricular activities are similar to those of parents of the 1980s subdivisions, explained in the next chapter, although hers go farther and are more consistent.

SUBURBAN YOUTH

We have seen the extent to which child-rearing and children's futures have been central to homeownership plans. Child-rearing practices have long provided insight into the relationship between the middle and working classes and the social mobility of families. In France schooling has come to be the focus of such analysis, and this tendency is especially strong in urban and educational sociology, which are often intertwined. The practices J-C Chamboredon and M Lemaire found in new housing projects in the 1970s[1]—middle-class families seeking distinction and morally condemning teenagers from the working-class families with whom they shared residential space—indeed worsened into stronger avoidance practices. Ultimately they manifest in residential mobility away from housing project neighborhoods or, if they stay, strict supervision of child sociability and educational strategies.

Children and teens' sociability may be controlled by family members or neighboring families with shared affinities, and may also be supported by associations offering supervised sports or cultural activities that are rarely attended by young people from working-class families.[2] Scholastic strategies may consist of flight from the neighborhood's assigned public primary or middle school district, requiring either a dispensation[3] to enroll children in other districts' public schools with better reputations or opting for private schools, usually meaning a Roman Catholic education.[4] Children can also be segregated within the public school system,[5] by guiding them toward the school's more selective classes through the choice of elective options that confer distinction (especially German and Latin).[6]

Although numerous studies analyze the sociability and trajectories of young people from the projects or their families' child-rearing and scholastic strategies, very few have turned the same kind of attention to young people growing up in the suburbs, as though neighborhoods of single-family homes are not just as influential on juvenile socialization. In fact, the material and social space of residential streets and subdivisions, as well as living in a single-family house, facilitate certain practices guiding juvenile sociability. The arrival of families with children of similar ages, often within a short time of each other, favors the establishment of neighborly forms of sociability in which children's activities occupy an important place. Juvenile socialization is closely connected to specific types of housing found in subdivisions, especially those designed around a common street or little square, as in the Poplars.

In the preceding chapters, we presented the parenting practices and concerns of several generations of parents in the Poplars, from the row-house pioneers to the families who moved in from a housing project. Now we turn to the viewpoint of the young people who grew up and live in the neighborhood, to see how they relate to their parents, their educations, their friendship networks, and their extracurricular activities. Although there is considerable sociological work on youth from the projects and how they are raised, little has addressed suburban youth growing up in housing developments in a comparable way. Yet subdivision streets' material and social spaces and living in a single-family home lend themselves to particular forms of youth socialization. To understand the processes at work in the construction of these adolescents' social identity, we must also take account of their self-perceptions compared with other social groups.

Analysis in this chapter focuses on a group of neighbors: three sibling groups who grew up on the same little cul-de-sac of one of the subdivisions built in the early 1980s named Partridge Terrace. Their parents were young couples with small children when they moved in; they held mid-level jobs, and a few were *cadres*. They predominantly have working-class backgrounds, and there are a fair number of immigrants among them. Of the Poplars's neighborhoods, Partridge Terrace ranks in the middle in terms of standing and price, putting it "between the Turks and the golf" as one resident put it—between the Old Poplars row houses and the New Poplars houses built in the 1990s and 2000s.

As we described in the introduction, these single-family homes, clustered into a village-style subdivision, were built along the fields behind the row houses in the early 1980s, and in turn saw more imposing new houses built on these fields that would henceforth mark the Poplars's boundary with farmland. The subdivision is composed of nine so-called terraces in the form of cul-de-sacs of ten to fifteen houses. The houses are freestanding or duplex, and usually have two stories and three or four bedrooms in a surface area of 100 square meters, with a 350- to 600-square-meter yard.

A happy coincidence led us to study Partridge Terrace, when one of us encountered a former student, Thomas Loiseau, on the street in the Poplars. Thomas was amused and surprised to see a "prof in Gonesse." After a long interview, he put the research team[7] in contact with his friends on the same street, and we kept in touch until 2007. Nearly everyone in this group of neighborhood friends was in a phase of occupational and residential transition. They were twenty to twenty-five years old when we met in 2004–5, and were still in school or had just finished and were looking for work. All but one (living and working in a neighboring town) still lived on Partridge Terrace, allowing us to comprehend the persistence of their neighborhood ties and the uncertainty of their social and career futures. Although their accounts of their childhood and teenage years were largely reconstructed approximations, they provide many specific indicators of their educational practices and activities. They also reveal commonalities and little differences in what appear to be very similar parenting practices.

GROWING UP IN A HOUSING DEVELOPMENT

The three sibling groups we met are surprisingly close in age: Marilyne and Thomas Loiseau were born in 1979 and 1981, and their sister in 1988; Stéphanie, Agnès, and Julien Bensoussan were born in 1979, 1981, and 1986; Delphine and Cédric Dumoulin were born in 1981 and 1985, and their little brother in 1995. Their parents all bought new houses from a developer that had built them on speculation between 1984 and 1986. They all grew up around the little circle of the cul-du-sac and speak readily of what seems to have been a happy time. Indeed, the little circle offered a physical and social setting that fostered an in-group feeling they all greatly appreciated.

The Little Circle

The "little circle" came up in all the interviews: their private house-lined street in the middle of the subdivision. The circle is where they formed ties with their "old buddies," as Thomas Loiseau called them. Each mentioned neighbors of the same age who had been, and sometimes still were, their best friends: Marilyne, Stéphanie, and two other girls of the same age (born in 1979) were inseparable until *lycée*; Thomas still had strong ties with a neighborhood family with three sons, one his age; Cédric and Julien were close throughout middle school. The circle was also a physical space for play, especially for bicycling and playing soccer. The older ones like Thomas also mentioned its surroundings, like the path leading to adjacent subdivisions or the cornfields behind the houses that extended the area of play until the New Poplars's more recent subdivisions were built there.

The strength of neighborhood friendships, which have lasted into adult-hood, is largely due to the similarity of family situations when they moved in and the subdivision's layout. The houses are placed very close to each other around the open circle, set off by low hedges that lend themselves to so-ciability. The design facilitated collective parental oversight, and the adults had common rules: children were not allowed to ride their bikes outside the little circle or take them on the "big street." Their children's memories also show that their play was closely related to their parents' social prac-tices: Thomas and Stéphanie tell how "the parents" took turns caring for the grass on the circle and the footpaths connecting it to adjacent circles, invited each other to dinner or "for drinks," and had little cookouts and parties in common spaces. Invitations between couples were additional occasions for children to see each other in the evening.

This sociability between newly arrived couples in the subdivision was largely contingent on their homologous family situations. Although this ap-parent similarity may mask their socioeconomic diversity, it is nonetheless rooted in comparable social trajectories, as with the row-house pioneers.

And the neighborhood is indeed diverse when it comes to occupation—laborers, a small business-owner, private- and public-sector employees and midlevel occupations, and *cadres* all regularly interact here. The neighbors nonetheless share working-class backgrounds and the experience of social ascension manifest in property ownership in the subdivision. Just like the row-house inhabitants twenty years their senior, they are also little-middles.

But as we saw in the introduction (and as detailed in table 3.1), these little-middles of the 1980s subdivisions are unlike those who moved into the

TABLE 3.1. Social characteristics of Partridge Terrace homeowners at time of study

Family (going around the circle)	Date of arrival; where moved from	Father's occupation	Mother's occupation	Biographical information, migration	Children
Bensoussan (younger)	1986, from an apartment building in Gonesse	Computer specialist in a bank	Primary school teacher in neighboring town	Both from Jewish families who came from Algeria in 1962	Stéphanie (1979), Agnès (1981), Julien (1986)
Dulac	Around 1985–1986	"*Cadre*"	"*Cadre*"		A daughter (1979?)
Georges	Around 1985	Air conditioning technician	Hospital administrator	Father from Réunion	3 sons, born in 1978, 1981, 1982
Bensoussan (elder)	1986, from the Cité du Nord	Retired pharmacy assistant	Retired, no occupation	Parents of M. Bensoussan, living in the first house; Algerian Jewish immigrants	Son lives on same street

Ponton	Around 1985–1986	Sporting goods salesman	Secretary in Gonesse	"French"	At least one daughter (1981)
Bourreau	Around 1996		No occupation	"French"	At least one daughter (1988?)
Dumoulin	1985, from a southern Parisian *banlieue*	Computing engineer	Employee in a management division	M. Dumoulin from Martinique	Delphine (1981), Cédric (1985), Jean (1994)
Loiseau	1984, from an HLM in a neighboring town	*Brigadier-chef* in the national police	Secretary in the Ministry of Justice, then midlevel *cadre* in a prison personnel division	Migrants from Martinique; returned there to live in 2000	Marilyne (1979), Thomas (1981), daughter (1988)
Boucher	1991, from a row house	Retired accountant	Retired former laboratory worker then librarian	Grew up in a neighboring town; her parents were small shopkeepers and his father in the national police	Two sons over forty live with them; another is a letter carrier on health leave. One daughter lives elsewhere.
Lepetit	Around 1985–1986	"Cop"	Load handler in Gonesse	"French"	At least one child
Kaldey	1990	Tailor	No occupation	Chaldean	Many children, including Joseph around 1981.
Amar	Around 1985–1986	Home-based business card business		"French Jews" from Morocco	Several children, including Sophie (1979)
Vim		Works at Charles de Gaulle airport	Employee of Parisian airport system	"Chinese"	
Flament		Retired	Retired	Come from the Nord Pas de Calais region of France	
Mazouz		Works for the Parisian airport system	No occupation	"Franco-Tunesian"	One daughter (1981), two sons (one in *lycée*)
Bout	Very recent			From Martinique	

Source: Interviews
Words in quotes are terms taken from interviews with informants describing former neighbors, which we were unable to further clarify with the people in question.

row houses in the 1960s and more closely resemble the families who relo-
cated from housing projects. Many of them have lived in publicly subsidized
HLM housing projects, and a significant number of them have experienced
immigration: among the first arrivals, four couples have at least one member from an overseas French department or territory (the French Antilles,
Réunion) and three are Jewish families from the Maghreb who migrated in
the 1960s, and families from Tunisia, China, and Turkey moved in later. In
addition, the percentage of public employees is very high, and unlike their
predecessors in the row houses, most of them pursued secondary studies, in
some cases rather far.

Parents of young adults living on Partridge Terrace thus all have trajectories characterized by upward mobility related to educational attainment or
steady public sector employment with internal promotion, and by migration
(from an overseas French department or territory or Algeria) followed by a
transitional period in an HLM in the Parisian periphery. This relative social
proximity was central to friendships forming between their children, as seen
in the three sibling groups we met.

> M. Bensoussan, father of Stéphanie, Agnès, and Julien, is a low-level computing
> specialist, and Mme Bensoussan is a schoolteacher in a neighboring predominantly
> working-class town. Both are the children of Jewish Algerian parents who moved re-
> spectively to Gonesse's Cité du Nord and Sarcelles in 1962. M. Bensoussan's father was
> a pharmaceutical assistant and his mother a housewife. The young couple had a house
> built at Partridge Terrace and left the Cité du Nord in 1986.
>
> Marilyne and Thomas Loiseau's parents are both from farming families in Mart-
> inique, a background where higher education was unusual. Both were schooled
> through middle school. He was a *brigadier-chef* in the police, where he started out as
> a patrolman, and she was a civil servant, an administrative employee in the Ministry
> of Justice, after having held temporary positions in a variety of agencies. They lived in
> an HLM (like those of their siblings who also migrated) before having a house built.
>
> M. Dumoulin, Delphine and Cédric's father, was also in computing, but as an engi-
> neer working for a subsidiary of AT&T. Mme Dumoulin was an employee in Renault's
> management services. Their families lived in the Parisian periphery and in Marti-
> nique, where M. Dumoulin is from.

Local Educational Strategies and Supervised Leisure-Time Activities

All of the children went to public schools until *lycée*, at which point only the
Dumoulins went to private school. They were districted for the Victor Hugo
Primary School nearest the row houses, now poorly reputed for the significant presence of Chaldean children. The distinction with the more respected
Emile Zola school was not as strong when they were children, but according
to Thomas Loiseau, fear of a "lower level" prompted his father to ask the
city council for a "little dispensation" so he and his elder sister could go to

Zola. The Dumoulin parents must have shared the same concern, because they also put their children in Zola school. The Bensoussan children went to their assigned school, Victor Hugo, perhaps because their mother (a school-teacher) did not want to go against the school district map.

The older children found themselves in the same classes in middle school thanks to a strategy their parents figured out: they enrolled the children in the sports option. This trick was based on the more common strategy of choosing a foreign language option, but seemed to better suit their children, who were not drawn to the "smart kid" classes: Thomas, for example, re-fused to pick German as his main foreign language because he did not want to be "with the smart kids." His attitude is reminiscent of that of Samira Ben M'Rad's son in chapter 2, who did not want to go to private school because it was full of "bourges" (bourgeois); it stems from a refusal to adopt a strategy of distinction and their attachment to an intermediate social position.

The sports option class was a little more supervised and had a lower en-rollment than other options, with a stable composition from year to year. The students had more time scheduled for sports, entered competitions, and took sport-related trips (like skiing). It was not the most elitist strat-egy, probably because many of the parents had low educational capital (the Loiseau parents quit school late in middle school, for example). But the sport option class, which did offer good educational conditions, was an ef-fective way to keep neighborhood children together, allowing Marilyne and Stéphanie, then Thomas and Agnès, to be in class together. They could walk to school and back with other neighboring classmates, which, as Thomas put it, "was a good deal" for subdivision middle-schoolers.

The choice of this option also reflects the prominence of sports in their scholastic and extracurricular activities. Indeed, beyond backing their chil-dren's schooling, parents on the circle all encouraged their children to take on several organized activities, so all did at least one club-based athletic activity from primary school until lycée, and sometimes beyond: tennis (Thomas, Ju-lien, Delphine, Cédric), basketball (Stéphanie, Agnès), dance and gymnas-tics (Marilyne), soccer and judo (Thomas). Delphine and Cédric's youngest brother, age ten, does horseback riding. Many also studied music at the Gonesse Music School or the conservatory in the neighboring town: violin (Marilyne, Stéphanie), piano (Delphine), guitar (Thomas, Cédric).

Parents encouraged their children to take up rather socially selective su-pervised activities (classical music, tennis, horseback riding, etc.) that were very time-consuming (sports practice followed by matches, music theory classes, musical practice, and concerts) and also competitive, with peri-odic evaluations. They made a considerable investment so that their teens could pursue these activities. They did not coach or preside clubs like some row-house pioneers did for the soccer and basketball clubs, but this does not mean they thought any less of these socializing activities. M. Loiseau, a policeman who often worked evenings, drove his children to their activities around Gonesse or neighboring towns during the week.

The parents' chosen educational strategy, typified by the sports option, could be qualified as relaxed. The Loiseaus continued their nonelitist bent in educational strategies when they moved back to Martinique just as Thomas was starting a *classe préparatoire,* two years of intense study for the entrance exam to a highly selective public university (*grande école*)—their departure could have been rather destabilizing for him at a time of considerable stress. He thought that his parents were still not very "clear" on how to navigate the educational system—for example, he first learned of *classe préparatoire* in his last year of *lycée,* from a teacher instead of his parents. But behind these more or less well-informed educational strategies remained a concern for assuring their children's academic success. They could also turn strict when children failed in school, as an example from the Dumoulins shows. When Delphine had to repeat her first year at the Gonesse public *lycée,* her parents sent her to a private boarding school in Normandy, near an aunt; likewise for her brother Cédric when he had to repeat his second year. And these educational strategies were accompanied by careful supervision of extracurricular activities, which also serves to control socialization.

We measure the relative effectiveness of parental supervision by the fact that their children's social circles continued to be largely based in the Poplars subdivisions and vicinity. The subdivisions thus seem to be the setting for a specific youth social life, deeply rooted in family homes.

Not Going Out Much, and the Subdivision's Appeal

The young neighbors around the Terrace were direct about their parents' control over going out during adolescence. In middle school, Thomas said, "I was young and my parents clamped down on me." He could only go to the closest movie theater, in the Cité du Nord. In *lycée,* he got to know Paris a bit, where he had only previously gone to see the dentist: he would go to the Châtelet shopping district with friends or "a girl" to "grab some Greek [*sandwiches*], go to the movies." But as he explained, these outings were rare because his parents did not let him go out often, and he had no pocket money.

Although some did imply these restrictions were a burden, none were particularly resentful of it. Actually, the draw of Paris does not seem to have been very strong when they were in *lycée,* and was focused more on shopping than cultural institutions. Marilyne mentioned "little trips to Paris, quick, on Saturday afternoons to go clothes shopping" or to the movies. Agnès began going to Paris for "crêpe trips" to Montmartre, but she did not hang around long. Thomas is the only one to have pursued his studies there, since the others preferred universities closer to home. He liked the Latin Quarter when he was a student, but not before, and always with a certain reserve. Only Julien, one of the youngest, explained that he goes to Paris "whenever the opportunity arises": "If you want to do anything interesting you've gotta go to Paris, not here." Interestingly, Cédric's girlfriend Laeticia (who he met in Normandy and was living with him and his parents in Gonesse) was the only one to say she dreamed of studying in Paris, "ever since I was little."

If exploring the capital (especially for cultural activities like museums, theater, or concerts) was not among neighborhood youths' favorite pastimes, this is likely because their parents, some with limited educations and most from working-class backgrounds, did not encourage them to do so or set an example by taking such cultivated excursions themselves. Their families did not seem to have very high aspirations to legitimate cultural appropriation, accounting for some of their children's disinterest in Paris.

So Paris only attracted these suburban youth for "quick little trips," and Gonesse—or more specifically its subdivisions—was their social hub throughout *lycée* and university. Thomas spent a lot of time with his neighbors, and parental restrictions do not seem to have been too frustrating. Marilyne always really liked spending evenings with her friends in Gonesse or going to parties, even if she "had to fight" over curfew. Stéphanie says she always preferred spending evenings with friends instead of big parties or nightclubs. They both said they had always spent a lot of time at one another's houses, talking and swapping the latest *lycée* or neighborhood gossip, and they would arrange it so one of their parents would pick them both up, which also helped them get parents' permission to do things: once again, indirectly, neighborly friendships structured social life.

Agnès described herself as something of a homebody; she spent a lot of time watching television at home or friends' houses (despite efforts to limit TV time when she was in middle school) and read occasionally. Julien and Cédric, the youngest boys, mentioned afternoons and evenings playing Play-station or watching soccer on TV with neighborhood friends, sometimes including Thomas. Family homes thus provided a space for adolescent and young adult sociability: parents seem to have tolerated and even welcomed their children's friends in their homes, and their children did not seem to want to cut themselves off or escape their parents. That Cédric and his girlfriend live in his parents' house is a prime example.

And yet the distance from Paris and the taste for spending time "at each others' places" in the subdivision does not mean that *lycée* and university students did not leave their immediate surroundings. The importance of drivers' licenses testifies to this, as a necessity for moving around without relying on buses or commuter trains heading to Paris or northward. After closely controlling their movement throughout adolescence, their parents then encouraged and helped them to get their licenses when they came of age. In addition to freeing parents from a certain amount of shuttling from place to place, the car is also more comforting than public transportation because it reduces contact between their children and other young people that could lead to aggressive encounters or bad social influences.

So, Agnès related that her big sister Stéphanie booked her hours of driving practice before turning driving-age so that she could get her license only five days after turning eighteen. Agnès got hers a month after coming of age herself, and their younger bother has his license, too. And once they had their licenses, their parents regularly let them drive their cars, as Marilyne and Thomas's parents did, too. Only the Dumoulin siblings, who were in Normandy through the end of *lycée*, had not learned to drive: their parents reproach them for it, so they are preparing for the test. Having a license indeed makes it easier to go to the university, the sports club, shopping, neighboring towns, and job interviews—but it is rarely used to go into Paris.

AMBIVALENT RELATIONS WITH YOUTH
FROM THE HOUSING PROJECTS

Relations with youth from the Cité du Nord and Cité du Sud was a recurring theme in interviews, as both of the housing projects are near the Poplars, their children partly attend the same middle schools, and they go to the same *lycée*. This relationship is a rather distant one, but subject to some ambivalence as well: although fear of violence between and with project youth dominates, this fear is sometimes mitigated by forms of social proximity between young residents of the urban periphery.

Close Neighbors with Limited Contact Outside of School

The Poplars borders the Cité du Nord, and the Cité du Sud is only a ten-minute walk away. They have their own primary schools, but until 1994, there was only one middle school for both the Poplars and the Cité du Nord. The neighborhood's older children went there: Marilyne and Stéphanie spent all four years there, and Thomas and Agnès the first two years. The old middle school was demolished and replaced with one for students from the Poplars and the Cité du Nord (Gérard-Philippe) and another for students from the Poplars, another development, and the Cité du Sud (Jacques Prévert, where subdivision children took the sports option). This is where they first met children from the projects, and to a lesser extent they maintained contact through *lycée,* primarily outside of school. The only students from the projects that attend the general *lycée,* facing the Cité du Sud and also built in 1994, are the ones that survive what Thomas called the "social creaming" process, but there are a lot of students from developments of single-family homes in neighboring towns. Middle school is thus the main period when suburban youngsters come into contact with their peers from the projects, with whom they have little previous contact.

The pastimes and social lives of subdivision children had given them few opportunities to meet children from HLM neighborhoods. They attended different primary schools, play was limited to the subdivision, and they had different extracurricular activities. Although the Cité du Nord's social center offered cultural activities, no one from the Terrace went there, preferring to study classical music at the conservatory or the music school.

Not even their athletic activities put them in contact with adolescents from adjacent neighborhoods. The tennis and basketball clubs trained in Gonesse center or other towns. There were impromptu soccer matches in the subdivisions' circles or sometimes Gonesse stadium, which has several fields. Julien and Cédric would meet up there with *lycée* friends, who were mostly from a neighboring town predominated by single-family housing. They only rarely played with *lycée* classmates from the projects or boys from the row houses, despite their proximity. Boys who frequented the recreation center, mostly from the row houses and often of Chaldean origin, played soccer in a free and informal style quite different from regulated club play. They usually played on a lot beside the gym where the boys living on the circles a few hundred meters away never went.

Because encounters with project or even row-house children before middle school and through extracurricular activities were rare, Terrace youths' friendships dating back to middle school or *lycée* were almost exclusively with children from adjacent subdivisions. For example, Marilyne and Stéphanie had a group of friends who were all neighbors, composed of four girls the same age from the circle, and some *lycée* friends from other developments in Gonesse or nearby. Thomas evoked "old buddies" from the circle and environs. Delphine introduced her two best friends from middle school and *lycée*—they are not from the circle, but one lived on a neighboring circle and the other in another Poplars subdivision. The two youngest, Julien and Cédric, were friends in middle school and mentioned other boys from the Poplars, especially the better-off subdivisions built in the 1990s by the developers Kaufman and Broad; their close friends lived in the recent subdivisions or adjacent neighborhoods, not in the projects or row houses. Only Julien, who went to Victor Hugo Primary School, mentioned old friends from these parts of the neighborhood and explained that going to another middle school and pursuing his studies cut him off from his row-house friends, especially Chaldean ones: "Some of them stopped going to school ... yeah. Well, the ones who live here, they pretty much did [the science *baccalauréat*]. In the row houses, they go for CAPs," lower-level diplomas certifying vocational training.

There is a clear compartmentalization process distancing neighborhood youth from those of the projects: if it began with differences in education and attention to extracurricular activities, it was reinforced in middle school through exposure to a great social distance, an experience they expressed by repeatedly decrying violent relations among youth from the projects, and between them and their suburbanite peers.

Fear of Violence and Practices That Create Distance

"Corner boys" and "college boys," to borrow the terms WF Whyte used to oppose gang youth and students,[8] do take the same classes for a few years, mostly in middle school. *Lycée*-aged, they mainly see each other around the building, which borders the Cité du Sud. Young Terrace residents' accounts of secondary schooling were heavily marked by references to violence between project youth (especially boys) and the toughest ones' exploits. These stories, somewhat stereotypical, may have come from the desire to teach a thing or two to the interviewers (perceived as Parisian students or teachers), and to show with a bit of bravado that they had personally suffered from a violent environment. But it is striking to see that the narrative of fear of aggressive encounters ultimately overwhelms mention of other relationships with project youth.

Every interviewee had a shocking tale from middle school, especially those who attended Gérard Philippe. Thomas laughingly recounted how surprised he was to find himself among students from the vocational *lycée* who were "seventeen to eighteen years old," and it was the "Far West," like "at the movies." He described the constant racket in his classroom his last year in middle school, where he "didn't work, not even once," and the spectacular forms of "shady dealings between the neighborhoods":

> Thomas: In middle school, I was small, but there was, like, a fight every day. A monitor got stabbed, there were guys who came with guns, with blanks, lead shot. They came in like that because they were looking for a guy, and they were shooting.

Agnès related the ambiance by describing the groups of boys who loitered outside the *lycée* and their latent aggressiveness.

> Agnès: They were always there, always at the middle school exit, the *lycée* exit, always hitting on girls, always giving people a hard time, they were always there.... The *lycée* was directly facing the Cité du Sud, they were under the breezeway watching, like, all the time.
> Interviewer: Did they do anything in particular or were they just there, just a presence?

Agnès: No, they were a presence, like monitors, who watched over the exit, watching what was happening.... It was more to say "there's a project across the way, watch out."

She went into greater detail when describing an episode when the Cité du Nord school bus was attacked by youth from the Cité du Sud:

Agnès: There is one story that marked me. It was 5:30, when *lycée* let out.... It must have been my second first year [*she repeated a year*], there was the Cité du Sud, too, and they came out with knives, all kinds of stuff, anything they could lay their hands on, rocks.... They started throwing rocks, empty bottles, all kinds of stuff at the Cité du Nord busses—the Cité du Nord is kind of far away.... And then everyone was running all over, it made a serious impression.... because everyone was there, girls...
Interviewer: Some girls got attacked?
Agnès: No, not particularly, it was ... like a warning, but it wasn't the people there who were the target; it was more to tell them, "You're on our ground, so you better watch out."

While Thomas and Agnès stuck to these rather general accounts of the ambiance and episodes that marked their generations' collective memory, Stéphanie Bensoussan and Cédric and Delphine Dumoulin spoke of aggressive situations and the resulting fear in a much more personal register. With little variation, they mentioned the same events (the boy from the projects who shot a gun in middle school "because of something to do with a scooter," the Cité du Sud's bus attack in front of the *lycée*), as well as the everyday strain of feeling afraid in the most ordinary of situations. This fear for them was associated with temporary departures from the neighborhood.

As we saw earlier, Cédric and Delphine completed secondary schooling at boarding school. Although both said this choice was motivated by their academic difficulties, each followed this explanation with a long account connecting it to fear of the violence in *lycée*. Delphine, the same age as Agnès, had very strong memories of the bus attack, which she said led to the decision to change schools:

Delphine: Private school wasn't a personal decision, it's our parents who sent us up there because, you should know, something happened.... They broke the bus windows, a girl had an asthma attack and got a bunch of glass shards in the face. I know I took off running; my neighbor—running ahead of me—he got beat up.... A neighbor who lives above us, he got beat up. Luckily he curled up in a ball on the ground. They were hitting randomly, they hit boys and girls, they had nothing to do with anything.
Interviewer: They were boys from ...?
Delphine: I have no idea. They were masked, they had baseball bats, that's all I know [*little laugh*].

They were also afraid of the walk between the *lycée* and home, which ran along the Cité du Sud:

> Delphine: I remember when I went to middle school I had like a fear of going ... There were days when I didn't want to go to school, because I didn't want to be seen by a group that got its kicks picking a daily victim. I didn't want to be the daily victim.
> Interviewer: Were your friends also afraid?
> Delphine: Yes, but it's, I think it's a fear each of us held in. I think it's like that in all schools. When you go to school, you don't want to be the one who's going to have trouble that day because someone's going to single you out as the victim. I think it's something everyone keeps to himself.
> Interviewer: Were there some who got hassled regularly or beat up by groups?
> Delphine: Not who got beat up, but they must have been seen as weaker, so easier. I know, for example, that when we went to *lycée* there's a stretch where there were always guys ... Well, I never got hassled there, but some [*did*]....
> Cédric: I'd always come home with my buddies, because I had buddies, well, one who lived at the top of the hill, I'd always come home with Julien Bensoussan. And there was another one a little farther and we'd come home all three because we were in the same class the first year in *lycée*, but after it was a little sad because my pals took the sciences track, but I had the bad luck to not get put with them, so sometimes I'd come home alone.
> Delphine: You got hassled once.
> Cédric: Yeah, once I got hassled by two guys, there was a tall black and an Arab who wasn't very tall.... I don't know where they came from.... They asked me if I had two euros, I said no, and I went on and all. I turn around to cross and then the guy comes back: "Hey wait up, we wanna talk to you!" They came and everything and they started to ... One of them was in front and the other was behind. The other he started talking to me, to put his hand on my coat. I go, "Let go, I haven't got anything." And the other, he starts saying, "You haven't got two euros? I bet you've got a cell phone!" ... And then the other who was behind, he started to take my bag and everything. I tell him, "there's nothing in there" and all. I take my bag back and I opened it because I didn't want him to take it, and he looked and the other took the calculator, it was a graphing calculator. And the big one he started saying, "Yeah, that's great, what do you do? You're just another nerd."... And he goes: "Yeah, we'll take that" and all. It's really to give people a hard time. The other one, he said: "What do you want me to do with that?" But I was really a little hurt when he said something, it was a little racist, what he said.
> Delphine: A little? A lot, right!
> Cédric: He gave my bag back, and he goes, "Yeah, whites are useless in this country!" And that really pissed me off at the time.

It is clear that fear here arises as much from *lycée* students' ("nerds") social confrontations and symbolic violence (insults, racism toward "whites") as from physical violence or theft, which are frequently cited reasons for fearing housing project youth that are also mentioned here. Although Delphine never experienced one of these dreaded attacks, and Cédric only a minor theft, their fear of being "mugged" or "beat up," kept active by project boys' presence on the path and their provocative attitude, had a prominent place in their accounts.

Julien Bensoussan, who walked with Cédric, did not share such a powerful fear with us, but the theme did dominate the entire interview with his eldest sister Stéphanie. Now a primary schoolteacher in the Cité du Nord, she was trying to get out, because "the more time goes on, the worse it gets." She related the ambiance at her middle school and *lycée* and listed off the bus attack, the fights between boys from the projects, the racketeering, the shots fired, the story of a friend who got "mugged behind the *lycée*" and showed up "in his undies." She added more personal experiences of attempts to steal her car at red lights—once in a neighboring town, once near her university. She feels "less and less safe" anywhere in the urban periphery.

After getting an undergraduate-level degree (*license*) in mathematics, she decided to leave the region for a teacher's training institute in Savoie to take the teachers' exam. At first she wanted to be a secondary-level math teacher, but she ultimately chose primary school to avoid finding herself in the same middle school environment she could not stand as a student. At the same time, her little sister Agnès, who she was very close to, had some problems with "some people from the Cité du Sud" she had gotten involved with. Her parents suspected they stole some money from her and had damaged her car. Stories of this episode are vague, but it was clearly a trying time for the family: "You're 600 kilometers away from the problem, but everyone calls you. Your father calls in tears, you mother calls in tears, your sister calls in tears, your little brother, who hears things he shouldn't have to hear at his age, because he's only fifteen." When Stéphanie tells the story, it reawakens her anxiety and permanent fear of being attacked.

These fearful references to project youths and accounts of their violent behavior in middle school and *lycée* demonstrate that after a very sheltered and protected childhood, the encounter was first and foremost experienced as dangerous, reinforcing the distance between them. But some subdivision youth's attitudes may be more nuanced, and their efforts to relativize this one-sided image allow a glimpse of some other kinds of relationships that were possible between these two worlds.

A Weighty Societal Image of Banlieue Residents

Stories illustrating fear of youth from the projects were often tempered or countered by later references to more empathetic relations. Even the most virulent of the Terrace neighbors said that they had never been attacked, or only in a minor way. Stéphanie acknowledged the gap between her experience and her fear: "I don't know if I'm paranoid or not, but I was suffocating here. Nothing ever happened to me, but I was always afraid something would happen." Cédric admitted that he went to *lycée* in Normandy "more for school reasons." Until his sister reminded him that he had been threatened once and had his calculator stolen, an incident that had slipped his mind, he felt that "for me personally, it's always gone well. No one has ever bothered me."

Thomas put his memories into more perspective. He talked about fights and confrontations between boys from the projects, and he described the position of subdivision kids like himself as being outside of that: it was "the movies" to him, and the Poplars had always been a "neutral zone." His sister confided: "I never felt unsafe here [*on the Terrace*], never." They both dismissed what some neighbors were saying about the doings of a Chaldean "gang" (passed along by the interviewers). Thomas thought it was "just for flash," "nothing at all," or "petty crimes," and that some friends and neighbors (Delphine and Cédric Dumoulin, Stéphanie Bensoussan) went overboard in their talk of aggressive incidents and how far they were from project youth.

In addition to relativizing tales dramatizing the most memorable episodes of their school years, some of these young people expressed a retrospective awareness of the social inequalities behind relations with their peers from the projects they only saw regularly in middle school. All of them described very clear forms of "social cream-separation" that persist despite the lengthening time young people from working-class backgrounds spend in school. Julien said his friends from Victor Hugo Primary School living in the row houses or the Cité du Nord have for the most part left school, and Thomas (who studied sociology) described *lycée* students from the Cité du Nord as "the exceptions" and explained that "it was a little bit ghettoized" between the general and technical *lycée* and the vocational *lycées* in surrounding towns. Agnès explained that the most aggressive youths "get thrown out [*of middle school*] fast," "they waited until they were sixteen and that's enough," so she thought their provocative and sometimes violent attitudes were "more like messing around, from, like, boredom" by "people who have nothing else to do."

Thomas thought boys from the projects loitered around the *lycée* for reasons other than settling scores: for many who went to a vocational *lycée* or had left school, it was a place to "hit on girls." Thomas seemed to have a kind of fascination for these boys he had been friendly with in middle school. Unlike several of his neighbors (Cédric and Delphine Dumoulin or Stéphanie Bensoussan), he was ambivalent and would not condemn their attitudes:

Thomas: I liked middle school. At the time I didn't wonder about who was going to BEP [*vocational school*] and who was going to *lycée*, y'know. I wasn't aware of the social cream-separation, basically. But I have a little trouble talking about it because I have a little trouble having an opinion about it.

Interviewer: What gives you trouble, is it related to the fact that it's memories and you didn't realize it at the time, or you can't make up your mind?

Thomas: Yeah, I dunno what to think about it. They were my pals, I tell you I finished middle school with those guys, so to characterize them, I'm forced to use certain words but it's not . . .
Interviewer: You mean, at the time you didn't put up a wall, they were just plain buddies?
Thomas: Yeah, we weren't buddies, friends, but they were guys you could talk to and really interesting.

He had very strong memories of these classmates, some of whom would later "go bad," and he spoke of them retrospectively with some emotion. Middle school can foster friendly relationships between youth from housing developments and the projects.

Moreover, housing project youth style often pervaded schools—as Thomas put it, "it was guys from the projects who inspired how we were." Subdivision boys often developed a taste for project-influenced music and clothing. Thomas, Cédric, and Julien listened to a lot of rap; Julien professed a preference for American rap and the "gangsta" style (Tupak and Eminem), and so did Cédric (Dr Dre and Eminem). Both described how their musical tastes evolved: Cédric discovered the blues, singer-songwriters, and lyric-driven rock in Normandy, and Julien found classic rock (Hendrix) at university. Their middle-school socialization included an acculturation to *banlieue* tastes diffusing from the projects to housing developments. While the 1970s and 1980s witnessed a growing "attraction for the student model [*that*] was likely a powerful factor for social and cultural change, by helping spread norms and behavioral styles to segments of youth distant from the social sphere from which students were recruited,"[9] we see the opposite trend among these 1990s housing development boys, attracted to working-class tastes and styles from neighboring projects.

Later encounters with peers from outside the neighborhood and *banlieue* and from other social groups would also lead subdivision youths to identify somewhat as *banlieusards* (a pejorative term for *banlieue* residents), which symbolically attenuates their distance from project youth a bit. They discovered that people in Paris or elsewhere in France thought they were similar to youth from the projects, although their entire upbringing had kept them at a distance.

Summer camp gave Thomas early exposure to how they were seen from the outside: upon hearing he was from Gonesse, children from other towns shot back, "Oh, Garges-lès-Gonesse, the *banlieue*!" But he became fully aware of this association while in Paris for a year of preparation for the entrance exam for selective universities. Heartily encouraged by a Gonesse *lycée* teacher, he had not given much thought to the social distance between him and the Parisian *lycée* students he would meet there: "I discovered another world, it was a world filled with the sons of professors and executives."

Although meeting such people had its good points, he suffered keenly from the academic gap between them, unable to "keep up with the pace." He always sat "in the front row," but despite his efforts, he quickly tuned out. He also felt as if the teachers mocked him: even one who "took [him] under his wing" had "labeled" him at first. He thought this experience made him "grow up" and was "a good life lesson," by making him aware of the distance with the upper intellectual classes that he had never had the chance to observe. As a young student who grew up in a subdivision a world away from the project youth living practically next door, he found himself a *banlieusard* in the Parisian world. He became close to a girl "who also came from the *banlieue.*"

Delphine and Cédric had a different experience because their confrontation with "another world" took place at the private Roman Catholic *lycée* where they finished their secondary education. Their account, punctuated by remarks by Laeticia, Cédric's girlfriend he met in Normandy, is revealing.

Delphine: [*little laugh*] Well, it's true that at the beginning it's not easy because when you come from the Paris area you're labeled right away.
Cédric: Yes, they immediately took me for hoodrat, because I was wearing a track suit.
Delphine: It was the same for me, and I was dressed normally.
Laeticia: Yeah, but that's normal, because Avranches is a tiny city, it's really deep in the provinces.
Cédric: There's only rockers! [*laughs*] Nah, I'm joking.
Laeticia: Here you see all kinds of people, all kinds of cultures, but in Avranches, there just aren't many people of color....
Interviewer: How did you know they took you for hoodrats? Was it things people said?
Delphine: Yeah, I got some remarks. When I got there I didn't talk a lot because I didn't know people. I'm usually pretty outgoing and I like talking with people, but they didn't really want to [*little laugh*] talk with me. They knew right away that I came from the Paris area, we didn't dress the same, everyone but me smoked [*little laugh*].
Interviewer: What did they say, for example?
Delphine: [*thinking*] I dunno, they said I seemed arrogant, because ...
Interviewer: Yeah, so maybe not hoodrat, maybe Parisian?
Delphine: Yeah, they were thinking Parisian, all that, they didn't even know I wasn't Paris-Parisian, that I was from the *banlieue*. After, when they learned I was from the *banlieue,* they went: "Oh, so she's a hoodrat, then!" [*laughing*] OK, fine. I said, "Yo, yo, no way! But it ain't no thing!"

This conversation exposes differences in the juvenile socialization of *lycée* students from a small Norman city and suburban housing developments near the projects: they are set apart by music, clothes, tobacco use, and speech patterns. But this distinction leads to the exclusion of youth from the urban periphery who non-Parisians perceive as "hoodrats" (*racaille*). This sometimes happens through mockery, and sometime through humor, as Delphine's "Yo, yo" (*Wesh, wesh*) story shows—she played the game to emphasize that she was not "Paris-Parisian," she was "from the *banlieue*." But relations can sometimes be more tense: Laeticia more directly raised the racist reactions they brutally encountered. The siblings are biracial (their father is from Martinique), and although this does not seem to have previously been an issue (all the more so because they are very light-skinned, to the point that Cédric could be taken for "white" by the youths stealing his calculator), they discovered a world where "people of color," as Laeticia said, "are out of place."

Such experiences made them aware of the cultural diversity around them growing up, and they are now very attached to it. Delphine emphatically decried the presence of "skinheads" in Avranches, and Cédric proudly listed his friends' diverse origins—Vietnamese, Algerian, Moroccan, "Israeli-Algerian," Cambodian—as well as his own (Antillean). Indeed since the mid 1980s, the village-style subdivision had drawn a significant proportion of families who were either immigrants or had roots outside of France. This diversity was a familiar and appreciated part of life in "the Paris area" for young people who grew up there, which was not the case for youth raised "deep in the provinces."

So relating to project youth and having shared places for childhood socialization (middle school, the city) coexist with distancing practices and fear of the most violent among them. This makes it possible, if only periodically, for friendships to develop with young people from neighboring projects who are already employed or who have pursued education. Case in point, when Delphine came back from Normandy, she reconnected with some friends from the Cité du Nord, including one she would see go on to see frequently who helped her find a part-time job in Gonesse and introduced her to others from the Cité du Nord, including students at the Gonesse nursing school.

Agnès met her friends in the Cité du Sud through Joseph, a son in the Chaldean family in the subdivision. As we saw earlier, the company she kept deeply worried her family when she had money problems and a difficult relationship with a young man from the project. She nonetheless kept her connections there and at the time of our interviews had a boyfriend she had met there in 2004. He was a forklift operator for an electronics company and seemed to have a steady job. Although such friendships and romantic relationships are rare, they show that in adulthood young people from the subdivisions and from the stable and educated fractions of the projects can develop social proximity, going against the tendency to hold each other at arm's length that predominated during middle school and *lycée*.

More generally speaking, the ambivalent image of these subdivision youths as *banlieusards* and the transformation of their relations with housing project youth over time are revealing of their socially in-between position. Their parents, with largely working-class backgrounds, histories of migration, and very diverse national origins, experienced a social ascent materialized in the purchase of a single-family home among other things. But despite their parents' watchful attention to their upbringing, pastimes, and education, these young adults are still faced with the challenge of taking these trajectories of ascension further. Their socially intermediary position runs up against the uncertainty of their social fates, which remain in flux even for those over twenty-five. Although their educations allow them to aspire to continue their parents' ascension, they do not shelter them from the risk of social downclassing either. Their protracted attachment to the neighborhood and parental homes could be interpreted as an indicator of this uncertainty and risk.

STAYING IN THE NEIGHBORHOOD:
THE SUBDIVISION AS REFUGE

The study revealed two basic residential patterns for young adults who grew up in the Poplars. Many left the neighborhood permanently as soon as they had the means, without any pangs of nostalgia, because the neighborhood did not fit their social aspirations. This was the case for Jérôme Deneuve, whose parents (a skilled worker become foreman, and an office worker become *cadre*) bought a single-family house from the 1920s in 1979. Thirty-one years old, working as a team leader for the postal service and aspiring to a *cadre* position, he had left his parents' house a few years earlier for a studio apartment he had bought and renovated. He was going to move "to the country" in a periurban town. Despite his parents' efforts, he had no desire whatsoever to take over their house because he and his companion wanted to leave "the *banlieue*" and eventually move to Brittany.

Inversely, other young adults from the neighborhood want to settle there permanently and hope to be seen as established. This was the case for several who grew up in the row houses, especially those from immigrant working-class families. Sami Krim is an example: son of an Algerian father (laborer) and a French mother (a former laborer turned office worker promoted internally to *cadre*), he was thirty-two years old and a civil servant in the national tax administration at the time of the interview. He hoped to buy his parents' row house when they retire, and was very attached to the neighborhood where he knows so many people. Paul Günes, a twenty-five-year-old student, grew up in a Chaldean family. He also wanted to defend the neighborhood's image, especially against anti-Chaldean prejudice. Like Sami Krim, he was active in the neighborhood council (discussed in chapter 5).

The young adults from Partridge Terrace do not come close to either of these scenarios: they do not reject the *banlieue* or scorn the neighborhood or family homes they are so fond of, but they are not extremely attached to the neighborhood either. None of them was invested in local life. Their trajectories were still in flux, and their drifting relationship to the neighborhood was an indication that they were in a transitional period when their social futures could still go in any direction. Rootedness in the family home and neighborhood seemed to be strongest among those experiencing situations of academic and occupational uncertainty.

Uncertain Occupational and Social Trajectories

Encouraged and helped by their parents throughout their schooling, the children in the three sibling groups who completed *lycée* all went on to higher studies, like most of their peers in the neighborhood (only one of whom went to a vocational *lycée* instead). But they seem to have been rather mediocre in secondary school, and several were held back a year (Agnès, Julien, Delphine, Cédric). All took an academic *baccalauréat* (in science or literature) save for Delphine, who took the technical *bac*. Their studies took them in very different directions afterward, some pursuing their studies rather high—or to be more exact, prolonging them for lack of a career plan, somewhat by default.

Marilyne passed the science *bac* specialized in biology then earned a DEA (Diplôme d'études approfondies, a degree roughly equivalent to a master's) in biology at the nearest university, but she did not know what to do next, so she got training to work in the pharmaceutical industry. This choice paid off, as she was hired the following year as "clinical research attaché" (a technical *cadre* position) in an American company.

Thomas had more trouble finding his way than his sister. After a year of *classe préparatoire* for exclusive university entrance exams, he started studying history then shifted to political science, where he was disappointed by the overly theoretical bent of the courses. He spent a year in Spain on the Erasmus program, where he did not work very hard ("I was kind of on the *L'Auberge Espagnole* program," he quipped, referring to a film about a house full of partying Erasmus students). Upon his return, he enrolled in a *magistère,* a high-level program of study combining coursework and on-the-job experience, in International Relations at the Sorbonne, but without knowing where it might lead him in the end. He was thinking of taking the civil service exam to join the Ministry of Foreign Affairs, although he knew that they are very selective. A year later, he did an unpaid internship for his program, working for UNESCO in South Africa, but he remembered it as a bad experience because he had to pay for all the travel himself and was treated like a simple "executant" in charge of the mail, and most of all because it did not lead to anything. At the end of this training in 2006, he vainly sent application letters to a great number and range of European and international organizations, associations, and NGOs, and the outcome discouraged him. To earn some money, he temped for the shops at Charles de Gaulle airport. His girlfriend, who he met on Erasmus in Spain, opted to do a DESS (Diplôme d'études supérieures spécialisées comparable with a master's) program in documentary filmmaking. She also had trouble finding steady work and was an intern in a small production company at the time of our interviews. In early 2007, Thomas decided to return to his job search seriously, expanding it to the field of communication as well as more commercial lines of work: "What I want is to work." Once again, all he managed to get was an internship, in a marketing firm specialized in real estate promotion. It was not really what he aspired to, but he hoped that it would lead to a real position because the eight months seeking employment, fruitless despite his rather prestigious training, had been very trying experience.

Stéphanie also took a year in *classe préparatoire* after the *bac* before enrolling in a regular university for a degree in Mathematics and Computing Applied to the Social Sciences. She did not like it, and since she had long "wanted to be a teacher" (her mother teaches primary school), she transferred to a teaching institute. Agnès studied history and was writing a master's thesis on "Amputation in the Eighteenth Century" when we met, although she was not sure that she would be able to pull it off. She was also unenthusiastically preparing for the civil service exam for teaching. In addition, some major health problems prevented her from sitting the exam the following years. As she put it, "I promised myself I'd stop after the *license* [undergraduate degree], but I can't." Julien had begun a program in Art and Events Staging that he found too focused on computing techniques, so he was planning on transferring to an applied math program, without really knowing what kind of work it might lead to.

As for Delphine, after getting a technical *bac* in administration and much indecision, she changed direction and, after three years of preparation, was accepted at the École Nationale Supérieur des Arts Décoratifs (the national decorative arts school), where she was studying textile design. Although it is a prestigious school, she chose a long program with unpredictable employability. Her brother Cédric and his girlfriend Laeticia enrolled in medical school in 2004, sort of on a whim. They both failed the exam to enter second year, and Cédric changed to architecture, which is also a long program with uncertain job prospects for those lacking the social capital so useful in entering the profession.

Their academic and occupational careers are thus marked by frequent middling results and, to various degrees, unrealistic social perceptions or at least a fuzzy conception of job opportunities (with the exception of Stéphanie, who teaches primary school). Drawing out their studies lets them avoid confronting the uncertainties of employment and occupational futures directly. Although all have university educations, and some might still hope to work as *cadre,* the possibility of occupational downclassing, in relation both to their educational levels and to their parents, is very real; the transmission of parents' social status to their children is anything but assured.

This uncertainty about future careers is reinforced by the fact that all of them have had side jobs since they began higher studies. Housed by their parents, who lend them cars as well, these jobs give them resources for autonomy. Thomas and his sister have frequently worked at the airport selling sandwiches. He has also worked in banks, spending over three months working for one full-time while his search for a job at his level of qualification went nowhere. Julien did private math tutoring during the academic year, and summers he sorted checks in the bank where his father worked. Delphine, Cédric, and Laeticia worked Saturdays (plus a weekday in Delphine's case) for a media distribution company, where they sorted magazines and newspapers for shipment; they said "it's like a factory job." Delphine's friend from the Cité du Nord told her about it, and she had worked there full-time during vacations for the previous three years. These odd jobs are for laborers or unskilled workers, and doing this kind of work regularly, especially for the Dumoulins who sort media weekly, has them navigating between very different social worlds: the world of universities and medical and decorative arts schools in Paris, and the factory world in a Gonesse industrial park. These young adults, who could be taken for housing development *"bourges"* (bourgeois) by youth from the projects, were at this stage of their lives in a fraction of the middle classes with frequent working-class contact.

Last, the extent of this career uncertainty is confirmed by their employed friends and neighbors' jobs. Marilyne referred to her close friends' situations: Stéphanie and Jeanne, primary school teachers in the Cité du Nord; Sophie, a neighbor on the circle, sales clerk in a shoe store in a nearby shopping center; a doctoral student in biology she met in school; and two brothers from an adjacent town introduced by a friend, one working in a temp agency and the other as a temp, after a failed attempt at a two-year post-*bac* technical degree.

Socially and career-wise, the youthful neighbors of Partridge Terrace still had wide-open futures, but they seemed to be closing in: although there were hopes for rising into the ranks of *cadre* and intellectual occupations, these hopes were sometimes rather unrealistically formulated, when they had not already been dashed. Their educational levels are overall higher than their parents', but their ascension seems compromised by a high risk of insecurity and a drop in social status by working below their level of qualification.

In that, their situation is more difficult than that of the row-house pioneer's children, and comparison of the situations of these two generations of suburban youth is illuminating. Children of row-house pioneers (presented in table 3.2), born in the 1960s, averaged less time in school. In the context of full employment while they were in school in the 1960s and 1970s, their parents' academic aspirations were lower than those of Partridge Terrace

TABLE 3.2. Academic and occupational characteristics of pioneers' children.

Family name	Level of studies	Current occupation
Boucher first child		Midlevel *cadre* at Air France
Boucher second child		Letter carrier
Boucher third child		Sales representative
Berger first child	Two-year vocational program, secondary level	Employee at the gas company
Berger second child	Technology *Baccalauréat*	Supervisory manager at the electric company
Vallès first child	Masters-level degree in environmental studies	Civil servant in subnational level government
Vallès second child		Specialized youth counselor
Pageot first child	*Baccalauréat*	*Cadre*
Pageot second child	*Baccalauréat*	
Morin first child	Middle-school diploma	Bank employee
Morin second child	Middle-school diploma	Employee at city hall
Morin third child	Middle-school diploma	Firefighter
Heurtin first child	Two-year vocational program, secondary level	Draughtsman in local-level government
Heurtin second child	Nursing school	Chief supervisor in a public hospital
Lenormand first child		Business-owner
Lenormand second child		Physical education teacher
Lenormand third child		Low-level employee at the national infrastructure agency
Lenormand fourth child		Mountain guide
Legris first child	Technical *Baccalauréat* and two-year degree in accounting	Accountant
Legris second child	Technical *Baccalauréat* and two-year degree in accounting	Buyer
Samson first child		
Samson second child		Nurse
Samson third child		Computing specialist

Source: Interviews.

parents. As employees of banks, the electric and gas company, and various public services, parents' opportunities to help their children get jobs would moreover allow their children to find stable positions at a time when unemployment was beginning to rise.

In contrast, the futures of the village-style subdivision children, educated in the 1980s and 1990s under the encouraging oversight of their parents, were much less certain, in spite of their higher studies. In this situation of uncertainty, the subdivision and family home provided roots and a protective shelter; their social lives and romantic relationships were still closely tied to them.

Extended Residency in the Family Home: Between Attachment and Constraint

During the study, many neighborhood youths in their twenties still lived on Partridge Terrace, including the three sibling groups discussed here (except Stéphanie, the teacher, living nearby) and most neighbors their age.[10] The three Georges brothers (aged twenty-three to twenty-seven), "old pals" from Thomas's childhood, were still there, as was another family the same age composed of Sophie (the shoe store clerk) and her younger brother, making five of the eight sibling groups whose eldest was born between 1979 and 1985. Other than Stéphanie, who lived in Savoie two years for school, none had lived in student housing: Marilyne and Thomas's father pressured them to move to student apartments when he returned to Martinique, but it was "too rough," and they preferred to stay in the house.

It is not statistically exceptional that they were almost all still in their parents' houses, as there is a gradual trend in delaying decohabitation.[11] In 1997, the median age for leaving the parental home was twenty and a half years for women and twenty-two for men, and the age of access to residential independence (housing no longer paid for by parents) was twenty-two for women and twenty-four for men.[12] These ages have risen slightly since, especially in metropolitan Paris. Like many young adults, those raised on Partridge Terrace stay at their parents' homes for largely financial reasons: other than student housing, no other kind of housing was within the youths' or parents' means. Cédric and Laeticia had wanted to rent an apartment in Paris, but gave up. Among people they knew, only peers from the upmarket Kaufman and Broad subdivision had had independent housing since leaving for school, like one of Julien's friends whose parents rented him an apartment in Paris.

But beyond the economic factor, the neighborhood and family home has a protective role for these young adults because of the many attachments they have there. Some have family ties in the neighborhood. Although Thomas and Marilyne Loiseau's parents have left, the Bensoussan children's paternal grandparents live on Partridge Terrace, and their aunts, uncles, and cousins in an adjacent town. Most importantly, they have friends in the neighborhood and the vicinity: they have at least partially maintained networks of childhood and teenage "buddies" and "girlfriends" that were built thanks to parental friendships, social proximity, and how they were raised. Neighbors still see each other regularly on the street, eat at each other's houses, and watch sports and eat out together. Cookouts sometimes bring them together in nice weather. Marilyne and Stéphanie are still close friends, and they also frequently see Jeanne, a colleague of Stéphanie's in the New Poplars subdivision from the 1990s. Agnès is friendly with Joseph and another neighbor from the circle. Thomas still sees his "old buddies."

The extent of this attachment to the neighborhood can be measured by the couples formed there. As we saw earlier, Agnès was seeing a young man from the Cité du Sud she met through a neighbor. Her sister Stephanie's situation is even more revealing of the strength of ties binding them to the neighborhood and Gonesse. Stéphanie left Savoie to return to Gonesse, where she had met a young man at a neighborhood friend's party. Meeting him led her to work in the Cité du Nord although she had left the Paris area precisely to get away from this kind of neighborhood.

Beyond the neighborhood itself, many of their friends still live in adjacent towns, so when they do go out, it is not far: movies in a multiplex, eating out (sometimes in Paris, sometimes McDonald's), errands in the shopping center, bowling nights, Gonesse nursing school parties, and the like. Several continue cultural or athletic activities in Gonesse or nearby: Marilyne still plays with the conservatory orchestra, and Agnès just stopped playing basketball with the local club. Julien, Cédric, and their subdivision friends from *lycée* regularly play soccer at the city field. Thomas sometimes goes out with his university friends in Paris, but still spends a lot of time in the neighborhood where he feels "calm":

> Thomas: Now I am starting to appreciate it a little, but I didn't like Paris, I'd get there and everyone was all stressed out and all. I really liked to come back to Gonesse, calm.

So these young people appreciated their family homes, with their yards and social networks, and they did not put down the neighborhood. And yet none of them wanted to stay there, by buying their parents' house after retirement or another house in the neighborhood. Marilyne and Thomas, living alone in the family house, had done nothing to appropriate the space, like rearranging or decorating. Moreover, Marilyne aspired to having a "place of [*her*] own" someplace else:

Marilyne: I don't know if we'll keep the house, but personally I hope to be settled down, with a job. With a little more security I could get an apartment, like, a little place of my own. For now this is good, but I hope I won't stay here forever. I've already spent a long time here, since '84, we've been here twenty years! So yes, I think there are always some regrets, but on this I don't think so. I don't really know if I'd really miss it. What I will miss is maybe my childhood at school.

Unlike the children of the immigrant families in the row houses cited earlier, not one had invested in neighborhood associative or political life. None had ever attended a neighborhood council meeting. Thomas, otherwise generally interested in political life, told us his only local activity consisted of identifying which neighbors had voted for the Front National the year of its breakthrough. He had a vague desire to attend a meeting for ATTAC, an alternative globalization organization, but had not taken the leap: "No, no, honestly, associations, not at all. I never had that kind of connection with the town."

Subdivision parents' child-rearing practices in the 1980s depict common but rarely studied ways of guiding youth sociability and education: it is not about keeping exclusively to one's kind or copying the distinction-focused educational strategies of the middle and upper classes with high cultural capital, nor does it involve attitudes of avoidance or flight from neighborhood public institutions, which are minority practices despite being mentioned frequently. These families took advantage of the material setting and protective relationships offered by their small subdivisions to guide their children's leisure time activities and friendships without entirely isolating them from children living in social housing nearby. They also made educational choices that fostered their children's success without being culturally elitist. These suburban youth thus experienced much better educational outcomes than most youth from the projects, from whom they gradually drifted even as they maintained an ambivalent relationship with them, all the more so as they found themselves labeled as *banlieue* kids as they grew up and ventured outside the neighborhood.

The family home, Partridge Terrace, and Gonesse constitute a setting that is "calm," a frequently recurring term that above all indicates people feel safe there. It let these young adults continue their studies while avoiding the uncertainty of their occupational futures. They do not imagine themselves staying long-term, however, nor do they aspire to reproducing their parents' lifestyles. The protracted in-group sociability in family homes and the housing development is a refuge for these young adults who find themselves on the cusp of a still very uncertain occupational future and at the crossroads of diverse social worlds: that of their families, from working-class backgrounds and in many cases immigrants; that of students, Parisians in particular; and last, even if it is more marginally the case, that of the projects and unskilled odd jobs.

NOTES

1. Chamboredon and Lemaire, "Proximité spatiale et distance sociale," 3–33.
2. O Masclet, "Mission Impossible. Ethnographie d'un club de jeunes," *Actes de la recherche en sciences sociales* 136–37 (2001): 62–70.
3. The public educational system is divided into districts in which children attend a given nearby school. The district map is redrawn regularly, a process involving local politicians' strategies and negotiations with the national education agency. It is possible to request authorization from city hall to enroll children in another school for family reasons or to enroll a child in a specialized program, but these authorizations are at the discretion of elected officials. See L Barrault-Stella, *Gouverner par accommodements. Stratégies autour de la carte scolaire* (Paris, 2013).
4. Since the 1990s, private schools represent approximately 15 percent of primary schools and 20 percent of middle and high schools. It is gradually rising in secondary education, from 20 percent to 22 percent in 2011 (Ministère de l'éducation nationale, *Repères et références statistiques* (Paris, 2014). Most private schools are Roman Catholic.
5. These internal inequalities have led some to speak of the process of democratic segregation in the school system. See P Merle, *La ségrégation scolaire* (Paris, 2012).
6. For more about the range of residential and educational practices, see Van Zanten, *L'école de la periphérie*; M Oberti, *L'école dans la ville. Ségrégation-mixté-carte scolaire* (Paris, 2007).
7. Especially two students who had participated in the second field school in October 2004, Emmanuel Comte and Fabien Brugière, who conducted five interviews with some young neighbors close to their own age.
8. W Whyte, *Street Corner Society* (Chicago, 1943).
9. J-C Chamboredon, "Classes scolaires, classes d'âge, classes sociales: les fonctions de scansion temporelle du système de formation," *Enquête. Cahiers du Cercom* 6 (1991): 121–43.
10. This study is not entirely representative, since we mainly saw those who had not left. Nonetheless, the study did allow us to confirm that the same holds true for many of the neighbors between twenty and twenty-five years old.
11. O Galland, "Entrer dans la vie adulte: des étapes toujours plus tardives, mais resserrées," *Économie et statistique* 337–38 (2000): 13–36.
12. C Villeneuve-Gokalp, "Les jeunes partent toujours au même âge de chez leurs parents," *Économie et Statistique* 337–38 (2000): 61–80. In fact, the whole journal issue is on the subject.

4

"THEY'RE VERY NICE, BUT . . .":
ENCOUNTERING NEW
FOREIGN NEIGHBORS

The persistent economic crisis affecting French society since the 1970s has damaged the cohesion of the society of wage labor[1] that was at its apogee after World War II. Mass structural unemployment concerns 10 percent of the working population, distancing a growing percentage of the population from the rights that come with contractual employment. Social assistance has expanded alongside unemployment-related insurance.[2] A minimum income was established for people suffering long-term unemployment, first called the RMI (Revenu Minimum d'Insertion), then the RMA (Revenu Minimum d'Activité), and most recently the RSA (Revenu de Solidarité Active). Concern for the most poor extends into their health care with the CMU (universal illness coverage). These social policies have led to divisions between more modest social categories, starting with certain political discourses in the 1980s and spreading into the general population. The Front National, followed by the more traditional right, denounce "welfare mooches" that "exploit" the system to the detriment of "the deserving." This system of opposition often tallies with an opposition between "the French" and "foreigners" or immigrants. The latter are also suspected of taking advantage of natalist French family policy, which grants all families a subsidy for each child (regardless of family financial situation); since the sum increases with the number of children, it can amount to significant disbursements for large families. The successive population waves in the Poplars have made such tensions felt in the neighborhood.

How to best qualify these tensions and divisions is subject to debate within the social sciences in France. Anthropologists have shown how the accusations made of "youths" or "foreigners" heard while researching among residents of stigmatized neighborhoods are intended to displace the stigma these residents feel as a result of the research situation.[3] Some sociologists have described the rising xenophobia of the working and lower middle classes and tried to explain it with the phenomenon of social downclassing,[4] while others prefer to deconstruct it by reacting to the way in which the media and policies end up identifying people with conservatism and a vote for the extreme right (see chapter 5). Modest social categories' intolerance of foreigners is even more subject to discussion given how it contrasts with the value that higher class categories in gentrified neighborhoods accord to diversity and cosmopolitanism.[5] Given all that, what are the relations like between little-middles and newer residents of foreign backgrounds in a neighborhood like the Poplars? Is there the xenophobia spotted in studies of the working-class world, or perhaps the same esteem for diversity as gentrified neighborhoods? Just what are neighborly relations between native-born French and immigrant small homeowners?

Families arriving in the Poplars neighborhood in the 1960s and early 1970s experienced an egalitarian ambiance while gaining access to the kind of housing and neighborhood that promised a better life in a good environment. But today differences and inequalities are more prevalent in neighborhood relations. The long-term residents who stayed in the neighborhood and some of the more recent arrivals are afraid of seeing resources they patiently acquired, be they their homes, skilled jobs, or educational degrees, slowly downgraded. These tensions emerged when a foreign population, Chaldean refugees from rural Turkey working as low-skilled labor, settled in the neighborhood. The remaining Poplars pioneers and some subsequent arrivals say that the neighborhood is not what it used to be, and its degradation began when "the Turkish families" moved in.

In fact, as we have seen, the row houses' population transformed gradually but continuously as soon as pioneers started to leave in the early 1970s. But for a long time, their successors were identified as French, with social characteristics that were barely distinguishable from their own. The population started to change in the late 1980s, when the proportion of foreign and poorer households (who often came from housing projects) increased dramatically. Although Turkish families only represented part of this change, they are seen as the new dominant population, as much numerically as symbolically. "It's become a Turkish neighborhood here," said a pioneer, expressing the earliest row-house occupants' collective sentiment that they are no longer entirely at home in the neighborhood.

When such long-term residents speak of "the Turks," it does refer to families from various regions of Turkey, but as a practical matter, Algerians, Moroccans, Pakistanis, and sub-Saharan Africans are also sometimes lumped into the designation. In practice, little-middles may use the label to denounce, sometimes virulently, populations they blame for the neighborhood's demotion, bad reputation, and everyday tensions. In so doing, residents identifying as French who could not or did not want to leave the row houses mentally draw a line between themselves and the others. On one side, there are people like them, "the French," the last representatives of a once-valued neighborhood that conferred prestige on its residents, and on the other, those who they perceive as inferior and/or different. We see, though, that their rejection of "the Turks" is only partial, and that time and time again they participate in building a reciprocal relationship. Relations between old-timers and newcomers are far from limited to complaints and discourses of rejection.

"SAVING HONOR"

Ethnologists like Althabe who observe relations between neighbors in high-rise public housing have given particular attention to the structure of the (frequently unsolicited) complaints they heard from residents.[6] Such complaints stem from the stigmatization of the place and serve as an outlet for tenants who find themselves in situations of class demotion. When face to face with a researcher from outside the local field, they usually blame the degradation on the young and foreigners. Criticizing their behavior is a way of protecting themselves from the blow to their self-esteem that comes from living in a low-prestige neighborhood. Through these complaints, they express the need for a symbolic redress of status, essentially a desire to "save their honor."[7]

This analysis also applies to some row-house owners. Many of them were concerned about our perception of the neighborhood, and thus themselves. "What do you think of the neighborhood?" an informant asked shortly after welcoming us into her home; as with others whose residential trajectory stopped here, she fears that the presumably negative image of the row houses coming from every direction devalues her social status.

Old-timers whose neighbors left en masse while they were stuck in the neighborhood experienced the arrival of foreign families as social demotion. Most who left had been planning on getting a single-story house or moving back to their home regions, but they had not planned on doing it so quickly. The arrival of Turkish and other families with foreign backgrounds precipitated their departure from a neighborhood they loved. But other row-house pioneers, too old to take on a new, heavy, long-term debt or lacking the means because of divorce or a low pension, could not follow in the footsteps of those for whom the neighborhood was ultimately only a transitional place on the path to a freestanding house and a higher residential status.

The arrival of foreign households poorer than their own consequently led to an intense revelation of their own low social status. In the decade during which departures accelerated, they became brutally aware of their social and residential limitations. Families with friendships going back many years severed relations, as those who stayed somewhat resented those who left, because their choice to live elsewhere dissipated the atmosphere of equality characteristic of the neighborhood's early years. Those who stayed were impotent spectators of their environment's transformation. If they still depict themselves as victims in interviews today, it is to assert their place in the neighborhood's upper strata, claiming to be (and objectively being) its last representatives. This discourse of victimization, of the "old-timers" enduring "the Turks," should thus be understood at least partially as a way of defending their social status.

Class Demotion, Denial of Equality, and Resentment of "the Turks"

A frequently arising theme in interviews with residents feeling trapped in their row houses is immigrant families' money. They cannot understand how "the Turks" could get houses like theirs so quickly. Those who spoke with us had to go into debt for twenty years to buy their houses and keep a very tight budget at the beginning, despite the houses' affordability. Seeing these families as much poorer than themselves, they cannot believe that they were also able to save up and take out loans, which would be tantamount to accepting that their situations are equivalent and making the new households' presence unremarkable, which many refuse to do. As a result, rumors constantly feed suspicion about "the Turks' money" and deepen the divide between them.

Many wonder, "How could they buy our houses?" In the 1990s, one of the answers circulating among "the French" was that "the Turks" had received 500,000 francs (76,225 euros) in assistance from the German government to get them to leave Germany. An array of clues gave credence to this claim: some had seen Turkish families arrive in Mercedes cars registered in Germany; others heard they spoke German. Many stories describe Turkish families arriving with suitcases of money and paying cash for their houses. As with many rumors, their strength lies in ignorance and a feeling of being under threat sparked by the arrival of foreigners. Seeing these households arrive in the political climate of the 1980s and 1990s, when the political party the Front National introduced its xenophobic propaganda (more on this in the next chapter), many residents thought that the French government was far too lax and welcoming compared with the German government, seen as rigorous and "pitiless." "France is becoming a trash can" became a sort of catch phrase.

Today, many old-timers mention this rumor, but with less conviction. The contacts formed with the Turkish families over fifteen years of cohabitation have toned them down. They now know that most of their neighbors did not come via Germany, and that some had lived in France for over ten years before buying a house. But better knowledge of the families still has not put an end to prejudice. Their money still raises questions: Mme Beauvais, who is not usually particularly hostile to her foreign neighbors, wonders how they could buy several cars and get the latest televisions when her pension as a retired insurance company employee only allows her to live decently if she "tightens the belt." We come across "French" residents who make sweeping accusations of foreigners who "take advantage of the system," such as M. Kergoat:

Interviewer: Were you surprised when you saw the people change, buying?
M. Kergoat: No, not surprised, I expected that. What surprised me is how they do it in such a short time. You worked your whole life to get here, and they get it in two or three years, there you go, it's done. It's not normal, shit! [*he raises his voice*]. There's something that's not right.
Interviewer: So you mean you don't know their occupations?
M. Kergoat: No, it's kept rather quiet. One of my buddies does Restos du Coeur [*a soup kitchen*] in Gonesse. And he was disgusted! He says to me, "Listen, I'm going to tell you about it because there are some who live by you, guys who have a nice brand-new Mercedes and trucks, and well, their little women, they come to get food and clothes at Restos du Coeur. I tell myself that it's not right that the town gives them coupons, there's that too. Do you know what the 412 is? It's a paper they give you to get hospital care. Well, you go to Gonesse hospital, you have people who go right through like that, You, you line up to wait and them, they go right through and it's free for them! And the pharmacist in the Poplars, she was telling me that 412s, there's a ton of them in the neighborhood. I think there's something that's not right. My daughter has a son and she doesn't get benefits, for example, and there are some who have eight kids who aren't even born here and who get them. What's going on here? Is that normal? There is something sick here!

In 1998, M. Kergoat sold his row house to buy a single-level home nearby. A long-term socialist sympathizer, he controls his reactions during the interview. Others are less circumspect in their rejection of the neighborhood foreigners. However radical their words, the sentiment that "the French" are suffering injustice—the feeling that the foreigners are given more help than they are—provokes hostility among a number of our interlocutors.

We stress that these are not poor people, but households that have experienced a small social ascension. Their denunciation of foreigners is not driven by the need to "avert exclusion" which is so frequent among the French poor,[8] but by a dread of social backsliding resulting from several factors. First, the row houses' long-term residents are mostly retired today, and leaving employment weakens social position in lower-ranking social categories, particularly for men. They lack the social capital that makes new outlets for activity available to aged members of higher social strata, so many spend retirement in the confinement of their houses and neighborhood, in isolation conducive to breeding ill will. In addition, physical aging generally increases the feeling of vulnerability, and the small homeowners we met are especially susceptible. They had to "make an effort" to pull themselves up socially, and many of them converted the values of virility acquired in their working-class backgrounds into an energy on the job that favored their promotion to floor supervisor or even an office job or a *cadre* position. This is the case for M. Kergoat, a seventy-year-old-son of an unskilled laborer who became a *cadre* in a computing company. Little-middles also generally possess an ambitious, competitive spirit that expresses itself in sports and leisure activities as well as work. Many hold leadership positions in sporting organizations and regularly practice a sport themselves (like M. Kergoat, who did calisthenics and ran), but aging has reduced this drive. What M. Kergoat says about foreigners who do not respect the rules and who cut in front of "the French" expresses the impotence that he currently feels.

In the second place, although the row-house pioneers could climb the ranks and avoid unemployment during their working lives, this is not so for their children, who are in generations living through economic crisis and weak growth. Louis Chauvel has shown that they are disadvantaged as a group compared with their parents, although their situations are quite varied.[9] As we mentioned in chapter 3, some were able to get employment in the public sector and escape job insecurity. M. Kergoat's children are married and have had stable work: his daughter is an accountant and his son a customer service representative in a large bank. But at the same time, his daughter, married to a skilled laborer who has experienced several periods of unemployment already, rents housing because they are unable to buy their own home. His son, who had a new house built west of Paris, has several side jobs alongside his bank job in order to cover his costs. While not failing, the family's children encounter more difficulties setting themselves up in life than their parents did, and their future is not entirely certain. "Everything's gotten harder" according to M. Kergoat, who is perfectly aware of the risks his children face. Even if they were able to escape the processes culminating in the "destabilization of the stable,"[10] the now-retired little-middles of the pioneering generation experience the weakening of careers and the rise in unemployment through their children. The vulnerability of loved ones also leads them to speak in such terms.

Last, their dread of social backsliding is clearly a direct consequence of the arrival of immigrant families in what some describe as a formerly "nice neighborhood." Home-buying made these pioneers' desire for social mobility a reality and made them feel relatively well-off. But those who still live there today feel the neighborhood is in decline. "It's like a housing project now," said both Mme Sanchez and Mme Samson, who particularly deplore the installation of a multitude of satellite dishes on most houses' facades, evoking the image of new immigrant ghettos symbolized by big public housing projects (see Illustration 4.1).

The demotion of the residential space is confused with the immigrants' presence, prompting little-middles to emphasize anything and everything that sets them apart. Bitterness colors pioneers' view of these families, and the only explanation they can find for their presence is the oft-repeated implication that they divert public money ("welfare money") to the detriment of others. Countless anecdotes evoke cases of "Turkish children" who "are outdoors at ten o'clock at night," "poorly dressed," and so on. For these small property owners who had limited the number of children they had in hopes of offering them better lives, immigrants' fertility is incomprehensible—

ILLUSTRATION 4.1. Satellite dishes on the Samsons' street. (Photo taken by author)

although some say it does help explain their access to homeownership by increasing child benefits. Even knowing how indebted their new neighbors are, doubt remains as to the source of their money, what they actually possess, and how they manage their budgets.

In the following excerpt from an interview, a manager at Secours Catholique (a Roman Catholic charity for the poor and disadvantaged) and his wife express their feeling that nothing is ever "really, really straight" with these families. Words like theirs are frequent in interviewees' discourse, and can be summed up in one phrase: "they gyp us."

> Mme Vallès: The arrival of this new population meant a lot of ink was spilled, because as a rule people didn't agree with the idea that this population has come, it's got to be said.... The old-timers were still opposed to the arrival of this population, and it raised a lot of discussion in neighborhood meetings, asking why they let them buy here, why this, why that. That dredged up a lot of things.
>
> Interviewer: They buy? They can buy their own houses, too?
>
> M. Vallès: I can't tell you how they do it. Or maybe they are in cahoots with the real estate agents to justify the possibilities of reimbursement or loans. We saw an example in the records: the interest rate dropped in the last few years, and they continue to be charged and to reimburse loans contracted with rates that are a bit exorbitant compared to those on today's real estate market. They haven't re-negotiated their loan, since it's possible....
>
> Interviewer: You see these records at Secours Catholique?
>
> Mme Vallès: Yes, for financial assistance.
>
> Interviewer: And when you ask them why they haven't refinanced their loan, what do they give as an explanation?
>
> Mme Vallès: That's very difficult. They always have a lot of arguments. Really, they don't take care of it, or they don't have money, or they don't have the time—it's never really, really straight, their stories.
>
> Interviewer: And you, how do you explain it?
>
> M. Vallès: Maybe they're poorly informed.
>
> Interviewer: Do you have the impression they understand the banking system?
>
> Mme Vallès: Yes, they should understand it. It's like when they say, "We don't understand what you are saying," but they actually understand very well, y'know. There's a lot of negligence on their part, y'know.
>
> M. Vallès: They take advantage of all the resources pretty well.
>
> Mme Vallès: Yes, and then, they sure know their rights.
>
> M. Vallès: For example, they were asking for assistance to send the children on vacation for three, four weeks in host families. The cost is fairly low, but they readily said, "I can't pay." They were told, "go see the social assistants, go see the social benefits office"—"ah no, I don't take social assistance," et cetera. The means are there, but they want to stay ... from fear, maybe, that someone will go sticking their nose in [*their affairs*]. I don't have a home cinema, but a lot of them have television sets.
>
> Mme Vallès: They have every comfort, there are some that want for nothing at all.
>
> Interviewer: Like you were saying, they have three cars.
>
> Mme Vallès: Yes. And then it's always negotiated, they never give automatically, you've got to ask them once they pay, you have to go back to ask for a check again. We can never manage to get the money. You have to ask them five or six times be-

fore they finally pay off all the children's vacation. And yet, like my husband told you, the cost is still far from being exorbitant. It's always so that it works for them, that they pay the least possible, that they have the necessary assistance. We almost think negotiation is a game for them. Real carpet merchants!

This couple's discussion undermines the rumors: neither high child benefits nor juicy schemes fill the coffers of these poor families who call on Secours Catholique for help. To the contrary, it reveals their great vulnerability to the banking system: they are incapable of renegotiating their debt to lessen their payments on an overpriced loan that absorbs the greatest share of their resources. They usually ask the charity for assistance with food and children's leisure activities. And yet M. and Mme Vallès persist in seeing them above all as "negligent" families who do not make the effort to manage their money better.

Their severity might arise from frustration because solutions exist, but immigrant families refuse to appeal to the social agencies that could provide them. But their severity also relates to the social difference between them. Poor fractions of the working classes quite typically fear and distrust social workers and their interference in their affairs because they threaten the little autonomy they have, let alone the common aversion to the dishonor of being a "social case."

M. and Mme Vallès are full-fledged members of the little-middle world, both distanced from their working-class backgrounds by their upward mobility. M. Vallès has a *baccalauréat* and worked his way from basic employee up to supervisor. His wife left her job when they moved into the first row houses in Gonesse. They have two children who respectively became a social worker and a supervisor for a municipal government. Effort and rigor are indispensable moral qualities for the Vallès', for whom the Turkish families seem negligent: their numerous children, their weak control over them, and the poor maintenance of their houses and yards all manifest what they interpret as laxity. They thus see their neighbors who come to Secours Catholique as the "bad poor" who refuse to conform to the norms of those who try to help them. On top of that, as charitable volunteers, they are additionally caught in a contradiction that feeds their suspicion: the poor who come to them are the ones who are damaging their neighborhood and ruining their small capital of respectability.

Dispossession of Place

Although long-term residents' opinions and practices regarding the newer arrivals vary according to several parameters we describe later, this new population nonetheless generally arouses the old-timers' disapproval. Thus far, we have largely attributed this rejection to the devaluation of the neighborhood resulting from the massive settlement of migrants from Turkey:

the perception of a drop in status was a decisive factor in rising resentment and more or less xenophobic remarks about the foreign newcomers. But the initial row-house occupants also feel a very concrete process dispossessing them of their residential space. This experience prevents them from feeling at home in the neighborhood anymore, and is another extremely important factor in "French" families' rising hostility to the immigrants.

The simple fact that there are foreign families living in neighborhood houses itself contributes to old-timers' isolation, as they find themselves living alongside kinds of people with whom they have previously had little real contact. Of the eighteen other families living on Mme Sanchez's little square, only one, an elderly woman living alone, is native-born French, and all the others come from foreign countries (mostly Turkey). We learned over the course of our discussions that she has cordial relations with some families, but it seems this is not enough to get her past feeling that she no longer knows anyone and is isolated. Families around the square used to be a rather united group and the children played together, and here as elsewhere in the neighborhood there was an ambiance of equality between families that offered them all a chance to be integrated into the neighborhood. The disappearance of this kind of neighborhood life has left a vacuum that is all the greater since the old-timers who stayed cannot recreate such dense exchanges with the new families. Too many differences separate them.

The children of Turkish families occupy the streets and squares today. The old-timers usually tolerate them, but they think they are too numerous and too noisy. As pioneers, they exercised great control over their own offspring, letting them play outdoors according to a rather strict schedule and only in front of the house. Squares were the children's territory, but the mothers watched over their games and playmates, and built their reputations as good parents through the surveillance of children's play. The Turkish families let their many and often very young children play more freely.

Some old-timers react to what they feel is a deterioration of their living environment. The noise is louder and more annoying at certain times of the year, like during school vacations, summer when children play outside well into the evening, and July 14, when firecrackers resonate throughout the neighborhood and make windows rattle. So Mme Sanchez has no compunctions about telling the children to stop playing from her window. Her tone is strict, and they usually obey. She seems to have taken the role of a sort of public guardian of her square, but the repeated yelling wears her out. She feels like she has to fight for her peace and quiet and fears the day when the teenagers rebel.

The long-term residents are also bothered by the noise of adults talking in front of the houses or in their yards, sometimes late into the night. Here again, summer is more conducive to protracted conversations in the cool evenings that may bring together members of neighbors' extended families.

Over the course of a few years, the core of neighborhood sociability has actually shifted, because Turkish families have rather extensive social networks while the old-timers have fewer occasions to get together in their yards, and with advancing age, less desire to do so. And when they are invited to celebrate marriages and births with their new neighbors, the prospect of mingling with them makes them too uncomfortable to accept. The myriad social and cultural maladjustments between the overly dissimilar resident groups are ultimately expressed in complaints about noise.

Their lives are paced differently, and they have different ways of arranging access to the house and using the yard. The original inhabitants say the neighborhood's charm was due to respect of co-ownership rules and the care each family devoted to its house and yard. They felt fully at home there because neighbors took care to neither put themselves ahead nor draw the disapproval of others. The gates and shutters were painted the same color, and the yards filled with grass and flowers showed how conscientious their owners were and supported the collective sentiment of homey well-being. But the common rules have been abandoned, and the new inhabitants are not all so assiduous in maintaining their houses. Many of them cannot afford to maintain the exteriors: the roughcast needs to be redone, and garden gates should be replaced or fixed. But income level alone is not enough to explain why their hedges are sometimes wild or bulky objects accumulate in front of the house. From the old-timers' perspective, "it doesn't cost anything" to keep things tidy. They believe the explanation lies in their culture of origin. "It doesn't bother them," said an interviewee who complains about his neighbor who never trims his hedges and who he considers "poorly groomed."

What's more, even when the Turkish families take care of their yards, they rarely use them in the same way as their "French" neighbors. A yard's primary function for the latter is to be decorative, requiring meticulous care, while the former mostly devote them to children's play. They have arranged them for easier upkeep, in many cases replacing the lawn with concrete and cutting down trees. Yards are more likely to be utilitarian: families cook their *pide* flatbreads in often rather cobbled-together outdoor ovens, and they stock the wood for this use in the garden (see Illustrations 4.2 and 4.3). These are all breaches of taste for their "French" neighbors, who lament these new uses that mar the pleasant view their upper windows used to offer.

> Mme Vallès: Yes, it's deteriorated, because, it's always the same, they don't always have the same way.... Yards, for example. The yards used to always be well kept, the lawn mowed, flowers, well that's not at all their style. They put a pile of junk inside, they pile up pieces of wood, they grow their tomatoes and onions, and they do meals in the back yard. That brings in a lot of junk, to say the least, it's no longer the little yards with well-kept lawns and all. It's true that there's deterioration, if we want to go that far. It's true, but to each his own culture and way of life.

ILLUSTRATION 4.2. The Samsons' yard: flowers and lawn. (Photo taken by author)

ILLUSTRATION 4.3. A yard that has been redone: concrete slab and grill. (Photo taken by author)

Even more than the noise and metamorphosis of yards, the new neighbors do some things that feed old-timers' feeling that their place is being taken away. The example that arises most often in interviews concerns all the cars that block sidewalks and access to their homes (see Illustration 4.4). To understand the intensity of conflicts on this subject, one must bear in mind that retiree households only have one car, but the Turkish (and many other foreign) families are large and some adult children still live with their parents, so they may have several cars. Moreover, the newer neighbors have many more visitors than the old-timers, who mostly only receive their children at home. The immigrant families have a much more extensive social life, especially the Chaldeans, who are part of a tight community bound by family ties. It is not the Turkish neighbors but rather their visitors that park badly and upset "the French."

These points are important because they force us to see that the long-term residents' "having it up to here" is not merely due to xenophobia. Their complaints are largely rooted in the differences between them and their foreign neighbors, in lifestyle as in family composition. But still, few try to reconcile these differences. Feeling superior, they are more likely to see the newcomers as an endless source of nuisance.

ILLUSTRATION 4.4. Cars crowding the streets and sidewalks. (Photo taken by author)

Those Who Left

Over the course of the study, it became clear that the inhabitants who had left the Poplars held a prominent position in interviews with the pioneers who remained in the neighborhood. These old neighbors seemed to play just as important a role as the new neighbors in the relationship interviewees had with their housing and neighborhood, so we sought some of them out to include their perspective. Because our research was focused on the Poplars, we chose people who had not gone far, and whose addresses were known. Several had moved to Arnouville, a bordering town long frequented by pioneers for a variety of activities (errands, religious practice, sociability) that is generally appreciated and considered pleasant. Others bought homes elsewhere in Gonesse. Here we analyze both the details of these relatively recent moves from the Poplars (in the late 1990s) and their consequences, in a context of climbing real estate prices and the row houses' specialization in populations of Turkish and North African origin.

The short distance of these moves (into another neighborhood of the same town or to an adjacent town) reflects, of course, the economic limitations constraining these households' real estate strategies, but it also indicates that in many cases, it was motivated more by fleeing a neighborhood situation they found intolerable than a desire to change towns or even type of housing. All cite the easy access to Paris and public transportation from Gonesse and Arnouville. By insisting on the forced nature of their departures in their interviews, they indirectly signal their attachment to their old house and neighborhood, the background and depth of which we saw in the introduction.

> Interviewer: When did you start to leave the Poplars? Because basically, what you just described to me, it wasn't bad. You only had one child, so it wasn't a question of space. When did you begin to think about it?
> Mme Heurtin: When neighborly relations completely degraded, because the plan we had for our life, that wasn't it.
> M. Heurtin: I tried … There's one person who moved in, and it just wasn't possible, noise until one or two o'clock in the morning. … The Laval's sold, two years before us, in 2002.
> Interviewer: And who did they sell to?
> Mme Heurtin: To an African family. With four children. And yeah, some neighbor problems that come on top of that.
> Interviewer: Noise issues?
> M. Heurtin: But noise at all hours of day and night. Gatherings with fifteen or twenty people.
> Interviewer: Every day?
> M. Heurtin: Almost every day. It became intolerable, you're no longer at home.
> Interviewer: What did this woman do for work?

M. Heurtin: I don't know, I have no idea. But the children were left alone, she didn't come home before one or two in the morning. The girls were all alone. She'd forget her keys, ring the bell for two hours. She'd have company, twenty to thirty people would show up all at once. They'd go to the garden with music. Well I had several exchanges with her, and then I said to my wife "Listen, if this goes on I'm going to lose my calm, this just isn't possible anymore."

Interviewer: So that was one element, because prior to 2002 you weren't thinking of selling?

Mme Heurtin: No, that wasn't our plan at all.... We were forced to. We wouldn't have left the Poplars if the situation had stayed the same. If we hadn't been faced with this noise problem, the permanent hassle, we might have done it, but not in the same circumstances.

Interviewer: You'd have left for the provinces?

Wife: That was more our style, but not even, you know. We were fine. We were good at the Poplars.

This is not an example of the comfortable social stratum that buys and sells easily according to their changing desires. For our informants, retired couples of relatively modest means, selling is costly business. The Bergers are nostalgic for their old house and tell of the difficulty in transforming a house bought after the age of fifty, a place with no memories, into a home. The departures, experienced in terms of force, are also touched by a sense of bitterness and indignation that emerge clearly in the following statement from M. Piazza, who arrived in the Poplars in 1989 and who resold in 2005.[11] He tenaciously resisted the interviewer, who seems to have cast doubt on the idea that neighborhood is "deteriorating." He also illustrates how much those who left draw criticism and blame. For the pioneers who stayed, the old neighbors who sold out are as much to blame as the new neighbors they associate with the neighborhood's deterioration.

M. Piazza: Well yeah, they gave [the Chaldeans] funding. What I'm going to say will be hard, but when you see people who work all their life and can't buy a house because they don't have the means, and that there are people who come from someplace else and you put several million [francs] on the table ... What has to be said about that is that it's also the French who play their game, at that level.

Interviewer: What do you mean?

M. Piazza: I mean that when people sell a house, they sell to whoever buys it. They don't try to find out who they're selling to. They sell it, too bad for the rest. Afterwards they'll criticize behind their backs, they'll say things about people. You've got to tell it like it is. They're going to criticize the new arrivals, the ones they sold to. They go someplace else, they're going to criticize. But at the end of the day you mustn't criticize, it's people themselves who create the situation, too.

The main consequence of departures was to demoralize those who remained and weaken the solidarities that had united the row-house residents.

Indeed, because they barely moved at all, those who left the Poplars occasionally run into those who stayed (at the supermarket, for example), regularly reminding those who stayed that departure and avoiding undesirable neighbors is a sort of norm. Having once forged a respectable neighborhood of lower-level *cadres* together, these old neighbors now embody the marginalization of those who remain, who now find themselves with neighbors who are entirely unlike their predecessors.

INTERACTION AND ITS LIMITS

After having shown the extent to which relations between the little-middles of the pioneering generation and their neighbors of foreign origins are marked by prejudice, rejection, and everyday conflicts, we would now like to turn to other aspects of these relations that are more positive and benign. Many exchanges have taken place over the years between the older households and their new neighbors with immigrant backgrounds. These exchanges have helped the long-term residents put up with their new neighbors, get used to them, and even have positive experiences with them. In the early 1990s, some contributions to P Bourdieu's *The Weight of the World,* which raises awareness of spaces of social suffering in France, showed that housing developments may harbor conflictual relations between neighbors and traces of xenophobia.[12] And in suburban developments located near housing projects (like the Poplars), interactions and positive relations integrating people into neighborhoods were also found between neighbors of diverse origins. Relating such cases helps us to understand how the temptations of racism and exclusion, very much present, may be moderated (if not entirely contained) by forms of tolerance and understanding.

What are these interactions like? What are their effects on the concerned families? Why, if they find them gratifying, do old-timers have such difficulty fully coming to terms with these relationships? We repeat that there is no great divide between residents inclined to rejection and those who are tolerant and understanding, nor is there one side spewing negative and racist discourse and another striving daily to include their new neighbors, as one might think.[13] Variations in the little-middles' behavior toward their foreign neighbors are explained as much by the situation as the people involved.

Getting Accepted

Neighborhood families of foreign origin, be they North or sub-Saharan African, Kurdish or Chaldean, or other, are intensely aware of their rejection by the old-timers and "the French" in general, and their concern for escaping neighborhood stigmatization crops up throughout interviews with these newcomers, primarily taken to be foreigners. It is especially noticeable among immigrant families coming from the projects and the Chaldean families. The will to fight prejudices takes the form of foregrounding moral values and occasionally distancing themselves from the most stigmatized families, but it may also take the form of practices aiming to foster good relations with the neighbors.

For immigrant families coming from metro-Paris housing projects, ethnicized neighborhood relations and stigmatization as foreigners are not new. M. and Mme Bonfo are both from Togo and work respectively as a stock manager in distribution and a nurse's aide in a retirement home. Their purchase of a Poplars's row house in the early 2000s was part of a trajectory of social ascension where first-time homeownership meant departure from the projects, whose state of degradation they cite in particular. But coming to this neighborhood where the presence of immigrants is more recent and limited means that they are much more strongly identified as foreigners— they are likely to suffer from the same stigma that they fled. M. Bonfo acts indifferent to possible signs of rejection and refuses to engage in a logic of distinction with the Chaldeans:

> You know, this story of rejection, honestly it doesn't matter much to me. I don't ask for anything at all, if someone in the neighborhood rejects me, I could give a damn about him, it's not a big deal, it doesn't stop me from living my life. If for example the person doesn't want to sell me the house anymore, it's not a problem, we'll find another. That is something you mustn't ever take on, because it gets too complicated.

So he does not want to "take on" these reactions of rejection, of which he has had his share, and prefers to "let it go." But he is not as indifferent to neighborly relations as this excerpt would have us believe. He regrets he does not know many people on the square (only his immediate neighbors and a neighbor who works on his house). He would like to be more up to date with the neighborhood council's activities. Although he is "not much of a handyman," he is also prepared to spend time on the house so that "the neighborhood will be beautiful," so he replaced the old gate with one in forged iron, which he says is easier to maintain than wood. He replaced the wire mesh fencing with a hedge to make it more "like home" and because it "gives it life." He's planning on planting a vegetable garden. And last, he was inspired by a neighbor to redo the facade of the house. "You know the gentleman who's all the way at the end? He did some work, it's not finished yet, but it's pretty. What we did, well, it draws a little bit on what he did. And, well, if the others don't do it, we can't force them, it's up to them." If he does not feel like he is in a position to criticize his neighbors for not maintaining their facades, he still appreciates that they do what they can so that the neighborhood will be "pretty." In this, he is fully in line with the legacy of the row-house pioneers.

The Chaldean families have more than their share of prejudices to fight. As we mentioned in the introduction, their immigration following persecution in Turkey was rather brutal, and they obtained political refugee status in France. They come from a very rural region, and most of the first generation has little formal education. After passing through a settlement center outside of Paris, some settled in the Parisian periphery to look for work, either first living in deteriorated housing projects like La Forestière in Clichy-sous-Bois northeast of Paris or buying a row house in the Poplars right away, with help from acquaintances in the area. The first to move into the row houses did not know the neighborhood and quickly felt they were held at arms length, sometimes to the point of hostility.

Although socially quite far from the old-timers, and lacking the cultural and relational resources of couples who emigrated long ago and are fairly qualified (such as the Bonfos), the Chaldean families nonetheless worked to dissipate the stigma attached to them and pacify relations with their neighbors, especially those who had lived there the longest. Interviews with Chaldean residents all insistently refute the negative stories that circulate about them in the neighborhood.[14]

Not one of the Chaldean families we met mentioned neighbors' reactions of rejection. To the contrary, interviews gratefully acknowledge France's recognition of refugee status (particularly by the fathers) and affirm that one "mustn't complain," as illustrated by this interview with M. Sabar and his adult son Georges, who was translating Aramaic for his father.

> Georges: Well, my father says we're happy here, we came here, we were most of all unhappy with the life we had in Turkey. What my father just said, is that if someone isn't the same religion as in Turkey, he can't live in Turkey.
>
> Interviewer: And in France, you don't have this kind of problem?
>
> Georges: No. [*father speaking*] My father, what he just said is that France is a big country, a country of freedom, where there are some of all the races, and there are no differences between the races. You understand what I'm saying? No difference between the races. And France, it pays for the handicapped, it pays for children, it pays for the blind, France doesn't hate anyone. No one who hurts France, it doesn't hate anyone. And what's more it's normal, even in a family, that someone who hurts your family won't be liked as much as the others. That's normal—it is.
>
> Interviewer: I don't know if all French are as welcoming as all that.
>
> Georges: You know, I have five fingers on one hand. Do you see two that are the same? But that's normal, that. [*Father speaks at length in Aramaic*]. So my father, he has a Jewish neighbor, he has an Arab neighbor, he has a Yugoslavian neighbor, French. Armenian, there isn't one of his neighbors. . . . he asked another one, "you, what are you? You, what region are you from? You, what do you do?"
>
> M. Sabar [*speaking forcefully*]: All of them very nice, it's not that in Turkey.

The will to "integrate yourself" (which takes place, for example, by Gallicizing first names and systematically seeking French citizenship) comes with a work on self-presentation that aims to counter oft-heard stereotypes. Indeed, we see in the next chapter how it may also be translated by a vote for the right, or even paradoxically for the extreme right. They mention how poor they were when they arrived, and their devotion to work. Georges Sabar, who left school young, was unemployed when we first met, and explained at length that he was ready to do "any kind of job." They all relate how they arrived without anything and were helped by people they knew who were already established in France. And Selma Yazïr, who works for an association of Chaldeans, is insistent in refuting the claim that families have many children in order to get welfare checks, insisting that it is the result of religious beliefs.

Fathers (who are also often grandfathers) insist on the need to strictly supervise children. This motivated them to establish nightly rounds following the excesses of the summer of 2005 (more on this in the next chapter) for which the young Chaldeans bore the blame. Ten or so parents assure that all children go home by a given time. About ten of these parents also attended a meeting at the middle school organized by the mayor in late April 2007 following some incidents between youth from the Poplars and the neighboring housing project, in order to express their concern for the safety of children on the way to school (as any parent) and offer to meet with parents from the Cité du Nord project to think together about how they might better supervise their children.

Several emphasize that they are neighborhood homeowners just like the others. Georges Sabar thinks that they reasoned "like anyone else," and that purchasing prevents losing money on high rent. Many had unsuccessfully applied for public housing. Perhaps anticipating our having heard the widespread rumor that they bought their houses in mysterious cash, they described their rather heavy long-term loans in detail, and explained that adult children contribute to payments. They stress attachment to the family and the importance of parents and children living near each other as central residential practices. They explain how there came to be such a concentration of Chaldean households in the neighborhood by stressing how important it is to help each other and for families to stick together, depicted as very positive values (the opposite of individualism).

Finally, owners almost "like the others," they report having good relations with their neighbors, who they describe as "very nice." According to Georges Sabar's father, "the neighborhood is ideal," relations with neighbors are very good, there is "no problem at all," and everyone gets along "like brothers." This harmonious image allows unflattering rejection and conflicts to be stifled. Some stories detail Chaldeans' good relations with the old-timers and their efforts to connect with them, largely focused on their houses. Selma Yazïr described the renovations made on a rather old-fashioned house that was "not very clean" on the ground floor: light-colored tile had replaced the wood inside and on the stairs, and a little terrace had been made in the yard. Moreover, many families had replaced the original stained or painted wooden gates with wrought iron fences that give houses a less "old-fashioned" look, as M. Bonfo put it, who had done the same.

Observation of the neighborhood confirms these efforts to embellish the houses: after a period when expenses had been devoted to interior work, many satellite-dish equipped facades were repainted, and window frames and glass replaced. There is garden furniture outside, decorations and welcoming messages ornament the doorway, and potted plants brighten up the entries. The second-story balconies are abloom with potted geraniums similar to those of older residents. These efforts at goodwill are also found in daily relations as families demonstrate their desire to prove their hospitality. Stressing that hospitality is part of their tradition, Selma explains how her family often offers food to its neighbors, following a common practice between Chaldean households. This practice began culinary exchanges with a Moroccan family on the same street, which brings them dishes in return. But she is proudest of the connection she made with the "old lady" on the square, an "old resident" who greatly appreciates visits from Selma's nephew.

Food and children seem to play a central role in establishing good relations and contribute to the development of everyday positive interactions. How do long-term residents perceive this goodwill? And what effect might these exchanges have on the cohabitation of long-term and newer residents?

ANOTHER FORM OF SOCIAL MOBILITY AT THE POPLARS: CHALDEAN FAMILIES BUY SMALL BUSINESSES

The portraits of retail business-owners presented below—all Chaldean men, mostly eldest sons—show different ways in which business ownership can serve as a path for social ascension for immigrant families.[15] If the Poplars still partially functions as a neighborhood of social ascension today, this is only so for a handful of its immigrant families, and their mobility differs greatly in form and amplitude from the mobility characterizing the other generations of little-middles studied in this book. A series of departures created favorable conditions for taking over some of the Poplars's small businesses: in 2005, several merchants who also lived in the neighborhood either retired (the owners of the hotel, the hair salon, and the bar/tobacconist) or invested elsewhere (the manager of a grocery store). These businesses' traits (small footage, low starting investment) made them accessible to these modest Chaldean entrepreneurs, permitting them to improve their occupational situations, and apparently their financial situations as well. This small social mobility cannot be disassociated from the family solidarities supporting it.

Alain Duman is forty-three and owner of the Poplars's hotel since 2005. He is married and the father of ten children, aged one to twenty-one, who live with him in a house fifty meters from the hotel. The second child of an illiterate peasant family that was chased off its land by Turkish authorities in 1984, he left Turkey in 1988 with his wife and two small children. Arriving in Mont-de-Marsan, the transitional town the government designated for receiving Chaldean refugees, he immediately started looking for work "to feed [*his*] family." He had a long string of temporary jobs in farming then in construction. The Duman family moved to Gonesse in 1994. Alain borrowed money from the bank to buy a house in the Poplars. He got work in the garment industry and was eventually hired in a permanent position doing a job requiring little training. In 1998, he invested his savings in the purchase of the General Grocery, located at the entrance to the neighborhood, supplemented by "a lot of money" (that is all we know) borrowed from the bank by mortgaging his house.

The store only started to be profitable in 2000. Alain then tried to expand it by transforming part of it into a take-out food business with the profits. This project caused some conflict with the person in charge of businesses at city hall, who suspected trafficking and feared an increase in noise problems at night. Alain finally decided to sell the business to set himself up elsewhere. After having looked toward Arnouville (which has a bigger commercial zone), he bought the Poplars's hotel (thirty-some rooms); he went into it with one of his nephews because the investment this time was far too heavy for him alone. Alain thus offers a profile of access to business ownership within the working classes: salaried work, progressive accumulation of savings, bank loan.

To understand how a laborer with few qualifications can both feed a large family and accumulate the savings necessary for commercial investments, we should point out the non-negligible contribution that various social services represent in terms of revenue for a family of this size. For example, in 2006, the child benefits for a family of ten children was 1,320 euros per month. This strategy for business ownership obviously also requires an unlimited investment in work: Alain works fifteen-hour days daily, the hotel being open from 9:00 AM to midnight, including Sundays. He admits he has not taken a vacation for eleven years—his children go visit family members when possible.

Alain hired two part-time employees. In the near future, he is planning to replace them with two of his children who recently got their *baccalauréats* and are pursuing higher studies (accounting for the eldest, law for the second), to limit the amount of money that goes out of the family as much as possible.

Georges Sabar has managed the grocery store on Ibis Square since September 2005. He is thirty-three and lives in a row house in the Poplars with his wife and three children. He has lived in the neighborhood for thirteen years, and he knows most of his customers personally. He is the eldest in a family of nine children (he had four brothers and four sisters), who all still live in the Poplars. He left school at sixteen to work in Paris with his father in the garment industry. For six years, like his brother, he passed his earnings on to his parents, who consolidated family finances to control expenses. Georges lived with his parents and siblings until the age of twenty-nine, when his father bought him a house. In 2005, his father reached retirement age and invested in the Poplars's grocery, handing its management over to his eldest son, who had been unemployed for five months. It was during an interview in the store during open hours that Georges indicated with his head (without literally saying so) that his father was the real owner of the store (he spends every day in the back room watching the store and his son on camera). In this case, it is the retiring generation that invests accumulated savings and provides employment to the working-age generation, which was previously unemployed or in an insecure position on the job market.

Georges does all the work in the store himself, and his work days have nothing in common with those he knew as a salaried worker: he is in the store from 9:00 AM to 9:30 PM, seven days a week. In addition, twice a week he gets up at 4:00 AM to drive his little truck to Paris's wholesale food market Rungis to stock up on perishable goods. His father sets his pay. The big investment decisions are the province of his parents and are aimed at conserving and developing family resources. Accordingly, in March 2006, Georges's father once again invested and bought the hair salon adjacent to the grocery, where he set up his eldest daughter (a trained hairdresser) as manager. Their business accession process has not yet run its course, and through it, we see how the family strategy gradually unfolds in the neighborhood space. It also cannot be dissociated from a family solidarity that, strong as it is, cannot be taken for granted.

In fact, Georges almost upset the family plans: he had wanted to marry a Spanish woman he met on vacation. A serious, sometimes violent, crisis erupted, his brothers physically stopping him from leaving several times. The father's purchase of a house for his son (where he lives with a woman who better suits family strategies), much like his purchase of the store, aims to settle the son down and attach him to the family plan. As for Georges, he has an ambiguous discourse on the sacrifice he made for his family, at once positive (he does it for the family, so the business will succeed) and negative (he works hellish days, earns little money). This raises questions about the reasons for such an investment in time and strength, but Georges brushes it aside by invoking the importance of family solidarity. This discourse may mask another possibility—that managing the store is also a more rewarding position for Georges. He expresses pride that he carries the family now, replacing his now-retired father. This is reinforced by the father's presence in the store all day long, which itself indicates the affective proximity he maintains with his son. Ultimately Georges holds a position as a local notable, someone known and recognized. He actually monopolizes the exterior signs of the success accumulated by those near to him: he's the one who is visible in and out of the store, while his father remains in the background. The qualities attributed to him personally are in fact the result of strategies for the conservation of family resources.

Multiple Interactions

Interviews with old-timers show the variety of interactions they have with the newcomers: greetings, gifts of food (couscous, stuffed grape leaves, or pizza from neighbors of Chaldean and North African origin, crêpes, batter-fried zucchini flowers, Twelfth Night cake in return from "the French"), lending each other a helping hand (be it filling out social services forms, reading official letters, doing home maintenance, or helping with homework, informally or through the charity Secours Catholique).

> M. Boyer: We're lucky—we are—to have rather pleasant foreigners. I tell you, they are all really charming. Take him, there [*he points through the window to a man returning home*]
> Interview: Where's he from?
> M. Boyer: From India.... They are really very nice. [*Gesturing to the houses facing his*] And then there, where there's a child going in, it's some Chaldeans, I think they're going to have their eighth child. They're really charming people, they bend over backwards to make us happy. We got bread twice a month, they brought tomatoes, cucumbers. We come back from vacation—we took off for two and a half months in a camper—we get home, we'd barely put our baggage down, and they have something to give us. They wait for us like we're part of the family. And then there, next door, that's some old-timers, and the next house it's people of Algerian origin, from, I'm not sure anymore, like almost in the desert. And it's the same, it's people, when they make couscous, we get couscous. The lady, when she comes back from Algeria, we have dates at their place because they still have land, with a date palm. We have dates every time, really very, very nice, we have nothing to complain about.

To read this, we are far indeed from a situation where people turn in on themselves, either among long-term inhabitants or immigrant groups. These interactions are the opportunity to discover another way of life and acquire firsthand information on neighbors who are subject to rumors and a source of worry. References to party invitations suggest that such occasions help get past the gossip and the temptation of rejection by making things like the circumstances of Chaldean migration known, as in this quote from an interview with the Boyers:

> There was a wedding there across the street, the Chaldeans. There was one that was trying to integrate herself, who was getting married and she wanted to invite us. In fact, most of the Chaldeans who are there, they are all from the same village that was flattened, it was destroyed. They told us, they were like chased, they all came here. They're refugees. They all know each other, they're from the same family. And when these people bought there in '90, they had cousins, family. Well, there was one for sale, so it filled up like that.

Interactions also affect how differences between people and families are perceived, beyond oversimplified categories like "foreigners" or "Turks."

Another extract gives a glimpse of the gradual discovery of language uses and children's difficulties adapting to school.

> Mme Boyer: And for two years, the two older boys had trouble at school, so in the evening, about three times a week, they came over and I'd help them do their homework. That worked out well until the day when they asked for the daughter. But wow, with the daughter it was hellish since even the alphabet, the letters of the alphabet, she didn't know it. And though I was really patient, you know, I tried to make a reading notebook with pictures, but no, impossible, I gave up. Plus at the same time I needed to go for my grandchildren, my daughter-in-law needed.... So I said "No, this isn't possible." And we stopped, you know, doing that. But the two boys, that was really good, they were making progress, they tried to work.
> M. Boyer: It's very hard because at home ... We make them speak French, but at home they speak Chaldean, and so it's hard.

Mme Sanchez, Mme Samson, and Mme Morin have also had children from Chaldean families over to help them with their school work, and several other kinds of interactions involve preschoolers (exchanged greetings, gifts of food, or candy). Remember that the new row-house residents have many preschool-aged children while the little-middle couples are aged and retired. Their own children are adults and, although they usually live nearby, they have their own families. These couples are thus both mentally and materially available for neighborly relations. They find themselves at an age when they might feel isolated or deprived of social relations, even if they have local forms of sociability (activities in associations, relationships with neighbors, and friends).[16] This availability allows them to build a social life with the new neighbors, and one of its most common manifestations is acting almost like surrogate grandparents: giving candy, helping with school work, supervising play. Several of the interviewed women say neighbor children call them "grammie." Some couples and women living alone (widowed or divorced) find an affection and human warmth in their relations with the Chaldean children that they would likely have missed if the neighborhood population had not changed.

Men's interactions revolve more around home improvement and yard work: as we pointed out in chapter 1, older-generation little-middle men enjoy tinkering, and they have the skills and tools to do it. Interactions between men lending each other helping hands was a component of the Poplars's early social life, and this same kind of sociability is possible with the new neighbors, but in an unbalanced and fragile way since the latter, poor in tools as well as skills, seem barely able to return the favor. Although masculine sociability is still organized around home improvement and maintenance in the Poplars, it is weakened by the differences in material and technical resources between men.

These exchanges go toward restoring the self-esteem of long-term residents whose social position is weakened by the neighborhood's transformation due to their peers' departure for a "real house" or a better neighborhood. In fact, by using and sharing their academic or technical resources, or even occasional advice and suggestions concerning house maintenance, these interactions refresh their superior social rank in relation to their new neighbors. The Boyers tell how their neighbor of Moroccan origin came to ask their advice on the type of material to choose when replacing his fence. Mme Boyer's account well illustrates the satisfaction felt in being placed in the position of guardian of taste for common spaces.

Although they do help make a friendly climate of improved mutual understanding that eases hostility and conflict, these interactions do not really challenge the ethnicizing gaze that separates the "foreigners" (or "Muslims," or "Turks") into a negative pole and blames them for the neighborhood's deterioration. Far from automatically weakening and suppressing this ethnicizing and excluding regard, the daily sociability between neighbors may, to the contrary, contribute to its revival and reinforcement, as we see next.

NEIGHBORHOOD PARTIES

Multiple residents mentioned neighborhood parties, which also contribute to these positive interactions.[17] As a parent, M. Hakimi (an urbanist from Iran who has lived in a row house since the 1980s) has organized several parties so parents of "different minorities" can meet each other. These parties were so successful that he went on to organize a neighborhood-wide party on the same idea:

M. Hakimi: A party really made an impression on us, two or three times when the kids were little. With parents from the school, we sometimes tried to have a party with a variety of representatives of the ethnicities that are here.... So, each one brings a cake. I swear, the first time there were—at a party that finished very late at night—between 180 and 200 people, a party, the dances were also very well organized, all that. That was an unprecedented evening, all the families came. After that, there was another time, thinking with some friends [*living*] behind us, we decided to throw a party. So I made a flyer that we put in all the neighbors' mailboxes and after, you know, it's really halting, like a child starting to walk. So I said to our friend behind us, I already have two or three tables that I put in the square behind, I called Alain. Even the neighbors who'd originally wanted to participate were a little hesitant, but then they came. We put out bottles of drinks and all that and I swear, we finished up at two or three in the morning with our almost multinational festivities! [*laughs*]

Interviewer: Everyone came?

M. Hakimi: Everyone from all the different parts, they came with their meal, their drinks. The Portuguese, they brought port, the Vietnamese brought spring rolls.

Interviewer: When was that, was it a while ago?

M. Hakimi: Yes, it was four years ago. It was really a great success, because at that moment people danced together, ate couscous, all that. And the Turkish women danced with the French, the French women danced with the others ... more like the French women who were dancing with the others (*laughs*). You see, that means we acknowledge each other, we talk with each other.

Contrary to other parties that consolidate the domination of a certain group of neighbors (often the old-timers) over collective spaces, this party's organizers were hesitant because they did not feel legitimate enough to represent the neighborhood given its ethnic diversity and state of tension. The goal of the party was actually to put different cultures, or "ethnicities," into contact with each other to encourage dialogue and mutual understanding. We find these same characteristics in the sidewalk party that took place a few years ago on Ibis Avenue, where the Samsons live. They talk about it enthusiastically. They organized the party with some neighbors to celebrate the fact that, after years of lobbying, the city had finally redone their pitted sidewalks:

Mme Samson: So there it was, they did our sidewalks. So everyone was happy. And people who don't belong to any associations, all that, a French, an Iranian, a Pole, who else took part in that? A Chinese. Who took part in that?

M. Samson: We all coordinated, and we said, "we're going to have a party."

Mme Samson: They put papers in the mailboxes—we said, since it's a small neighborhood, we all made a specialty of our own!

M. Samson: We danced.

Mme Samson: We danced Turkish! At first we'd put on tapes, of ours. And then, all at once, there were some grown kids who took off, and they came back with Turkish cassettes. Well, we danced the sirtaki, we danced all that. We ate Chinese, we ate Iranese ... Iranese or Iranian? We ate Turkish, stuffed grape leaves, we ate French, I'd made some things. And I did mention that—I make savory breads, you know, with ham inside—I'd made it with turkey breast that time. And I put right on it "without pork," because, well ...

This party illustrates one form of neighborly relations at the Poplars that should not be overshadowed by conflicts and practices of rejection. It took place to celebrate the intervention of a third party, the city, in the life of the street, rather than marking the power of one group of neighbors over the space. As in Omid Hakimi's party, all the residents coordinated to organize it, and it provided an occasion to interact that valued everyone's identity, through culinary specialties as well as music and dance. The resident network's configuration explains the nature of this party. On the Samson's street, the Turkish families are in the majority and are well networked through social and family ties, and they function as the "established" group, while the four "French" households are effectively "outsiders."[18] Despite having lived there forty years, in a way, they feel like they were abandoned by their neighbors who moved away one by one. Their relative lack of clout prevents "the French" from getting their conceptions of residential uses accepted. If the sidewalk party made such an impression on the Samsons ("it's a book's worth!" they warned us before telling us about it), this is primarily because it embodied the hope that different conceptions could coexist. Everyone could learn to accept the others' uses of residential space, through dialogue instead of force, without renouncing their own expectations. Yet this party only took place once, one of the organizers having moved away ("because of the Turks, because he couldn't sleep anymore," Mme Samson specified). Omid Hakimi also tells how the party on his square was not repeated and went on to mention a conflict between two families, Chaldean and French, following the latter's complaints about the noise made by the Chaldean children. He tried to act as a mediator between the families, both of which he finds "very good" and "very obliging," but without success.

Interactions Without Real Futures

Many studies have found that children and child-rearing are subject to tension and conflicts over norms in socially heterogeneous residential settings, and the Poplars in the 2000s is no exception. It is attenuated, however, by the fact that the neighborhood is home to both parents and grandparents, and the aging old-timers see the children as much as grandchildren to pamper as children to be raised. So in this section, we would like to highlight another area of practices that merely curb sociability without sparking conflict and ill will. The rationales behind the previously described interactions between little-middle households and certain neighbors of Chaldean or North African origin do not defuse inclinations to stigmatize or reject these neighbors as foreigners. We found that occasions for interaction often end up blocked or stalled, and reciprocal feelings of distrust resurface. Ways of eating (mealtimes and foods) are especially susceptible to be embarrassing, and may weaken the impact of the encounters and relationships they are intended to encourage. Mme Samson tells how she had invited her Chaldean neighbors to share a Twelfth Night cake. Invited for 5:30 in the afternoon after having eaten lunch late as is their habit, they ate practically nothing that she had prepared. "I thought I was inviting them for a snack. I thought they'd have eaten at noon, like us, we could have spoken about it. I'd made a fruit salad and all that, so we'd have the time to really . . . enjoy it."

The Boyers also express their discomfort when confronted with these little moments of misunderstanding:

Mme Boyer: The relations have to stay friendly, but we can't, uh, go to their place, invite each other. We don't have the same ways of living.
M. Boyer: I'm ready to lend him a hand.
Interviewer: But why? I don't understand, what could happen if you went?

Mme Boyer: Oh, well, they're going to offer us a coffee or who knows what, and we'll feel obligated to, maybe, to do the same thing and we don't want to find ourselves there.

Interviewer: Because you'd be bothered to invite them to have coffee at your place?

Mme Boyer: No, but they don't have the same lifestyle, it's entirely different.

M. Boyer: When I went to Turkey, we fell into step with the others, you know, with the Turks.

Mme Boyer: Well yeah, but we were on vacation, that's different. But when we came back ... We'd made a film there in Turkey. Well Thérèse and Naïma, we showed them the film on the TV, they came over. Things like that, it's different. They saw it; "Yes, it was like that at home when we were children." ... But the relations aren't ... Neither eating nor "come have a coffee." It's not the same, I find, it's not the same thing. After, you're too... a little obligated.

Interviewer: Yes, you're afraid of getting into a cycle, which gets away from you.

M. Boyer: That's it.

Mme Boyer: Already, the wedding we went to was an experience.... But it's not relations like you can have with the French.

M. Boyer: The other day, he wanted to invite us to his brother's wedding, last Thursday. Well, I say "No, it's not my culture."

Mme Boyer: Well, the Algerians next door, it's the same, they are charming, those people, really. They do Ramadan, at the end of Ramadan there's a couscous. She comes back from her country, after the holidays, there it's the same, we're going to have dates from their place.

M. Boyer: They're nice, y'know.

Mme Boyer: And how many times has she said to me "But come with your husband, come eat." Well yeah, but no! We're happy they give us couscous, we thank them in our way, but we wouldn't go eat at their place, with them—that goes beyond our relationship.

Interview: So how did you thank them, then?

Mme Boyer: Well, for example, we come back from vacation, we bring a box of cookies from Brittany, something like that. When Sabrina was little, it was more gifts for her, for the little one.

M. Boyer: But on the other hand, they are really very nice, y'know.

Mme Boyer: They are charming. And the gentleman, at the beginning ... Her, she spoke French poorly but she tried to speak it, and the first time we saw her she borrowed a table from us because she didn't have a table in the house. We tried to find what could work, ok. We had trouble understanding that was what she wanted. Fine, now she's made great progress. But him, from shyness, he'd turn his head away a little, he didn't say hello to us. And now that he's gotten a little confidence, he stops when he comes back from work. He's really very, very nice.... The son, it's the same when he comes. And the oldest girl, she had two little ones, well we gave a gift for the baby when it was born.

M. Boyer: See, it's little gestures that don't cost anything.

Interviewer: It's true that it isn't easy to build relationships like that with people.

M. Boyer: You can't ...

Mme Boyer: No, then, what could be right for them isn't necessarily ...

M. Boyer ... right for us. No, we don't have the same culture [*laughing*]. We don't have the same stomachs!

The Boyers said this at the very end of an interview, and the Samsons' quote comes from the third interview. In front of academics who interview them in their homes, they emphasize the positive side of sociability with the new neighbors at first. But encouraged to open up by the length of the interviews and the confidence that they build, they also finally speak of the failures and limits of these good relations with their Chaldean or North African neighbors. We end up understanding that all these gifts of food, initially seen as positive, can also come to be irritating because they are too frequent, arrive at a bad moment, or simply do not suit the recipients' taste.

Such accounts clearly communicate the seeming impossibility of deepening interactions, especially through that most essential form of exchange, eating together. It is easy to imagine that the newcomers trying to build relations in the neighborhood might be hurt by these refusals of invitations to eat or to simply come into their homes. Beyond long-time residents' reticence, they are also afraid of doing something wrong, making faux pas, and embarrassing everyone. "What could be right for them isn't necessarily ... right for us," the Boyers explained, referring to the uncertainty about the behavioral norms they should adopt in interactions with Chaldeans or North Africans.

In chapter 1, we evoked the alarm of certain women (Mme Samson, Mme Sanchez) upon discovering the very strict sexual division of roles observed in the homes of their Chaldean or Togolese neighbors, including the husband's authority and the wife's submission. Sociability gets blocked as much over male-female relations as over foodways, where differences of "culture" (as M. Boyer put it) return to center stage. And on a more mundane level, linguistic challenges also make it far more difficult to get into a cycle of exchange. Communication with people who do not speak French or speak it poorly is weaker and ripe for misunderstanding and complication.

The experience of failed encounters reactivates and consolidates the ethnicizing discourse that reinserts cultural difference between "them" ("the foreigners") and "us" ("the French") into neighborhood relations. The examples we just gave testify to this cultural difference, or to be more exact, to these lifestyles that introduce pitfalls into neighborly sociability. But contrary to interpretations put forward by the interviewees, this cultural difference alone is not enough to explain the extreme difficulty in developing a cycle of interaction and a unified residential group. Cultural difference is intimately associated with the social distance between the little-middles and their new neighbors. The tenuous nature of this social distance and the challenge of coming to terms with it have made it virtually impossible for old-timers to successfully overcome cultural differences and accept and appreciate their new neighbors in the way that certain inhabitants of old gentrifying neighborhoods have done, in word if not in deed.[19]

On top of that, although there is a gap in cultural and academic resources between the populations—long-term residents remind us that some of their new neighbors cannot read or write—the old-timers only have limited resources themselves. Note that the women who enjoy helping Chaldean children with their homework only do so through primary school, never beyond. And their prior experiences in school, work, and cultural practices were such that they had never had the chance to learn to mix with people from different ethnic backgrounds or lifestyles. Last, neither their socialization nor recent local political history inclines these little-middles to a left-leaning sensibility, which is found in gentrified neighborhoods. Ultimately, their relations with their new neighbors remain deeply ambivalent.

The Ambivalence of Relationships with Foreign Neighbors

Although the old-timers sometimes admit that the neighborhood is getting better and materially improving, they still affirm their distance and reservations vis-à-vis these new neighbors, most often through judgments of taste. Thus, Mme Samson credits the Turkish families with improved upkeep of the neighborhood ("Actually, the Turks keep things up better than some of the French a few years back ... doing the tile, in the courtyard, in the yard, they've done it for their fences, so that was more tidy right away")—but at the same time, she laments an aesthetic degradation: cement instead of trees and flowers, imposing gates with posts instead of painted wooden fences. And if, as we saw, the Boyers are pleased that their neighbors of Chaldean, North African, and Indian origin decorate the facades of their houses for festive occasions, they may also criticize the excess and exuberance of some of their efforts in veiled terms, as Mme Boyer does in speaking of her Indian neighbors' decorations:

> Oh, the Indians, it was pretty! All the way to the top! I don't know how they managed to go put the lights above the upper windows. That made the whole house ... it was pretty. You'd have thought it was, was Las Vegas! It was really a thing that blinked everywhere. Whereas us, we also put up blinking lights, but on the tree, y'know.

When speaking of the ambivalence of their relationships with foreigners, we want to draw attention to the fact that these little-middles do not espouse the raw xenophobia found in certain working class families,[20] nor do they raise ethnicity to a new status as in certain fringes of the urban middle classes. The following extract from an interview with the Samsons puts this ambivalence at the heart of relations with foreign neighbors into sharp relief. The Samsons' behavior toward their neighbors is marked by compassion and tolerance stemming from their Roman Catholic socialization, found among many of the neighborhood pioneers. But they are also tempted by xenophobia and the urge to reject.

> Mme Samson: And then an Armenian family came, then two Armenian families, three Armenian families. Fine, little by little the others, Turkey, Iraq, the problems with Iraq; an Iraqi family arrived, got his cousins to come, got his big brothers to come. And now, well, fine, I don't want to do racism, because, I'm not saying I'm racist, since I'm poorly placed, since I'm in Secours Catholique, an association that takes care of exactly these people here. But it's getting hard, it's getting very hard. They are very nice! Very very nice!
>
> M. Samson: Very very nice!
>
> Mme Samson: I broke my hand: "Oh! You can't make dinner!" They brought me things to eat and all that. But there are nine children across the street. There [*indicating a house*], not there, that's another of the old-timers like us, but the other house, they work until two o'clock in the morning.
>
> M. Samson: Ah yes, but the work, well, they party too.
>
> Mme Samson: They have a lot of parties and all. And, well, when we had our children we didn't realize it! We must have made noise for the neighbors! The neighbors never complained, since they had children too.
>
> M. Samson: Yes, but still, they went to bed early.
>
> Mme Samson: We were used to it—then after, it was almost too quiet, we were all old. There, happily, now it's good, the neighborhood has come back to life with all these young children. We can't complain, we have a neighborhood. They are very nice.
>
> M. Samson: Oh yes, they are very nice.
>
> Interviewer: You broke your hand, and then?
>
> Mme Samson: The lady, she'd sent one of her children.... It's a Chaldean. The little one showed up with a pot, "you can't make anything to eat. Mommy brings you something to eat."
>
> Interviewer: Ah yes, so that's why, when you say they're nice ...
>
> Mme Samson: Obviously, they live a lot among themselves, we have trouble integrating them.
>
> M. Samson: There's no doubt that. They come alive at eleven o'clock at night.
>
> Interviewer: Ah yes.
>
> Mme Samson: And summer is really a pain.
>
> Interviewer: Yes, maybe we don't realize it, now, since it's winter. It's more summer ...
>
> Mme Samson: In the summer, when we sleep with the windows open, they have cookouts until two, three in the morning. And the sound rises, eh, since we're on the second floor. Otherwise we like it here, since we're staying here. We deliberately did work to grow old here; our children are here, our children are married, they're at the Poplars too. So it's not so bad as all that!

In a disconcerting progression, their words skip from expressions of sympathy and motives for satisfaction ("very, very nice," story of the gift of food illustrating helping out, "a neighborhood that's come back to life," "we can't complain," "we like it here") and signs of understanding (many children are inevitably a source of noise and you are more sensitive to it when you no longer have small children yourself), to more or less direct reproaches and criticisms ("it's getting very hard," "they party," the children go to bed very late, "it's really a pain").

Mme Samson herself helps with schoolwork through a Secours Catholique program and visits families of children with academic problems to urge them to get them such help. She speaks at length of her anxiety at going to knock on her Chaldean neighbors' doors and the tactics that she has gradually developed to earn their confidence. She refers to the work on herself (self-persuasion, "launching" herself, finding the right self-presentation) that is involved in developing close contacts with neighbors of Turkish origin. Words and practices addressing cohabitation with the new neighbors seem contradictory and ambivalent because sociability in a residential setting with so many vivid differences (demographic, cultural, social, and economic) seems to be anything but natural. Unlike homogeneous residential contexts, nothing is taken for granted: distrust, embarrassment, and misunderstandings threaten relations here more than elsewhere. Bourdieu's expression "sociability work" is particularly suitable in this instance[21]: skills like prudence, tact, and cool-headedness are necessary for deeper social relations to develop.

Other than her own fears, Mme Samson also has to overcome the disapproval of other old-timers who are hostile to these new neighbors. She is not the only one to have developed relations with the newcomers—other women such as Mme Sanchez or Mme Boyer do the same, with no relation to Secours Catholique. But one of her experiences demonstrates that her attitude is not widespread. She recounted how the owner of the neighborhood's central café-tobacconist made some "comments" to her, saying "You take care of those people—there's too many of them!" causing her to slink away with her head down. Through her exchanges with children and their families, Mme Samson acquires notoriety and recognition measurable in gifts of food and the exchange of innumerable greetings, from which her husband also benefits. But while speaking with evident pleasure of these signs of recognition that brighten the time spends out and about in the neighborhood ("it's intense!"), she emphasized the hostility of some old-timers who are disinclined to break the ice and take on such sociability work.

I'm going to tell you something. There are some who, well, I'm not going to be ... I'm no better than anyone else, eh, I've got a little bit of a little devil in me too. But they say it's up to them to say hello! It's up to them, when they arrive, to speak to us. I don't know how many times I've said to some people I know well, since we've known each other for a long time, "Listen, it's up to *you* to speak to them!" Because it's got to be said that when you arrive like that, you're completely lost, eh. If you don't go talk to them, they aren't going to dare to speak to you. We do that right away.

In the interview, Mme Samson sets herself apart from some residents who are reticent to develop exchanges with foreigners, people she knows well and with whom she seems to have discussed the subject often. She says that the newcomers on her street are "well integrated." Having mentioned the street prompts her to count off the "five families that are left" ("like in Asterix," she added, referring to the classic comic books about the Gauls resisting the invading Romans) and describe neighbors' more or less direct pressure to sell. She seems to put aside her interpersonal relations to put herself in a position to think of the neighborhood as a confrontation between two ethnic groups. But after setting herself apart from the old-timer's ways of seeing things, she seems to come back to it and finishes by expressing fear of losing her identity: "Sometimes we are a little bit afraid, still, because ... Not fear of them, not that, but fear, us, of losing us, our identity! We ourselves are going to be obliged to live at their pace." The ambivalence and contradiction are even more flagrant at the end of the interview. After describing this sociability work and demonstrating that they understand their neighbors' history and living conditions, and after describing the range of practices to integrate them, M. and Mme Samson lapse into the eternal rebukes made of "foreigners": not working, being "on welfare," "being expensive for France," "not integrating themselves." After having said that, Mme Samson describes herself as being a "little demon," ultimately objectifying the ambivalence of her behavior herself.

This chapter thus supports the idea that residents' ambivalence toward foreigners is connected with the little-middle lifestyle. Residential downclassing certainly leads to an interpretation of neighborhood decline from the arrival of the foreigners and to forms of rejection related to these concerns. But tensions also come from different lifestyles, which stem as much from differences between each population's stage of life as they do cultural differences. And these tensions do not prevent neighborly relations and exchanged favors that lead to gradual forms of acceptance. Studying actual relations in everyday neighborhood life thus provides nuance to what might initially appear to be xenophobia.

It is important to describe this ambivalence, this unstable relationship to those who are seen as foreigners, because it is too often glossed over with attributions of racism or oversimplifications that obscure the complexity of neighborly relations in these housing developments in greater Paris that, as we discuss in the next chapter, are being won over to "the Le Pen vote." These households are from the pioneering group, whose formation and decline we have already described. We found that the ambivalence of individual statements is often an echo of debates that agitate the pioneers in general, their sentiment of belonging paradoxically intensifying as the group weakens. The following examples show that attitudes seem to be shared among the couples. M. Legris joined us after an interview with Mme Legris, and we said we would like to meet Mme Samson. Mme Legris said she was a "neighbor" and a "friend," and they know she has good relation with Chaldean families. The husband then explained, in veiled language, that the Samsons disagreed with him and his wife about what to make of the transformation of the neighborhood's population. With irony and irritation, he made fun of Mme Samson, saying "At any rate, she thinks everyone is nice!" But his wife defended her, maintaining that she is "tolerant."

For these little-middles having experienced modest occupational success (to be weakened later by economic crisis in some cases), the 1960s purchase of a house in a cute neighborhood with a good local reputation and well-employed neighbors was the main symbol of their success and social ascension. The collective construction of a local domestic culture also contributed to this sentiment. But the crumbling of this culture under various factors downgraded their social status, and finding themselves neighbors with large Chaldean or North African families only makes that fall seem worse. Starting a cycle of exchange with these new neighbors is ultimately tantamount to renouncing their social ascension, already worn and weakened simply by living together.

These little-middles' thus have a very different relationship to their residential space's reputation than residents of gentrified neighborhoods have with theirs. They cannot distance themselves from the neighborhood's reputation because it is the very basis of their social position. They cannot reverse the stigma that has come to be associated with their neighborhood since the immigrant households arrived, discernable in the discourse of neighbors who have moved away, other inhabitants of Gonesse, and even municipal authorities. The only remaining way to defend their social honor, based as it is on a modest success manifest in suburban homeownership, is to refuse overly intimate or frequent interactions with the new neighbors.

As for the Chaldean families, they are concerned about giving a good image of their community, and those we met emphasize their desire to integrate and how well they get along with the neighbors. At first they seem to deny that there are tensions and expressions of rejection, but they do sometimes eventually indicate their awareness of it and how it hurts them. Take the example of Claudine Ramirez, a former resident of the neighborhood from a Jewish family from Sarcelles who works on the cleaning staff at Gonesse hospital. Citing fear of seeing her property value decline as her reason for leaving, she admitted that the warmth and generosity of her Chaldean neighbors was not enough to make up for their excessive lifestyle differences. She describes her neighbors' sadness when she sold the house, asking: "Is it because of us?" This concern with preventing further stigmatization of one's community was also evident in how Paul Günes, a young resident of Chaldean origin, related to us. In his second interview in October 2005, he asked us to further explain our research objectives for fear that we might give a stereotypical image of his group. We explained that we were not focused on Chaldeans but were interested in the life stories of all neighborhood residents. He seemed reassured at the time, but upon reading our report in late 2006, he confided that he had been hurt by old-timers' harsh words to neighbors with foreign backgrounds. When he spoke at neighborhood council meetings, his words manifested how he suffered from his community's stigmatization: whenever the occasion arises, he brings up the history of his people, the persecutions they suffered, and their respect for family solidarity. By doing so, he hopes to reduce the prejudice against them by making these foreigners more familiar. We develop this further in the next chapter, which pursues how these neighborhood tensions may be translated in politics and voting—among the old-timers and newcomers alike.

NOTES

1. Castel, *From Manual Workers to Wage Laborers.*
2. N Duvoux, *Le nouvel âge de la solidarité. Pauvreté, précarité et politiques publiques* (Paris, 2012).
3. G Althabe, "Le quotidien en procès," *Dialectiques* 21 (1977): 67–77, and C Calogirou, *Sauver son honneur: Rapports sociaux en milieu urbain défavorisé* (Paris, 1990).
4. A Sayad, "A Displaced Family," in *The Weight of the World,* ed. P Bourdieu et al., trans. P Ferguson et al. (Stanford, CA, 1999), 23–36; Beaud and Pialoux, *Retour sur la condition ouvrière*; I Coutant, *Politiques du squat* (Paris, 2000).
5. S Chalvon-Demersay, *Le triangle du XIVᵉ, de nouveaux habitants dans un vieux quartier de Paris* (Paris, 1984); C Bidou-Zachariasen, ed., *Retours en ville, des processus de "gentrification" urbaine aux politiques de "revitalisation" des centres* (Paris, 2003).
6. Althabe, "Le quotidien en procès."
7. Calogirou, *Sauver son honneur.*
8. L Gruel, "Conjurer l'exclusion, rhétorique et identité revendiquée dans les habitats socialement disqualifies," *Revue française de sociologie* XXVI, no. 3 (1985): 431–53.
9. Chauvel, *Le destin des générations.*
10. Castel, *From Manual Workers to Wage Laborers.*
11. The trajectories of the Piazzas and their neighbors the Heurtins, who also left for Arnouville, have been further analyzed by J-P Hassoun in a report on the Poplars study for the Ethnology Mission of the Ministry of Culture ("Vendre son pavillon, quitter les Peupliers," in *Pavillonnaires de la banlieue nord: Une ethnographie des petites mobilités sociales,* ed. M Cartier et al. (Paris, 2006), 407–41.
12. We are thinking particularly of the chapters by R Christin, "Everyone in a Place of Their Own," in *The Weight of the World,* ed. P Bourdieu et al., trans. P Ferguson et al. (Stanford, CA, 1999), 37–45; and Sayad "A Displaced Family," 23–36.
13. Studies conducted in the United States have shown that where racism is concerned, what people say does not automatically correspond with what they do. See the syn-

thesis of the work of RT La Piere in H Peretz, *Les méthodes en sociologie: L'observa-tion* (Paris, 1998); and chapter 8 in J Chapoulie, *La tradition de Chicago, 1892–1961* (Paris, 2001).

14. The first interviews among members of Chaldean families were conducted in 2004 by A-P Wagner, J-C Hassoun, and two students, V Braconnay and A Ouss. Contact was made via the *Association des Assyro-Chaldéens de France* (AACF, Assyro-Chaldean Association of France) in Sarcelles, which put them in contact with selected families. These circumstances led them to present an image of immigrants trying to "integrate themselves" in France and in the neighborhood, omitting any mention of neighborhood tensions. Interviews were subsequently carried out with adult children and adolescents without their parents present.

15. This case was studied in depth by C Dherbécourt, "La difficile sortie des classes po-pulaires pour les Assyro-chaldéens: De petites ascensions sociales par le biais du commerce de quartier," in *Pavillonnaires de la banlieue nord: Une ethnographie des petites mobilités sociales,* ed. M Cartier et al. (Paris, 2006), 258–71.These profiles rep-resent a phenomena of social ascension via business ownership among the working classes, especially those of immigrant origin, which has been somewhat neglected in French historiography until recently, with the exception of A-S Bruno and C Zalc, *Petites entreprises et petits entrepreneurs étrangers en France, 19e–20e siècles* (Paris, 2006).

16. Recall that sociability decreases with age, and that this process is accentuated far-ther down the social scale (F Héran, "La sociabilité une pratique culturelle?," *Éco-nomie et Statistique* 216 (1988): 3–22).

17. This case was analyzed in great detail by Marichalar "Vers le bon voisinage: Enquête ethnographique sur les entrepreneurs de la morale résidentielle" (Master's thesis, ENS-EHESS, 2006).

18. N Elias and J Scotson, *The Established and the Outsiders: A Sociological Enquiry into Community Problems,* 2nd ed. (London, 1994).

19. See in particular Chalvon-Demersay, *Le triangle du XIVᵉ* ; and Bidou-Zachariasen, *Retours en ville.*

20. For an analysis of a neighborhood conflict with overt racism between a work-ing-class woman and a family of Algerian origin, see Sayad, "A Displaced Family." The work of Beaud and Pialoux (*Retour sur la condition ouvrière*) shows just how present the temptation to xenophobia is in the factory setting today, among laborer groups that are weakened and divided.

21. P Bourdieu, "Le capital social: Notes provisoires," *Actes de la Recherche en Sciences Sociales* 31 (1980): 2–3.

A VOTE OF THE
WHITE LOWER CLASSES?

The 2007 presidential elections revealed a striking electoral contrast between housing developments and housing projects. The majority of
housing development residents voted for the mainstream-right candidate
Nicolas Sarkozy, who touted a political right "freed of its complexes" and
advocated strongly neoliberal economic policy, particularly repressive approaches to public order, and very restrictive immigration policy, whereas
HLM residents more often chose Ségolène Royal, the Socialist Party candidate whose discourse emphasized social justice (her campaign was built
around a call for "a fair order"). The media made much of these contrasting
voter tendencies along residential lines in 2007, and it continued to draw
journalists' attention in subsequent elections because it seemed to reinforce
a range of other social and ethnoracial oppositions: single-family homeowners are described as belonging to the middle classes, while residents of subsidized HLM projects are "poor" or "excluded"; the former were said to be
French in both nationality and background, while the latter were foreigners
or of foreign backgrounds. These images contain a grain of truth: the chasm
between homeowners and housing project residents is even greater than it
used to be as social housing has gradually concentrated the most economically diminished fractions of the working classes. Indeed, the latest available
study from INED (Institut national d'études démographiques) of the reality
of discrimination attests to the fact that a majority of Africans and Magrhe-
bians were living in public housing in 2008.[1] Last, these journalistic analyses

give credence to the now-classic image of a social and electoral opposition between the "lower white" classes, socially anxious and hostile to foreigners, and residents of the "ghetto," or at least the most segregated neighborhoods, who supposedly see a progressive vote as possible self-defense. Our observations of Poplars residents' political behavior also partly point in this direction. A large number of residents of this little-middle neighborhood has certainly shifted to the right and extreme right.

But at the same time, our study is a call to reject partial analyses and over-simplification.[2] For one thing, although this neighborhood has registered a rising vote for the right (and the extreme right in the 1990s), the left is far from absent. In Gonesse, the Socialist Party became the leading political force in the 1980s, and the Socialist mayor since 1995 (reelected in 2001, 2008, and 2014) largely owes his seat to voters from the Poplars. Suburban homeowners' votes thus cannot be homogenized and automatically classified to the right—doing so would deny the vote of its history and prevent us from examining the circumstances and complex factors determining voters' position on the right-left spectrum. Second, the conservative vote in the neighborhood, which had long been neither right nor left, has been present since the mid 1980s. But the minorities' own vote—the electoral choices of new homeowners from non-French backgrounds that have become French citizens—is increasingly coming to resemble the wider neighborhood trend, so the rightward shift cannot be summed up as being the vote of "lower class whites." Such a local scene is ideal for studying the forms of political participation chosen by naturalized citizens and native-born French of immigrant backgrounds.[3]

These circumstances have led us to organize this chapter around two main issues. The first is taking a deeper look into the reasons behind variations in the homeowners' votes, at least insofar as they can be observed based on our study in the Poplars,[4] and trying to identify the factors influencing the shift of many of them toward the right and extreme right. The second issue is to understand how residents who are ethno-racial minorities identify with this conservative vote, despite belonging to the very groups it targets.

A POLITICALLY DIVERSE AND ACTIVE NEIGHBORHOOD

The Poplars's electoral results in the 1990s through the 2010s are heavily marked by the mounting vote for the right and far right, especially in national elections like the presidential election. Jacques Chirac, the candidate for the mainstream right party Union pour un Mouvement Populaire (UMP), and Jean-Marie Le Pen, the head of the far-right Front National, led the first round in both 1995 and 2002, Le Pen even placing ahead of Chirac in all the neighborhood's polling places in 1995. Closer examination of more recent election results reveals residents' voting practices are more complex and contradictory than what this period indicates, and this complexity is further accentuated if we look back several decades.

First of all, the successive generations of residents have been electorally divided, so the neighborhood's election results have often shifted from one election to the next. Although it is difficult to identify general trends, there is no ambiguity in the significant turnout of registered voters in the Poplars: such high participation is typical of the little-middles.

Suburban Homeowners' Civic Engagement

The Poplars's high and persistent voter turnout is a striking specificity of voting practices in this suburban housing development. Turnout is at or slightly above the national average and has been consistently higher than citywide rates from the 1950s to the present, especially compared with polls in housing projects.[5] Obviously, turnout rates depend on the intensity of the campaigns and fluctuate from one election to the next, with the greatest gaps in presidential elections. This contrasts starkly with voter turnout tendencies in public housing neighborhoods, where abstention has risen steadily since the late 1970s due to the decline in forms of social integration and political mobilization in such urban areas.[6] It is a strong indicator of its residents' social position over the generations: this electoral civic engagement shows that they cannot be grouped with the working classes of the HLM housing projects, even if they remain close. These households' social and cultural resources, though they are modest, are enough to hold off the *cens cache* (hidden political domination)[7] that often distances working-class voters from politics, even when parties or civic groups try to represent them.

Most row-house pioneers, even those with low educational attainments, have had educations giving them access to cultural resources different from those of their original social backgrounds; the educational levels of families arriving since the 1990s, although not high, are rising. Most importantly, first-time homeownership in a neighborhood of upward mobility comes with a different relationship to the future and the social world than that of working-class neighborhood residents. The little-middles are not characterized by skepticism or indifference, which are at the heart of working-class relations with politics.[8] Moreover, the row-house pioneers' attachment to an "atmosphere of equality" (see chapter 1) or the burning desire for conformity and social recognition in the neighborhood expressed by more recent generations moving in from the projects (see chapters 2 and 3) favor respect of a social norm of civic behavior, voting being a sign of successful social and local integration. This civic engagement expresses households' will to take control of their social and political environments as they were able to take control of their ascendant socioeconomic trajectories.

This participation and civic engagement also have to be put in relation with the local and interpersonal activism that sustains it. As we have seen, residents' involvement in local associative networks goes far back: home-owners' associations, athletic associations, church groups, and school parents' associations are all settings in which neighborhood residents frequent each other and the prominent local figures that run such organizations, some of whom also serve as relays to the municipal council. Indeed, it is striking to see that the neighborhood has always had several elected officials among its residents, in every council, left or right, since the end of World War II.

~~~

A NEIGHBORHOOD RUN BY ELECTED
MUNICIPAL OFFICIALS WHO LIVE THERE

The archives tell us that the municipal officials in place 1947–1971, elected from the MRP-SFIO[9] (Christian Democrat-Socialist), always included Poplars residents: six of twenty-three in 1953 (an employee of the national train network, an agricultural accountant, a floor supervisor, a school principal, a commercial director, a woman without occupation).

The next group of officials, from 1971 to 1995, identified as "independent" before being connected with the right (the Rassemblement pour la République party, RPR). From the outset, it included row-house pioneers invested in local associations who were solicited to join the slate for this very reason: M. Lenormand, who was active with the Scouts, served from 1971 to 2001, then M. Morin, head of the basketball club, served from 1977 to 1995. Both were deputies. In the 1980s, other residents invested in the homeowners' associations of more recent subdivisions came on board.

The Socialist Party-Communist Party coalition, led by the new mayor Jean-Pierre Blazy, won the election in 1995, 2001, 2008, and 2014. It also recruited in the neighborhood, especially through the school parents' association, the FCPE. So, in 2007, the city council included four elected members of the majority who lived in the neighborhood, three who grew up or worked there, and two members of the opposition living in the Poplars—nine of twenty-seven elected officials in all. The 2008 elections were the occasion to include some newer neighborhood residents, including a young man of Chaldean descent who we return to at the end of the chapter.

~~~

The presence of local political figures in the neighborhood—who in most cases came to assume political functions through investment in civic life—encourages residents' electoral participation and strengthens the feeling of having some control over their environment and being able to make themselves heard. Even if it only rarely leads to engagement in a political party, civic engagement is one of the leading characteristics of the political practices of the Poplars's little-middles, setting them far apart from residents of working-class neighborhoods. It is even more striking because it is shared by voters who, beyond their common civic engagement, express divergent political orientations in the ballot box.

A Neighborhood Long Neither Right Nor Left

It is remarkable that voters to the right and left (including Communist voters) have coexisted in this neighborhood for decades without a strong majority emerging,[10] which goes to show how oversimplistic it is to assume that there is a connection between voting for the right and homeownership. Of course the neighborhood's population has changed over time, and it is very difficult to analyze the factors influencing the electoral orientations of residents of the 1950s, 1960s, and 1970s based solely on these general results. But it is possible that the diversity of social origins—spanning all fractions of the working classes (agriculture, labor, commerce, trades) and several regional origins (North, West, greater Paris)—might work in favor of this heterogeneity, some remaining faithful to a leftist laborer identity while others have internalized more conservative values.

The 1980s witnessed a left-leaning vote in the Poplars: the Socialist Party, which was supplanting the Communist Party, lead the 1986 regional and legislative elections, then the 1988 presidential election and the legislative elections that followed. But this vote to the left coexisted with a right-leaning local-level vote for city offices: the right-leaning slate without party affiliation won in 1983 and again in 1989 (though by a small margin).

This mayor's victory, won thanks to residents who voted for the left in national-level elections, is a reflection of a particularity of local elections: due to local issues and the personification of elected offices, local elections at least partly escape partisan predispositions and national divisions, especially among the least politicized voters.[11] In the Poplars, this situation reveals how weak the rationales of party and activist loyalty actually are, because candidates positioning themselves outside of the political party system and emphasizing local activities and individual skills are able to succeed there.

The Breakthrough and Establishment of the Front National

In this setting, where political oppositions are relatively euphemized, the vote for the Front National is all the more striking for its rapid emergence. It began with the 1984 European elections, when the Front National garnered 17 and 19 percent of the vote in the Poplars's two polling places (as compared

with 11 percent France-wide, where the breakthrough was of a lesser degree). It was the start of a continuing progression lasting over twenty years,
frequently surpassing 25 percent.[12] How to understand the strength of the
vote for the extreme right since 1984, and its persistence in this neighborhood that had been characterized by its strong electoral civic engagement
and a vote shared between the left and right? It is subject to national and
regional influences, of course, but it is also rooted in social factors specific
to the city and neighborhood. It must be resituated in "everything that roots
the Front National vote in everyday social and political practices"[13]: that is,
partly in the social history of a neighborhood of social promotion that has
become a place of downward mobility for some, and partly, too, in a particular local political configuration that helped the extreme-right vote progress
and become commonplace.

   In-depth studies of the Front National remain rare, but the few there are
highlight the variety of processes that drive it, the social milieus that support
it, and the degree to which this vote is politically informed. At least one in
four voters is estimated to have voted at least once for the Front National
since the early 1980s.[14] The focus on the working-class fractions of the Front
National electorate not only results in the overshadowing of other kinds of
supporters,[15] but sometimes leads to rather simplistic generalizations about
social downclassing as well. Several studies have shown that both occupational and symbolic downclassing in the 1980s and 1990s played a key role in
the development of the extreme-right vote among some laborers and basic
employees that could be interpreted as a reaction to social insecurity and
disqualification.[16]

   The little-middles we studied in the Poplars are not as affected by occupational downclassing and weakening social positions as the families of laborers
and basic employees are, especially those who find themselves relegated to
housing projects around Paris. Such weakening exists, however, both in the
working world[17] and in uncertainties about the academic and career futures
of their children. The departure of neighbors and their replacement by newcomers seen as dragging the neighborhood downhill fed a strong sentiment
of declining status among long-time residents, while families who moved to
the Poplars from HLMs also have a fear of downclassing commensurate with
the extent of their efforts to get out of the rapidly degrading projects.[18]

   The downward mobility felt by longtime row-house residents and feared
by new subdivision owners alone is insufficient for a thorough analysis of
the chronology and pace of the Front National vote's progression in the
neighborhood, however. It is related to a specific local political context that
corresponds to the radicalization of part of the local right and the growing
legitimacy of a discourse stigmatizing foreign newcomers, gradually focusing
on "the Turks" (this is in contrast with some HLM neighborhoods, where it

corresponds to the fraying of the relatively few left-leaning political party or union organizations).

Indeed, the right-leaning municipal council of the 1980s helped legitimize the extreme right and its discourse on immigration, leading to what even a right-leaning former official described as "radicalization." For one thing, as he put it, it regularly "expanded" to include people who "extoled the virtues of the FN [*Front National*]" in the municipal majority. For another thing, it actively and openly stigmatized Turkish families by implementing a policy of preemption for houses put on the market in the Poplars—a rather rare policy for a housing development—to prevent them from moving in (a policy that would moreover be continued for a time by the subsequent Socialist-dominated council).

After a period of division within the local right, the head of the slate leading the 2001 municipal elections was an open proponent of the hard right: he was known locally as a shopkeeper and for having won a legal case against the state in 1992 over the "dearth of police forces" in the HLM neighborhood where his pharmacy is located. His discourse on security fustigates the delinquency generated by "ghettos" and promotes a local alliance of "all the parties of the right,"[19] with no exceptions.

The local establishment of the Front National and extreme-right networks in general has also gone toward making extreme-right positions commonplace. Gonesse's Front National results are inflated by the presence of two apartment buildings primarily for police officers: the Cité du Nord voting district where they are located has had the highest Front National results in the city since the 1980s, and until 2004, another police housing unit voted at the Emile Zola poll, where the Front National also has high results. These apartment buildings are likely to include Front National activists or sympathizers, especially given that the candidate for the extreme-right "independent" slate in the 1989 municipal elections was a policeman who also held a seat in the Independent Professional Federation of Police (FPIP), a union with close ties to the Front National. There is another Front National figure present locally, as well—Jean-Michel Dubois, member of the party's political bureau and president of the Val d'Oise federation, representing the French department where Gonesse is located. He was a candidate in local elections in 2004 and made it to the second round, at which time he had very high results in Gonesse and the Poplars in particular, garnering 32 to 38 percent of the vote in the three polling places.

In sum, there are distinctly political factors that created favorable conditions for the extreme right's breakthrough and enduringly high voting levels in the Poplars, in the form of a diffuse and well-established politicization within classic local right-leaning networks that have become more radical and a local presence of Front National or extreme right activists. This context lent legitimacy to xenophobic speech and representations. The vote for extreme-right slates is thus an indicator that the permissible discourse on "Turks" and "foreigners," despite a general ambivalence, now also includes racist stereotypes.

Xenophobic Discourse Becomes Commonplace

Our interviews only allowed an indirect approach to talking about the Front National vote. Few openly acknowledge having voted for Le Pen or his party's candidates, but there are exceptions: M. and Mme Deneuve are a retired midlevel insurance *cadre* and a skilled laborer living in a house from the 1920s; a neighborhood shopkeeper; a couple of retired municipal employees (a road-maintenance worker and cleaning worker); and Mme Legendre, a retired accountant living in a row house since 1984.

These residents drawn to the Front National are also repelled by it because of the discourse coming from the left and right alike decrying its danger for democracy. This vote is even less tenable for them because they are aware that it could lead to conflicts with friends and family. Although the Front National corresponds to their radicalized social and political attitudes, they also see it as a dangerous party that puts all immigrants in the same basket and advocates violence. In addition, they cannot totally identify with a political orientation whose violent language debases them and whose policy goes counter to their social ascension and the self-restraint it presupposes. This most likely explains why most would not openly admit having voted for the Front National in interviews, as it would have run the risk of having their social status reduced to the category "Front National voter." But even if "it's not something you talk about," as one interviewee put it, many still let their Front National sympathies be understood and are even less shy in communicating their rejection of neighborhood foreigners in xenophobic terms, as we saw in the preceding chapter. Their discourse on the neighborhood's "colonization" by foreign families "on welfare" picks up many discursive formulations from the extreme right.

Xenophobic discourse is focused on "the Turks" (meaning the Chaldean families) while the figure of the "good" or "worst" foreigners alternates among people of other backgrounds (Maghreb, sub-Saharan Africa, Asia, etc.). As we saw in the preceding chapter, complaints about large families arriving in the 1990s concerned practical aspects of cohabitation (poor yard maintenance, presence of satellite dishes, noise, etc.). But they also make generalizing representations of these Turkish families as a whole, much less based on actual experiences, supporting the idea that they "will never integrate themselves." The incompatibility of their lifestyles is consequently sometimes described in extreme ways: "they" hang out the laundry and pile up mattresses to air in the windows in a messy way intolerable in France; "they" "break down the walls" between row houses to "live fifty together," and "their" houses are of such dubious cleanliness that they have "rats."

Although most residents know that many of these families are Christian, when stereotypes come into play, this may be glossed over in favor of other preconceptions. People may decry their "Muslim" practices: they "slit sheep's throats" in their gardens for parties (M. Kergoat) and veil their women with no respect for secularism (*laïcité*; M. Kergoat, M. Ronsart). Beyond complaints stemming from dispossession of the everyday living environment, the old-timers' discourse about "foreigners" is sprinkled with generic and imagined themes that echo those popularized by the Front National.

Some of the more recent arrivals also speak virulently against "the Turks," a discourse even more explicitly rooted in a feeling that there is an "invasion" of "foreigners" that goes well beyond the Poplars. Many of these residents have lived in HLMs, and they see this alleged invasion as a phenomenon touching all of French society, so their discourse of vast generalizations is more politicized along these lines. They claim a right to live amongst themselves, among "the French," which makes them want to protect themselves from "foreigners" by, for example, limiting their ability to move into the neighborhood by refusing to sell them houses or appealing to public authorities.

M. Collin, aged about forty, grew up in central Gonesse and bought a house in the Poplars in 1997. He thinks that the city is "degrading" overall, and that even a previously peaceful neighborhood like the Poplars is now affected, especially due to the departure of the old residents and their replacement by foreigners. Partisan of a strong response to this development, he thinks they need to "clean house" and evict the young Chaldeans who hang out in the neighborhood, especially on the little circle right in front of his house: "I won't leave because of them, no question about it, even if I have to go get a gun!" As he sees it, this development is largely to blame on the city hall, which gave up the policy of preemption when it should have done everything in its power to make sales to "Turks" "get dropped."

The frequency of this discourse in interviews attests to its local legitimacy, spurred both by the political legitimacy established by the local political right and by the permissibility of neighborly relations. The refusal to stigmatize racism and the Front National vote by residents who are otherwise very eager to personally set themselves apart from it, even among some who still vote for the left, is striking proof of this mundane acceptance.

While it is true that some residents, often from fractions of the middle classes the most endowed with cultural resources and politically oriented to the left, set out to condemn the extreme right vote and rejection of the Chaldeans (especially in the neighborhood councils), most residents refuse to condemn Front National voters. This refusal in some cases may come from the fact that they themselves have already voted Front National, but it also concerns voters who, while taking a very clear distance from the Front National themselves, refuse to do the same to their neighbors voting for it.

For instance, several practicing Catholics or sympathizers of leftist political parties say they are against the extreme-right vote while at the same time showing considerable tolerance for their neighbors voting Front National. As we saw, the Samsons, row-house pioneers, have successfully formed good relations with their foreign neighbors, Chaldean in particular. Because of these good relations and their Christian socialization, they bemoan their neighbors' actions rejecting foreigners and encourage them to "reach out to them" so that these relations go well. Unlike most of their old neighbors, they believe that the Chaldeans have rather "well integrated" themselves. In the first interview with them, Mme Samson was the one to raise the subject of the Front National vote by recalling in an alarmed tone that "here in the Poplars, there's 24 percent, even 26 percent Le Pen!" But after having told how a neighborhood storekeeper, known for his extreme-right sympathies, chastised her for "taking care of those people," she hastened to add that despite his "strongly held opinions" he is "very nice" and "you have to put yourself in his position." When the conversation returns to the Front National vote in the second interview, she and her husband confirm their tolerance of Front National voters and their refusal to assume antiracist postures that could put them in an awkward position with some neighbors and friends.

> Interviewer: Do you think the Le Pen vote has declined?
> Mme Samson: I don't know. We avoid talking about politics.
> Interviewer: Why?
> Mme Samson: Well, because there's always trouble. How to put it; it would cause trouble, and we are for people getting along, we are friends with everyone, so you see ... One time someone gave me a "Don't touch my pal" hand,[20] so I wore it a day just like that, and I took it off. I said to myself "No, you take care of everyone, don't fret about whether the person in front of you is a pal or not a pal! (*laughs*) I know people who I'm sure vote for the Front National. Others vote Communist, others vote Socialist, others vote I don't know how, I couldn't care less, or the kind of religion, we try to be friends with everyone. So we don't talk about things that risk upsetting people. It's not worth it. Everyone has his political opinion and that's that.
> M. Samson: And anyway, yeah, that's it, to each his opinion and that's that.
> Mme Samson: To each his opinion, they should be respected, and that's that.

This idea that one should "put oneself in the position" of Front National voters and that "all opinions are respectable" cropped up repeatedly, also among people who vote to the left. M. Kergoat, who moved into a row house in 1967, then to a village-style subdivision in 1998, describes himself as close to the Socialist Party. He mentions his father's past as a Communist and resistant during the war, and asserts his refusal to vote for the Front National or extreme right. And yet he also stresses that "Le Pen has some good ideas" and "tells the truth," although he "keeps bad company." He also laments that you can no longer express certain "opinions" about foreigners without "going to jail."

Fear of downward social mobility fed by the degradation of nearby housing projects and the arrival of families from the projects in the neighborhood has helped the Front National vote gain ground. Made legitimate by the hardening of the local right that was already well established in the neighborhood, this vote has also been sustained at high levels by the mild condemnation it receives from neighbors.

THE SUBURBANITE VOTE SHIFTS RIGHT

This growing attraction for a hard right that castigates immigrants and people on welfare contributed to Nicolas Sarkozy's success in the neighborhood in the 2007 presidential election, an event we found rich for analysis.

An Unspeakable Vote for the Right

Although nationally N Sarkozy was positioned well ahead of the Socialist Party candidate S Royal, who he bested by 5.3 points, this gap was much less important in Gonesse where barely a point separated the candidates (32.7 percent over 31.4 percent; the remainder was distributed between other parties' candidates). This weak margin is a reminder that the city's political balance is such that neither the left nor right are in a hegemonic position.

To better understand the diversity of Poplars residents' electoral choices, we administered a questionnaire at the exit of the neighborhood's Victor Hugo poll and conducted several interviews about voting during the 2007 election period.[21] Because of the contours of the voting districts, this poll's registered voters included a significant number of row-house residents and a heavy proportion of voters living in the recent New Poplars subdivision, a social heterogeneity that led us to choose this poll out of the three in the neighborhood. Of the 858 voters who came to vote on 22 April 2007 (out of 1,022 registered), 368 agreed to respond to our questionnaire, which is 43 percent of participating voters that day (with a response rate of 50 percent among people actually solicited).[22] This figure allows us to discuss the voting behavior of Poplars residents, but it also leads us to question the refusal of half the voters we approached.

A significant share of voters came as a family: husband, wife, children of voting age or below. Televised news did little to show the diverse backgrounds of voters in greater Paris, and even less in the northern suburbs: French of Turkish, Asian, Maghrebian, and African origin turned out to vote in numbers in the poll we studied. These immigrants and children of immigrants become homeowners willingly answered our questionnaire in most cases. They performed their civic duty solemnly and often timidly, and did not want to shirk the additional duty we imposed on them. But they were also troubled that their French was not better and uneasy in the rather school-like situation in which we placed them, seated at a table with paper and pen, reading questions we came to realize were formulated with language that was difficult for them to understand. Wives often delegated the task to their husbands, or parents to their children who are students.

While these newly French families, along with young voters who were also numerous that day, agreed to divulge their vote, neighborhood retirees were much more reticent: people over sixty represent only 7 percent of our sample. Immigrants and young voters seem to have been less hesitant to fill out our questionnaire, which they might have seen as additional proof of their conformity with expectations, a gauge of national legitimacy or civic maturity. But the retirees began their electoral lives well before opinion polls and voting questionnaires became common. Some reacted violently, not believing the promise of anonymity and proclaiming that this kind of survey "shouldn't be allowed" because it is "not legal" to ask people to tell how they voted. The good rapport we developed with some during interviews, instead of lifting their reticence, seemed to the contrary to have reinforced their fear of being reduced to their vote. In addition, those who voted for the Front National—which we do not mean to imply was the case for everyone who avoided us—doubtlessly also had difficulty admitting their vote. This reticence is a consideration in explaining Sarkozy supporters' lower response rate: fewer than one in three Sarkozy voters at the poll (88 of 311) filled out a questionnaire, compared with one in two Royal voters (130 of 256).

Private-Sector Employees at the Core of a Mainly Working-Class Vote

If we look at the vote in terms of socioeconomic categories, private and public sector *cadres* and midlevel employees responding to the questionnaire voted more often for S Royal and F Bayrou than N Sarkozy. Their vote is in stark contrast to that of their neighbors who are basic employees, many of whom lean distinctly more to the right. Among all basic employees, those in the private sector seem to be the most "to the right": 44 percent of them voted for N Sarkozy, compared with 28 percent for S Royal, and 5 percent for F Bayrou. Public sector employees were more likely to keep their politics to themselves by leaving the question on who they voted for blank:

18 percent of basic employees and 15 percent of midlevel employees filled out the questionnaire but skipped that question. These figures must be put into relation with the percentages of these categories having reported voting for N Sarkozy, 5 percent among midlevel employees and 0 percent among basic employees of the public sector—results so low that a bias appears obvious.

These figures actually reveal the nearly unspeakable character of such a vote among public employees, especially those in lower-level jobs. As a city hall employee put it, "voting for Sarkozy when you're a public employee is like shooting yourself in the foot." N Sarkozy's proposal to reduce the number of civil servants, a move long advocated by the right, received a lot of media attention during the campaign, and the neighborhood's low-level public employees seemed to take it as an attack on who they are. We are reminded of an informant who mentioned frequent fights with her sister-in-law, a secretary in the private sector, who incessantly criticized "civil servants" who "don't do anything and have tons of privileges," signaling a spreading social jealousy among the lower fractions of private-sector employees.

The contrast with the Poplars's pioneer generation is striking. The public-private split drew very little resentment in the 1960s and 1970s, when public enterprises and agencies, in the words of one informant, "recruited with a vengeance." Coming from a private-sector employee, the word "privilege" denounces a world become rare and unattainable that offers advantages, job security chief among them. In the current sociopolitical climate critical of civil servants, public employees won over to the Sarkozy camp, probably of a split mind themselves, may have been less likely to declare it.

Frustrated Middle-Class Aspirations: A Strong Impetus for a Rightward Shift

Some of the modest homeowners saw N Sarkozy as an opportunity to protest what they saw as a threat to themselves and their children's futures. In the interviews conducted during the three years prior to the presidential election, some of them were openly hostile when speaking of the Turkish families in the row houses, who they often associated with the world of housing projects and criticized for not trying "to integrate themselves" and dragging down the "quality" of the neighborhood. They also repeatedly complained of the youths seen smoking joints and blasting their music in the neighborhood. Their talk of immigrants and youth in part reflects what the televised media say about the *banlieues* in general: these small homeowners "right up against" the housing projects are inclined to pick up certain stereotypes and want to protect themselves from a more or less imagined reality by calling for greater severity.

For some, this troubled relationship with the *banlieue* is expressed in a rejection of "the environment." Mme Hancel, a thirty-two-year-old mother of three and homeowner in the New Poplars, said in a 2005 interview that she was "disgusted by the *banlieue*." She dreamed of leaving for "the provinces" (that is, to leave the Paris region) as soon as possible, because she believed they offer a better life, or at least one that is more "calm." This is a common aspiration among these small homeowners for whom "the provinces" would allow shelter from the "chaos." In the interview, Mme Hancel quite openly complained of the behavior of immigrant populations at the Poplars. She showed no concern that she might appear "repressive" or even "racist." She considered the presence of "the Turks" to be "abnormal" and felt they created a "ghetto" in the neighborhood. She did not show the verbal caution we encountered in more highly educated neighborhood residents or those more attuned to antiracism. Her bluntness can be partly explained by the fact that she left school very early, after a very low-level vocational certificate (CAP). Additionally her "mixed" origins (her father fled Vietnam in the 1960s) seem to give her license to condemn recent immigrants while sheltering her from any charge of racism. She is not politicized, voting "for the mayor" (a Socialist) in municipal elections without knowing which party he is in. "For me, politics, I force myself to go vote! It bores me to death, except when I hear taxes are going up—now that's revolting! Then you hear me complaining." Her discourse on taxes places her somewhat to the right, as do her perceptions of public order—two years before the presidential election she said she preferred N Sarkozy "for everything to do with security."

Mme Hancel had been laid off from her job as a beautician and went on parental leave with the birth of their third child. She wanted to return to work by going into business for herself, but she could not afford to open a salon. Her husband, who has a vocational *baccalauréat* degree, is a technician at Citroën. Thanks to their savings, they were able to buy an apartment and leave the HLM neighborhood where they had first lived together. The sale of this apartment, along with a 1-percent employer loan and another 0-percent loan, then allowed them to buy a house in the New Poplars in 2000 (before she was laid off) with three rooms, a living-dining room, and a small yard. But mortgage payments are compounded by other expenses—property and local taxes, the water bill, and worst of all, heating—while their income has declined. On top of that, their house is too small for a room for each child, so they are thinking about building an extension. Although they chose Gonesse because Mme Hancel has ties there (her father still lives in the subdivisions from the 1970s and 1980s, where she grew up), it was also because they could not do any better. The price of real estate prohibits them from buying a house in the nearby towns that have become middle- and upper-class territory. The dissatisfaction stemming from the gap between the Hancel's actual resources and their plans to improve their living conditions, which she refers to as living "a normal life," is behind her "disgust for the *banlieue*" and her appreciation of N Sarkozy and his agenda.

More visible and accentuated in the recent New Poplars subdivisions than they were in the row houses in the era of the pioneers, the objective resource inequalities between households further weakens the lower strata of homeowners who, like Mme Hancel, fear being trapped in the neighborhood. Dual-income households and midlevel employees, *cadres,* and professionals are indeed more numerous in the New Poplars than they were in the row houses thirty or forty years ago, due to the proliferation of academic qualifications and rising female employment.

At the same time, the relationship to money and consumption has changed profoundly between the generations. While the pioneers carefully and haltingly explored the world of mass consumption, younger homeowners are much more solicited to consume goods and services (cars, vacations, leisure-time activities, etc.) at a high level, if only by exposure to more affluent neighbors. This rising cost of entry into the middle classes can cultivate frustration in some modest homeowners, a corollary of the "triangular" social consciousness identified by Olivier Schwartz: an "us" caught in the middle, based on a distance from those "above" and a rejection of those "below," foreigners and the poor alike.[23] Refusal to live with "foreigners" and fear of seeing the neighborhood turn into a "ghetto" are expressions of the mixed feeling of superiority and devaluation that has become frequent for part of the population.

These small homeowners at the threshold of the middle classes thus identified with N Sarkozy's neoliberal discourse that praised the "deserving" in order to better put them in opposition to recipients of public welfare assistance. Some informants interviewed well before the presidential election returned to the theme of "merit" time and time again to foreground their "efforts" to "develop in society" and condemn the "welfare-dependent." With these words, they express a refusal of solidarity, feeling they are abusively taxed to pay for social policies destined for others.

In an interview in June 2005, Patrick Jarreau, a thirty-seven-year-old nurse's aid in a public hospital, thus decried the "welfare-dependent," who he considered guilty of not looking for work and "taking from the [*social*] categories who can pay." He believed that too many people choose the "easy option" of unemployment and public assistance to avoid having to "earn their living." He pointed the finger both at foreigners benefitting from family benefits and the "unemployed who are indeed French" who live "at someone else's expense." To raise his household's modest income and be able to finish the interior of their house, he regularly moonlights (doing garden work, plumbing, and mechanics), allowing the couple to buy contemporary upscale furniture and putting them closer to the "comfortable" fraction of the neighborhood's middle classes.

Patrick's wife, a schoolteacher, is the daughter of an engineer and a math teacher who gave them considerable financial help when they started out. The Jarreaus are closer to the middle classes and more inclined to identify with them than couples where both members are employed and from the working classes. Accordingly, Patrick and his wife have ties with four families on their street (of which the men are bank *cadre,* owner of a construction business, manager of a security business, and jeweler) and sometimes go on vacation with them. But they cannot keep up with the lifestyle of these neighbors-become-friends, especially when it comes to vacations. Lack of money crops up constantly in Patrick's speech. He thinks "they put too many limitations on the desire of the French to earn more money." He would like to "work more" by doing overtime at the hospital, but he cannot "because of the thirty-five hours" employment law that forces him to "moonlight" even though "the hospitals are understaffed."

We saw Patrick Jarreau and his wife when they came to vote, but they declined to fill out the questionnaire, and he was very reserved—probably because his (and his wife's) civil servant status made him reticent about revealing his vote. In our interviews, he said he was "disappointed" by "politicians" and was waiting "to see what Sarkozy [*would*] do." He explained that he had voted blank ballots in presidential elections since he had reached voting age, and had voted "for the mayor" since moving to Gonesse. And if he was clear that he had never voted Le Pen "because he's crazy," it was to immediately go on to say that he "nonetheless [*has*] some very strong opinions" about "immigration and all that." Interested in politics but uncomfortable talking about it, throughout his speech he seemed to be for order and security, suspicious of unions, and above all opposed to immigration and the "welfare-dependent." Beyond his case, it seems that in the neighborhood, the Sarkozy vote came partly from some small homeowners at the cusp of the middle classes who had interiorized a primarily economic model of success that they shared with their business-owner or private-sector *cadre* neighbors, but lacking the means to make it happen or the assurance of being able to do so in the future.

Alongside people's feelings about the neighborhood and its population changes, children's futures (educational in particular) also seem to play a role in the little-middles' rightward shift. During the study, some parents went into antiteacher diatribes, accusing them of only paying attention to the "good students" to the detriment of their children. Mothers think their children are "impressionable" because of their "mediocre level" and would like teachers to pay more attention to them. Above all, a large number of parents described the public schools attended by children from immigrant

families as schools to avoid at all costs, so, like parents of the middle and upper classes, some parents with low educational levels tried to escape them by
requesting dispensations and choosing rare academic options. Mme Hancel
was thus able to arrange for her children to go to a primary school other than
Victor Hugo, attended by the neighborhood's Turkish children. She thinks
that Victor Hugo's level is very low and feared it would prevent her children
from getting an "average" education.

The spread of these avoidance strategies into the neighborhood's academically modest categories testifies to a rising anxiety in face of scholastic
difficulties. Comparison with the previous generation is revealing: in interviews with pioneers, there is nearly no mention of fear of children not
doing well in school. Perhaps they had forgotten it by the time of the interview, or perhaps they were not worried about the level of the schools,
which were less socially and ethnically diverse at the time. It seemed most
likely to be because higher studies used to be less essential to career potential than they are today.

But as we saw in previous chapters, today's parents' cultural and scholastic
ambitions are sometimes disappointed. Indeed, even if they are more stra-
tegic than past generations, parents with limited educational experience are
still less effective than parents with more academic resources. Thus, Mme
Hancel did not think her son should take German as a primary foreign language option, thinking English would be much more useful "for his future."
She went on to tell us that she is mad at her neighbor, a parents' association
representative, who said she had made the wrong choice: "When he found
out that I hadn't put my son in the international class or whatever that thing
is, the European thing at the middle school: 'How's that, Guillaume isn't taking German? I don't understand!'" Less aware of strategies for placing their
children on the path to success, parents lacking educational capital are more
exposed to the risk of "bad classes" and want the scholastic institution to be
stricter. N Sarkozy's conservative discourse on school values—full of discipline and respect for authority—could have answered the expectations of
these mothers who are awkward with scholastic institutions. Because their
children are more susceptible to the vagaries of the social composition of
classes and often frequent children from other social backgrounds, they are
particularly inclined to revere the "good old methods," as one interviewee
put it, especially in middle school, which many think is the riskiest period
for falling under bad influences.

The threat of downclassing, the depreciating environment, and the fear
of being trapped in the neighborhood and contaminated from below, especially through children's education, all contributed to the Sarkozy vote by
pushing some preexisting rightward inclinations even further. The examples
we presented indeed show that this vote made sense to voters socialized in

weakly politicized but generally conservative milieu. This tendency is also found among a portion of voters who are immigrants or descended from immigrants who live in the row houses or recent subdivisions of the New Poplars.

The Right-Wing "Immigrant" Vote

We did not intend to study the political choices of neighborhood families from foreign countries or descended from foreign-born parents when we set out on this study. The issue emerged late in the research, upon seeing how voting results had developed in the Poplars, with a constant rise in Front National and UMP votes despite the significant reduction of the number of former residents and the rising share of voters with immigrant origins in the neighborhood. To look more closely at this phenomenon, we interviewed several and tried to learn more of their vote through our questionnaire. Coding their origins was something of a stumbling block. We could have asked voters' nationalities prior to naturalization and where they were born, and asked French-born voters where their parents were born, but we were concerned that this would discourage many from responding. We did ask questions about their religious orientations, however, a very indirect indicator of origins that is a classic in French exit polls.

Voters in the polling place we studied were thus asked to declare the extent of their religious belief and then, for the faithful, to indicate (by checking a box) if they were Catholic, Muslim, Jewish, Protestant, Chaldean, Hindu, or other. By classing the Chaldeans among religions, we aimed to set them apart from other Catholics, but our clumsy choice earned us severe criticism from some voters from Chaldean backgrounds who were outraged that we had confused religion with ethnic group, and even more so because we had arbitrarily singled Chaldeans out from other Catholics, raising the chances of reinforcing their stigmatization.

Paul Günes, a law student, was especially angry. As we described in the previous chapter, he defends his ethnic group's image by any means possible, especially against the negative perceptions held by long-term neighborhood residents and some elected officials (the mayor chief among them). On top of that, he is on the board of the Assyro-Chaldean Association of France in Sarcelles, which has close ties to the Socialist Party, so he had no choice but to reject our attempt to expose Gonesse Chaldeans' very conservative political orientation. But he was far from being the only person to resist our request. Although voters from non-French backgrounds, particularly the Maghreb, more often than not answered the question, they do not seem to have found it intrusive or contrary to their desire to not be singled out and set apart from other French citizens.

Coming during a highly symbolically charged presidential election and in a situation where individuals are increasingly defined by their ethnic or religious affiliations, in a way our religion question was a trap for these French citizens who are endlessly tied back to their origins. Not answering meant denying their pasts, but answering ran the risk of their being reduced to their religion and supposed difference. In interviews, voters with Algerian or Moroccan parents indicated in myriad ways their desire to be seen "like everyone else" and "blend into the crowd," and their refusal to be pigeonholed. They moved to the Poplars specifically to get out of stigmatized neighborhoods and reaffirm a personal identity that had long been crushed by association with housing projects and the low view society generally has of their world.[24]

In our sample (which admittedly was small, especially concerning the number of representatives of each religion), rather clear differences appear according to the declared religion: thus "Muslim" voters (71 respondents) were much more numerous in declaring a vote for S Royal (62 percent) and, to a lesser extent, F Bayrou (21 percent), and "Catholic" (143 respondents) and "Jewish" (18 respondents) voters' ballots went more frequently to the right (for the former, 23 percent for N Sarkozy and 22 percent for F Bayrou; for the latter 61 percent for N Sarkozy). A proportion of "Catholic" voters declared themselves Chaldean; of twenty-three, fifteen said they voted for N Sarkozy and four for J-M Le Pen.

Religion is an imperfect indicator for summing up a collection of parameters (migratory history, the international political situation, local and nationwide discourses about them, values) in order to factor them into interpretations of political preferences. It sidelines other equally influential factors, such as family situation, job type, vision of the future, or children's situations. Some light can be shed on the electoral oppositions among the neighborhood's "French from someplace else" by offering several possible interpretations of why some of them (Chaldean in particular) vote for the right, based on interviews conducted several months preceding and immediately after the first round of the presidential election.

The Sarkozy vote first seemed to be an anti-Muslim vote. Some Chaldean voters, traditionalist Catholics who fled persecution in their home region near Turkey's Iranian and Iraqi borders, are opposed to Muslims. Marie Yalap, a business school student, has so much difficulty in accepting what her parents' friends in the neighborhood say on the subject that she was uncomfortable talking about it. Socialized in what she describes as a leftist family, she is among the handful of Chaldean children who refuse these oppositions rooted in Turkish history that are endlessly revived by televised images. She stresses the role satellite television and Aramaic language networks play in perpetuating this legacy: they broadcast the image of a clash of civilizations between Islam and the rest of the world that deeply frightens parents with little or no formal education who themselves were victims of persecution. Another indicator of the spreading sentiment of Muslim threat, a group of children who loitered at our questionnaire table at the polls said they wanted to "throw out the blacks and Arabs that aren't Christians" and saw N Sarkozy and J-M Le Pen as men up for the task.

Another possible interpretation of the vote is to look at it in terms of insecurity, lived and felt in different ways. Marie Yalep puts it this way:

> Sarkozy, he actually rubs people the right way. I mean, he tells them, "Today there are problems in the *banlieue,* we're gonna put all those hoodrats in prison, we're gonna get rid of them, we're gonna clean it out with a water jet," and that also seduces them. There are a lot of them who have already voted for Le Pen, they're thinking, "Sarkozy isn't as extreme, maybe we'll vote for him." And people think the hoodrats are the Arabs, y'know, well, the Muslims.

In Gonesse, as at the national level, public safety concerns rank third among public preoccupations, behind unemployment and poverty. The great majority of respondents claimed they were afraid for their children in public transportation (79 percent), in leisure areas, at school (72 percent).[25] Although these rates are comparable with those in other cities of metropolitan Paris, they are significantly higher than results from metropolitan Lyon, France's second-largest city. Gonesse may have one of the highest burglary rates, but the Poplars has long been sheltered from inter-youth violence, including the 2005 riots. At the urging of the city's Socialist mayor, who was inspired by American community policing, citizen vigilance networks have been established in the neighborhood. For example, Chaldean men organized neighborhood rounds, and elected officials and some residents watched over public buildings during the 2005 riots.

Despite this left-leaning public safety policy, confrontations between young people erupted in 2006, leaving a young man from the Cité du Nord paralyzed when a youth from the Poplars shot him in the back. In the following months, tensions simmered, and there were recurring confrontations, especially around the middle school and in front of the church attended by the Chaldeans, located in the Cité du Nord. Then on Easter Monday, a public holiday in France that fell barely two weeks before the first round of the presidential election, the situation degenerated—shots were fired, adults got involved. In response, a public meeting with the mayor was held between the elections' first and second rounds, and a Chaldean father stood up to speak. He said that Chaldean parents, like other parents, were hesitant to send their children to the assigned middle school for fear that they might be attacked on the path to school: "A kid who can't go to school because of safety [*problems*]? It's unacceptable." And so it would seem that Chaldean families felt increasingly unsafe in the months leading up to the presidential election because of the mounting violence between young people from the Poplars and Cité du Nord public housing. They complained of insults as they left church in the Cité du Nord and damaged cars in the parking lot.

Burned cars, frequent fights, hateful language, cell phone theft, and comparable incidents feed a wider demand for order in this group as in others. M. Sabak, a father we interviewed after the first round of the election who voted for N Sarkozy after having voted Le Pen in 2002, said he wanted "to have done with the rioters" and praised N Sarkozy's efforts as Minister of the Interior for having successfully reduced delinquency in the neighborhood. Interviewees of Chaldean origin acknowledge that their children's behavior leaves something to be desired: young adults loiter in front of businesses, hang out in playgrounds, dabble in petty trafficking, drive fast on neighborhood streets. Until recently, sons of neighborhood Chaldean families sought work immediately after quitting their studies, usually in small garment workshops where their fathers worked, thus not provoking much talk. The youngest are now more likely to end up on "the slippery slope." The garment industry no longer offers as much work, and the youngest are less inclined to accept reproducing their fathers' positions by becoming laborers. Parents' eroding ability to control their own children is another impetus for calling for greater severity from the state. M. Sabak is thus upset that "people don't want to work anymore," adding: "beyond that, it's drugs, joints, stupid stuff—you have to earn respect, you've got to punish those who don't want to work."

This radicalization of political behaviors also manifests concern about preserving the "neighborhood calm" to prevent the departure of more fortunate Chaldean families. Remember they started arriving over twenty years ago, and today some of them hope to leave a neighborhood that they, like the older residents, think is on a downslide. The row houses will end up being transitional housing on the path to a quieter neighborhood that will allow them to leave behind the intra-ethnic ties that have become less necessary with the passage of time in France and the laying down of roots. But their departures would threaten the ecology of families who do not have the same possibilities for mobility: like the small "French" homeowners before them, they are especially motivated to "preserve the neighborhood."

Through the Le Pen vote and the more recent Sarkozy vote, a share of voters of Chaldean descent is trying to correct the image given to their group by affirming they are people who "deserve" to be French. "We are in France and we are French," "we came here to stay permanently," said M. Sabak, who contrasted his ethnic group to "foreigners who take advantage of France" and "go back home." "We do everything for France," and "we succeed," unlike other immigrants who remain loyal to their home country and do not make the necessary efforts to "integrate themselves well."

M. Sabak grew up in a small village near the Iraqi border, which he left for the lack of opportunities it offered him as one of the few village children to have gone to middle school. He fled to Istanbul where he found work as a steward in an Armenian church. When the opportunity arose in the early 1980s, he joined his seven brothers and sisters already in France and obtained political refugee status. He went through shelters and then was housed, with his wife and seven children, in an HLM apartment in the Cité du Nord. In 2001, he bought a row house in the Poplars, with the help of his eldest son (a trucker) and his wife (who worked in the schools). He had been a textile trader until he had an automobile accident, a year earlier. His life course more or less reflects that of other Chaldean neighborhood residents who arrived in France in absolute destitution and in twenty years managed to acquire property, an object of great pride.

Abandoning all hope of return also brought this group to an accelerated "Frenchification": in addition to investing their savings in the country where they live, they quickly requested naturalization and systematically gave their children French Christian first names and modified their own. At the same time, these "exemplary" immigrants (in terms of assimilationist norms) often have trouble with the French language and remain attached to their cultural traditions. By promoting their civic and economic rootedness in French society, they try to set themselves apart from other immigrants. Being Christian is also a resource in the competition pitting them against Muslims. This explains why some of them might have thought of J-M Le Pen as a way to radically demarcate themselves from Muslim immigrants. In 2007, they seem to have seen N Sarkozy as a more legitimate ally in their quest for distinction: like other neighborhood residents who voted for him, they set themselves apart from "immigrants from the projects" by asserting themselves as "homeowners" and "deserving people."

In contrast with the past, the Poplars today is inhabited by little-middles who are now distinctly to the right, arriving there through a variety of processes contingent on their group affiliations. But while a majority of voters opted for N Sarkozy, we were still struck by how involved leftist activists were on the 2007 election day, when volunteers like Mme Fayard, elected official from the Socialist Party, and an elected Communist who is a long-running neighborhood activist predominated among poll workers. Other leftist sympathizers joined them to count the ballots that night, while activists and sympathizers from the right were all but absent. Facing the impression of a massive shift to the right, we were reminded that there is not only a non-negligible voting block for the left remaining in the neighborhood, but a network of left-leaning activist residents invested in local life as well.[26]

On top of these election-day observations is the fact that although the Poplars moved to the right in national elections over the 1990s, the left has had good results in local elections since 1995. This observation spurs us to nuance the impression of suburban neighborhoods' massive and persistent shift to the right, at least for this neighborhood whose past political hetero- geneity we have already discussed. One wonders if the left's successes in leg- islative and municipal elections might be related to local political options for public security and the "grassroots activism" that today may be more com- mon in neighborhoods of little-middle homeowners than in working-class HLM neighborhoods, which now seem more economically and politically neglected.

The Rightward Shift of Small Homeowners: A Shared Reality

Although our analysis of electoral practices and political engagements re- mains exploratory (due to the fact that it was not central to our initial re- search plan), it ultimately holds an important position in our study overall.

First of all, fluctuations in the neighborhood's voting patterns could be read as an indicator of the transformation experienced by these successive generations of little-middles who became homeowners in the outskirts of Paris. After long being split between the left and right, with a majority for the Socialist and Communist Parties, the neighborhood vote shifted right- ward, although Socialist/Communist slates still win elections. This new bal- ance is not a simple reversal of roles, however, because it now includes a newly established vote for the Front National. This vote for the extreme right reveals the extent to which a discourse rejecting "the Turks" and foreigners in general has become legitimate, but it is also related to efforts to take a distance from the poor and people "on welfare" who are seen as downclass- ing the neighborhood and its inhabitants, especially those who have been there the longest and feel trapped there. Some migrants also contribute to the rightward shift in this housing development. When people from Chal- dean backgrounds vote for the right and extreme right, it is an expression of anti-Muslim sentiment that reflects both a desire to fight the disorder de- grading the neighborhood's reputation and a strategy for assimilating into French society chosen by refugees without hope of return.

Our study suggests that these same elements are also largely found among the Sarkozy voters that we met in 2007. The dissatisfactions born of the gap between the hope of acceding to the middle classes and the lack of economic means for making it become reality influenced a proportion of the neigh- borhood's homeowners to vote for the right. Comparison with owners of the previous generation is quite instructive in this regard, as the row-house pioneers voted to the left, even though homeownership was not easy for them. The neighborhood at the time was home to an "ambiance of equality" that favored social optimism among even the most modest of them and prevented positions from hardening. There is no longer such an ambiance in the Poplars. New, strong, and palpable forms of social competition and division now tip the balance clearly to the right. This does not mean that the vote to the left has collapsed—it remains important, especially in local elections, and is related to an attachment to the current municipal council as well as the presence of left-leaning people invested in neighborhood life who embody alternative trajectories among the little-middles. Although their activism takes place partly in local institutional contexts such as the neighborhood council where tensions between neighbors come to a head, it is mainly manifest in the everyday work of micro-activism among their family and friends in the neighborhood, where its contributions are still rather limited.

NOTES

1. See especially J-L Pan Ké Shon, "Ségrégation ethnique et ségrégation sociale en quartiers sensibles. L'apport des mobilités résidentielles," *Revue française de sociologie* 50, no. 3 (2009): 451–87.

2. For a rigorous analysis of how suburban homeowners vote, see J Rivière, "Le vote pavillonnaire existe-t-il? Comportements électoraux et positions sociales locales dans une commune rurale en cours de périurbanisation," *Politix* 21, no. 83 (2008): 23–48; V Girard, "Explaining the Periurban Right-Wing Vote: 'Social Frustrations' of Low-Income Households or the Reshaping of the Working Classes?" *Metropolitics*, 2012; V Girard and J Rivière, "The Grandeur and Decadence of the Suburbs. Looking Back on Three Decades of Analysis of Social and Political Change," *Metropolitics*, 2013.

3. For a comparison with the American situation on this subject, see D Reed-Danahay, "From the 'Imagined Community' to 'Communities of Practice': Immigrant Belonging among Vietnamese Americans," in *Citizenship, Political Engagement and Belonging*, ed. D Reed-Danahay and C Brettell (New Brunswick, NJ, 2008), 78–97.

4. We thank Annie Collovald for her comments on this chapter.

5. This is based on the municipal archives that were made available to us.

6. C Braconnier and J Dormagen, *La démocratie de l'abstention* (Paris, 2007).

7. D Gaxie, *Le cens caché. Inégalités culturelles et ségrégation politique* (Paris, 1977). The notion of *cens caché* (hidden *cens*) refers to the historical right to vote granted only to people who paid a particular tax (the *cens*), which limited voting access to rather financially well-off people; this system existed until 1848 in France. The "hidden" *cens* nudging many voters into abstention today is cultural rather than economic.

8. In addition to Braconnier and Dormagen, *La démocratie de l'abstention,* see O Schwartz, "Sur le rapport des ouvriers du Nord à la politique. Matériaux lacunaires," *Politix* 11 (1991): 79–86; A Collovald and F Sawicki, "Le populaire et le politique, quelques pistes de recherche en guise d'introduction," *Politix* 13 (1991): 7–19; and B Pudal, "Politisations ouvrières et communisme," in *Le siècle des communismes*, ed. M Dreyfus et al. (Paris, 2001), 513–21.

9. MRP: Mouvement républicain populaire; SFIO: Section française de l'Internationale ouvrière.

10. As shown by analysis of election results since the 1950s (municipal archives).

11. J Briquet and F Sawicki, "'L'analyse localisée du politique': lieux de recherche ou recherche de lieux?" *Politix* 7–8 (1989): 6–16.

12. In view of this growth, the 2002 results were less spectacular (at the national average), although the canton-level elections of 2004 resulted in a runoff election between the Socialist Party and the Front National. It was not until 2007 that the Front National's score dropped significantly, as it also did at the national level.

13. A Collovald, Le *"populisme du FN,"* un dangereux contresens (Paris, 2004), 162.

14. Collovald, Le *"populisme du FN,"* 119–62; P Lehingue, "L'objectivation statistique des électorats: que savons-nous des électeurs du Front National?," in *La politisation,* ed. J Lagroye (Paris, 2003), 247–78.

15. C Traïni has shown, for example, how the theory of the working-class and urban character of the Front National vote has masked its strong implantation in well-off small and medium-sized towns and cities in southern France: "L'épicentre d'un 'séisme electoral.' Le vote Front national en région PACA," in *Vote en PACA. Les élections 2002 en Provence-Alpes-Côte d'Azur,* ed. C Traïni (Paris, 2004), 21–48.

16. Of the many analyses along these lines, we single out those analyzing the phenomenon over the long term: Beaud and Pialoux, *Retour sur la condition ouvrière,* and their chapter "Pourquoi la gauche a-t-elle perdu les classes populaires? Petit retour sur l'histoire," in *A gauche!* (Paris, 2002); and G Michelat and M Simon, *Les ouvriers et la politique: permanences, ruptures, réalignements. 1962–2002* (Paris, 2004).

17. P Bouffartigue, "Le salariat intermédiaire sous tensions," in *Le retour des classes sociales. Inégalités, dominations, conflits,* ed. P Bouffartigue (Paris, 2004).

18. For uncertainties about children, see chapters 3 and 4. For more on the processes of social weakening and residential downclassing, see chapters 1, 2, and 5.

19. As reported by an article devoted to the subject in *Figaro Magazine* in January 2001.

20. *"Touche pas à mon pote"* is a slogan from the antiracism association SOS Racisme, whose logo—the slogan written inside the outline of a hand in a "halt" gesture—appeared on pins, T-shirts, and other media from 1985 onward.

21. Céline Braconnier and Jean-Yves Dormagen were kind enough to share the questionnaire they developed for their survey of the Cité des Cosmonautes, which greatly informed our own.

22. We started distributing the questionnaire around 9:30 AM, after we ourselves had gone to vote, at which time, a little over 100 people had already voted.

23. A Collovald and O Schwartz, "Haut, bas, fragile: sociologies du populaire," interview by S Grelet, F Jobard and M Potte-Bonneville, *Vacarme* 36 (2006): 50–55.

25. On these reservations about "ethnic reduction," see also P Simon and M Clément, "Comment décrire la diversité des origines en France?" *Population et sociétés* 425 (2006): 1–4.

26. Local surveys from 2005 on victimhood and insecurity; E Didier et al., *Enquête locale 2005 sur la victimation et l'insécurité: Gonesse* (Guyancourt, 2006), CESDIP, "Etudes et données Pénales" collection.

27. In this regard, it is interesting to observe that city officials identified and approached Paul Günes and Marie Yalap, the two Chaldean young people whose progressive tendencies we have mentioned, during preparations for the 2008 municipal elections, which were marked by an initiative to open the local political field to minori-

ties. A breeding-ground for candidates, the Poplars is a potential site for political socialization and building a feeling of belonging, and apprenticeship in citizenship for new generations of residents, immigrants, or their descendants. See on this subject M Cartier et al., "Promotion et marginalisation des élus de la 'diversité' dans une commune de banlieue parisienne," *Politix* 91 (2010): 179–205, and for a comparison with the American situation on this subject, see D Reed-Danahay and C Brettell, eds, *Citizenship, Political Engagement, and Belonging: Immigrants in Europe and the United States* (New Brunswick, NJ, 2008).

APPENDIX

1

INTERVIEWS CITED IN THE BOOK

Pseudonym	Which part of the neighborhood they live in	Date(s)	Interviewer(s)
M. and Mme Deneuve	Old single-family houses (garden-city period)	2004 2005	Pascal Marichalar, Alice Richard, and Yasmine Siblot Pascal Marichalar
M. Collin	Old single-family houses	2004	Maud Vu Van Kha, Marie Cartier, and Yasmine Siblot
Mme Verrier	Old single-family houses	2004	Pascal Marichalar and Alice Richard
Omid Hakimi	Row houses	2004 2005	Maud Vu Van Kha and Alice Richard Isabelle Coutant
Sabar family	Row houses	2004	Aurélie Ouss, Vincent Braconnay, and Anne-Catherine Wagner
Georges Sabar	Row houses	2004 2005	Aurélie Ouss, Vincent Braconnay, and Anne-Catherine Wagner Clément Dherbecourt
Yasïr family	Row houses	2004	Aurélie Ouss, Vincent Braconnay, and Anne-Catherine Wagner

(continued)

Pseudonym	Which part of the neighborhood they live in	Date(s)	Interviewer(s)
Paul Günes	Row houses	2004	Aurélie Ouss, Vincent Braconnay, Jean-Pierre Hassoun, and Clémence Patureau
		2005	Isabelle Coutant
		2007	Isabelle Coutant and Olivier Masclet
M. and Mme Samson	Row houses	2004	Pascal Marichalar
		2005	Marie Cartier and Nicolas Renahy
		(twice)	Pascal Marichalar
Marie Yalap	Row houses	2007	Olivier Masclet and Marie Cartier
M. Sabak	Row houses	2007	Isabelle Coutant, Olivier Masclet, and Yasmine Siblot
M. and Mme Vallès	Row houses	2004	Delphine Roy and Olivier Masclet
M. and Mme Garcia	Row houses	2004	Pascal Marichalar and Jean-Pierre Hassoun
M. Ronsart	Row houses	2004	Olivier Masclet
M. and Mme Boyer	Row houses	2005	Marie Cartier and Olivier Masclet
Dominique Legendre	Row houses	2006	Pascal Marichalar
Mme Sanchez	Row houses	2004	Marie Cartier and Olivier Masclet
		2005	Marie Cartier and Olivier Masclet
		2007	Yasmine Siblot
M. and Mme Berger	Row houses/ Recent subdivision	2005	Marie Cartier and Isabelle Coutant
		2007	Marie Cartier and Isabelle Coutant
Mme Legris	Row houses/ Recent subdivision	2004	Pascal Marichalar, Delphine Roy, and Marie Cartier
Mme Pageot	Row houses/ Recent subdivision	2004	Pascal Marichalar
Luc Robin	Row houses/ Apartment building	2005	Nicolas Renahy
M. and Mme Morin	Row houses/ Recent subdivision	2005	Yasmine Siblot

Pseudonym	Which part of the neighborhood they live in	Date(s)	Interviewer(s)
M. Lenormand	Row houses/ Recent subdivision	2005	Yasmine Siblot
Mme Boucher	Row houses/ Recent subdivision	2005	Yasmine Siblot
M. and Mme Guissard	Building from the 1930s	2005	Yasmine Siblot
M. and Mme Piazza	Row houses/ Recent subdivision	2005 (twice) 2006	Jean-Pierre Hassoun Jean-Pierre Hassoun and Yasmine Siblot
M. and Mme Heurtin	Row houses/ Recent subdivision	2006	Jean-Pierre Hassoun
M. Bertaux	Row houses/ Recent subdivision	2005	Olivier Masclet
M. Kergoat	Subdivision from the 1980s (village-style)	2004	Dagmara Drazewska and Olivier Masclet
M. Robert	Subdivision from the 1980s	2004	Jean-Robert Dantou and Dagamara Drazewska
M. and Mme Péruchot	Subdivision from the 1980s	2004 (twice)	Pascal Marichalar Laure Lecoat and Laeticia Strauch
M. and Mme Largent	Subdivision from the 1980s	2004 (twice)	Vincent Chabault Dagmara Drazewska and Laeticia Strauch
Thomas Loiseau	Subdivision from the 1980s	2004 2005 2007	Emmanuel Comte, Fabien Brugière, and Yasmine Siblot Emmanuel Comte, Fabien Brugière, and Yasmine Siblot Yasmine Siblot
Maryline Loiseau	Subdivision from the 1980s	2004	Emmanuel Comte and Fabien Brugière
Stéphanie Bensoussan	Subdivision from the 1980s	2004	Emmanuel Comte and Fabien Brugière
Agnès Bensoussan	Subdivision from the 1980s	2004	Emmanuel Comte and Fabien Brugière
Julien Bensoussan	Subdivision from the 1980s	2005	Emmanuel Comte

Pseudonym	Which part of the neighborhood they live in	Date(s)	Interviewer(s)
Delphine and Cédric Dumoulin, Laeticia	Subdivision from the 1980s	2004	Emmanuel Comte and Fabien Brugière
Samira Ben M'Rad	Subdivision from 1990–2000 ("golf-course" houses)	2004 2005	Jean-Robert Dantou, Dagmara Drazewska, and Marie Cartier Marie Cartier and Olivier Masclet
Mme Germain	Subdivision from 1990–2000	2004 2005	Jean-Robert Dantou and Laure Lecoat Laure Lecoat and Olivier Masclet
Nadia Dhif	Subdivision from 1990–2000	2004 2005	Olivier Masclet Olivier Masclet and Nicolas Renahy
Karima Dhif	Subdivision from 1990–2000	2005	Olivier Masclet
Jean-Luc Thomas	Subdivision from 1990–2000	2004	Laeticia Strauch and Nicolas Renahy
Mme Fayard	Subdivision from 1990–2000	2005 2007	Olivier Masclet and Yasmine Siblot Isabelle Coutant and Yasmine Siblot
Patrick Jarreau	Subdivision from 1990–2000	2005 2005	Olivier Masclet Marie Cartier and Olivier Masclet
M. and Mme Perret	Subdivision from 1990–2000	2004	Marie Cartier, Laure Lecoat, and Laeticia Strauch
Mme Hancel	Subdivision from 1990–2000	2005	Olivier Masclet
M. and Mme Sorel	Subdivision from 1990–2000	2007	Olivier Masclet
Michèle Yacine	Municipal policy liaison officer	2003	Marie Cartier, Isabelle Coutant, and Olivier Masclet
Mme Hernandes	Primary school principal	2005	Nicolas Renahy, Yasmine Siblot, and Anne Catherine Wagner
Alain Duman	Hotel owner	2004 2005	Samuel Neuberg, Clément Dherbecourt, and Jean-Pierre Hassoun/Clément Dherbecourt
Jean Duman	Convenience store manager	2005	Clément Dherbecourt

APPENDIX

2

DOCUMENTS AND SOURCES

ARCHIVES

Private archives of a common-interest development of single-family row houses, 1965–1986
Departmental archives, nominal data from the 1968 census
Municipal archives, boxes 18 W 3 to 40, electoral data for the 1947–1995 period

STATISTICAL DATA

INSEE, Census data from 1990, 1999
INSEE, financial data, 2001
Gonesse City Hall, Elections department, electoral data
Gonesse City Hall, Urban planning department, "Declarations of the Intent to Alienate" (*Déclarations d'Intention d'Aliéner*) 1988–2005, which were used to create an original database

DOCUMENTS

Le Gonessien, the municipal newsletter
City of Gonesse, neighborhood council meeting minutes
Reports from the association Elélé, 1997, 1999
City of Gonesse, Urban and social study conducted by B de Lataulade, 2001

Plaine de France (land use planning agency for zone northeast of Paris), "Le parc pavillonnaire ancien fragile" (Single-family housing stock old, weakened), June 2004

City-Quality Initiative Contract between the City of Gonesse and the General Council, 2002

City of Gonesse, City Contract 2000–2006, 2001

BIBLIOGRAPHY

Althabe, Gérard. "Le quotidien en procès." *Dialectiques* 21 (1977): 67–77.
———. "La résidence comme enjeu." In *Urbanisation et enjeux quotidiens. Terrains ethnologiques dans la France actuelle*, edited by G Althabe, C Marcadet, M de la Pradelle, and M Sélim, 11–69. Paris, 1993.
Anderson, Robert T, and Barbara Galatin Anderson. *Bus Stop for Paris: The Transformation of a French Village*. Garden City, NY, 1965.
Avanza, Martina, Gilles Laferté, and Etienne Penissat. "O crédito entre as classes populares: o exemplo de uma loja em Lens." *Mana. Estudo de Antropologia Social* 12, no. 1 (2006): 7–38.
Backouche, Isabelle, Fabrice Ripoll, Sylvie Tissot, and Vincent Veschambre. *La dimension spatiale des inégalités. Regards croisés des sciences sociales*. Rennes, 2011.
Balazs, Gabrielle, and Abdelmalek Sayad. "Institutional Violence." In *The Weight of the World*, edited by Pierre Bourdieu et al. Translated by Priscilla P Ferguson, S Emanuel, J Johnson, and S Waryn, 492–506. Stanford, CA, 1999.
Barrault-Stella, Lorenzo. *Gouverner par accommodements. Stratégies autour de la carte scolaire*. Paris, 2013.
Beaud, Stéphane. *80 % au bac ... et après?: Les enfants de la démocratisation scolaire*. Paris, 2003.
Beaud, Stéphane, and Younès Amrani. *Pays de malheur! Un jeune de cité écrit à un sociologue*. Paris, 2005.
Beaud, Stéphane, and Olivier Masclet. "Des 'marcheurs' de 1983 aux 'émeutiers' de 2005. Deux générations sociales d'enfants d'immigrés." *Annales* 4 (2006): 809–43.
Beaud, Stéphane, and Michel Pialoux. *Retour sur la condition ouvrière*. Paris, 1999.
———. "Pourquoi la gauche a-t-elle perdu les classes populaires? Petit retour sur l'histoire." In *A gauche!* Edited by the A Gauche Collective. Paris, La Découverte, 2002.
———. *Violences urbaines, violence sociale*. Paris, 2003.
Berger, Martine. *Les Périurbains de Paris: de la ville dense à la métropole éclatée*. Paris, 2004.
Bidou, Catherine. *Les aventuriers du quotidian*. Paris, 1984.
Bidou-Zachariasen, Catherine, ed. *Retours en ville, des processus de "gentrification" urbaine aux politiques de "revitalisation" des centres*. Paris, 2003.

Boltanski, Luc. *The Making of a Class: Cadres in French Society.* Translated by A Gold-hammer. Cambridge, U.K., 1987.

Bonvalet, Catherine, and Anne Gotman, eds. *Le logement une affaire de famille.* Paris, 1993.

Borges Pereira, Virgilio. *Classes e Culturas de Classe das Famílias Portuenses. Classes sociais e "modalidades de estilização da vida" na cidade do Porto.* Porto, Portugal, 2005.

Bosc, Serge. *Sociologie des classes moyennes.* Paris, 2008.

Bouffartigue, Paul. "Le salariat intermédiaire sous tensions." In *Le retour des classes sociales. Inégalités, dominations, conflits,* edited by P Bouffartigue, 113. Paris, 2004.

Bourdieu, Pierre. "Le capital social. Notes provisoires." *Actes de la Recherche en Sciences Sociales* 31 (1980): 2–3.

———. *Distinction: A Social Critique of the Judgment of Taste.* Translated by Richard Nice. Cambridge, MA, 1984.

———. *Les structures sociales de l'économie.* Paris, 2000.

Bourdieu, Pierre, Salah Bouhedja, Rosine Christin, and Claire Givry. "Un placement de père de famille. La maison individuelle: spécificité du produit et logique du champ de reproduction." *Actes de la recherche en sciences sociales* 81–82 (1990): 6–33.

Bourdieu, Pierre, and Monique de Saint-Martin. "Le sens de la propriété. La genèse sociale des systèmes de préférences." *Actes de la Recherche en Sciences Sociales* 81–82 (1990): 52–63.

Bourgois, Philippe. *In Search of Respect: Selling Crack in El Barrio.* New York, 1995.

Braconnier, Céline, and Jean-Yves Dormagen. *La démocratie de l'abstention.* Paris, 2007.

Briquet, Jean-Louis, and Frédéric Sawicki. "'L'analyse localisée du politique': lieux de recherche ou recherche de lieux?" *Politix* 7–8 (1989): 6–16.

Bruno, Anne-Sophie, and Claire Zalc. *Petites entreprises et petits entrepreneurs étrangers en France, 19e–20e siècles.* Paris, 2006.

Calogirou, Claire. *Sauver son honneur: Rapports sociaux en milieu urbain défavorisé.* Paris, 1990.

Cartier, Marie. *Les facteurs et leurs tournées. Un service public au quotidien.* Paris, 2003.

Cartier, Marie, Isabelle Coutant, Olivier Masclet, and Yasmine Siblot, eds. *Pavillonnaires de la banlieue nord. Une ethnographie des petites mobilités sociales.* Report for the Mission à l'ethnologie, Ministry of Culture and Communication, Paris, 2006.

———. "Promotion et marginalisation des élus de la 'diversité' dans une commune de banlieue parisienne." *Politix* 91 (2010): 179–205.

———. "From the Petite Bourgeoisie to the Little-Middles: An invitation to put small social mobility into question." In *The Routledge Companion to Bourdieu's 'Distinction,'* edited by Philippe Coulangeon and Julien Duval, 63–77. Oxford, 2014.

Castel, Robert. *From Manual Workers to Wage Laborers: Transformation of the Social Question.* Translated and edited by Richard Boyd. New Brunswick, NJ, 2003.

Chalvon-Demersay, Sabine. *Le triangle du XIVe, de nouveaux habitants dans un vieux quartier de Paris.* Paris, 1984.

Chamboredon, Jean-Claude. "Construction sociale des populations." In *Histoire de la France urbaine,* edited by M Roncayolo, 467–501. Paris, 1985.

———. "Classes scolaires, classes d'âge, classes sociales: les fonctions de scansion temporelle du système de formation." *Enquêtes. Cahiers du CERCOM* 6 (1991): 121–43.

Chamboredon, Jean-Claude, and Madeleine Lemaire. "Proximité spatiale et distance sociale." *Revue française de sociologie* XI, no. 1 (1970): 3–33.

Chapoulie, Jean-Michel. *La tradition de Chicago, 1892–1961.* Paris, 2001.

Charmes, Eric. "Entre ouverture et fermeture: les rapports à autrui dans les tissus périurbains." In *La société des voisins*, edited by B Haumont and A Morel, 109–21. Paris, 2005.

Chauvel, Louis. *Le destin des générations. Structure sociale et cohortes en France au XXe siècle.* Paris, 1998.

———. "Le retour des classes sociales." *Revue de l'OFCE* 79 (2001): 315–59.

Chenu, Alain. *Les employés.* Paris, 1994.

Christin, Rosine. "Everyone in a Place of their Own." In *The Weight of the World*, edited by Pierre Bourdieu et al. Translated by Priscilla P Ferguson, S Emanuel, J Johnson, and S Waryn, 37–45. Stanford, CA, 1999.

Coing, Henri. *Rénovation urbaine et changement social. (l'îlot n°4, Paris 13è).* Paris, 1966.

Collovald, Annie. *Le "populisme du FN," un dangereux contresens.* Paris, 2004.

Collovald, Annie, and Frédéric Sawicki. "Le populaire et le politique, quelques pistes de recherche en guise d'introduction." *Politix* 13 (1991): 7–19.

Collovald, Annie, and Olivier Schwartz. "Haut, bas, fragile: sociologies du populaire." Interview by S. Grelet, F. Jobard and M. Potte-Bonneville. *Vacarme* 36 (2006): 50–55.

Coulangeon, Philippe. *Les métamorphoses de la distinction. Inégalités culturelles dans la France d'aujourd'hui.* Paris, 2011.

Coutant, Isabelle. *Politiques du squat.* Paris, 2000.

Cuturello, Paul. *Dialogues de propriétaires. De comment le devenir à comment le rester, deux décennies de stratégies d'accession à la propriété du logement (1978–1995).* Paris, 1997.

Cuturello, Paul, and Francis Godard. *Familles mobilisées. Accession à la propriété du logement et notion d'effort des ménages.* Paris, 1980.

Daubresse, Marion. "La reprise de l'accession à la propriété." *INSEE Première* 913 (2003): 1–4.

Debrand, Thierry, and Claude Taffin. "Les facteurs structurels et conjoncturels de la mobilité résidentielle depuis 20 ans." *Économie et statistique* 381–82 (2005): 125–46.

de Singly, François. *Le soi, le couple et la famille.* Paris, 1996.

Dherbécourt, Clément. "La difficile sortie des classes populaires pour les Assyro-chaldéens: De petites ascensions sociales par le biais du commerce de quartier." In *Pavillonnaires de la banlieue nord: Une ethnographie des petites mobilités sociales*, edited by Marie Cartier, Isabelle Coutant, Olivier Masclet, and Yasmine Siblot, 258–71. Paris, 2006.

Didier, Emmanuelle, Sophie Névanen, Philippe Robert, and Renée Zauberman. *Enquête locale 2005 sur la victimation et l'insécurité: Gonesse.* Guyancourt, 2006.

Dubet, François. *La galère. Jeunes en survie.* Paris, 1987.

Duvoux, Nicolas. *Le nouvel âge de la solidarité. Pauvreté, précarité et politiques publiques.* Paris, 2012.

Elias, Norbert, and John Scotson. *The Established and the Outsiders: A Sociological Enquiry into Community Problems,* 2nd ed. London, 1994.

Epstein, Beth. *Collective Terms: Race, Culture, and Community in a State-Planned City in France.* New York, 2011.

Fassin, Didier. "Riots in France and Silent Anthropologists." *Anthropology Today* 22, no. 1 (2006):1–3.

Faure, Alain, ed. *Les premiers banlieusards.* Paris, 1991.

Felouzis, Georges. "La ségrégation ethnique au collège et ses conséquences." *Revue française de sociologie* 44 (2003): 413–47.

Fourcaut, Annie. *Bobigny, banlieue rouge*. Paris, 1986.

——. *La banlieue en morceaux. La crise des lotissements défectueux en France dans l'entre-deux-guerres*. Paris, 2000.

Galland, Olivier. "Entrer dans la vie adulte: des étapes toujours plus tardives, mais resserrées." *Économie et statistique* 337–38 (2000): 13–36.

Gans, Herbert. *The Levittowners: Ways of Life and Politics in a New Suburban Community*. New York, 1982.

Garbin, David, and Gareth Millington. "Territorial Stigma and the Politics of Resistance in a Parisian Banlieue: La Courneuve and Beyond." *Urban Studies* 49, no. 10 (2012): 2067–83.

Gaxie, Daniel. *Le cens caché. Inégalités culturelles et ségrégation politique*. Paris, 1977.

Girard, Violaine. "Explaining the Periurban Right-Wing Vote: 'Social Frustrations' of Low-Income Households or the Reshaping of the Working Classes?" *Metropolitics*, 13 June 2012, http://www.metropolitiques.eu/Explaining-the-periurban-right .html.

Girard, Violaine, and Jean Rivière. "The Grandeur and Decadence of the Suburbs. Looking Back on Three Decades of Analysis of Social and Political Change." *Metropolitics*, 18 September 2013, http://www.metropolitiques.eu/The-grandeur-and-decadence-of-the.html.

Gojard, Séverine. "François de Singly, *Le Soi, le couple et la famille*." *Genèses* 27 (1997): 164–65.

Gollac, Sibylle. "La fonction publique: une voie de promotion sociale pour les enfants des classes populaires?" *Sociétés contemporaines* 58 (2005): 41–64.

Goody, Jack. *The European Family: An Historico-Anthropological Essay*. Oxford, 2000.

Gouirir, Malika. "Ouled el kharij: les enfants de l'étranger. Socialisation et trajectoires familiales d'enfants d'ouvriers marocains immigrés en France." Doctoral diss., Université Paris-X Nanterre, 1997.

Grafmeyer, Yves. *Les gens de la banque*. Paris, 1992.

Grafmeyer, Yves, and Françoise Dansereau. *Trajectoires familiales et espaces de vie en milieu urbain*. Paris, 1998.

Grignon, Claude, and Jean-Claude Passeron. *Le Savant et le populaire. Misérabilisme et populisme en sociologie et en literature*. Paris, 1989.

Groux, Guy, and Catherine Lévy. *La possession ouvrière. Du taudis à la propriété (XIXè–XXè siècle)*. Paris, 1993.

Gruel, Louis. "Conjurer l'exclusion, rhétorique et identité revendiquée dans les habitats socialement disqualifies." *Revue française de sociologie* XXVI, no. 3 (1985): 431–53.

Guenif-Souilamas, Nacira. *Des beurettes aux descendantes d'immigrants nord-africains*. Paris, 1999.

Halle, David. *American's Working Man: Work, Home and Politics among Blue Collar Property-Owners*. Chicago, 1984.

Hassoun Jean-Pierre. "Vendre son pavillon, quitter les Peupliers." In *Pavillonnaires de la banlieue nord: Une ethnographie des petites mobilités sociales*, edited by Marie Cartier, Isabelle Coutant, Olivier Masclet, and Yasmine Siblot, 407–41. Paris, 2006.

Haumont, Nicole. *Les pavillonnaires: étude psychosociologique d'un mode d'habitat*. Paris, 2001.

Héran, François. "La sociabilité une pratique culturelle?" *Économie et Statistique* 216 (1988): 3–22.

Hoggart, Richard. *The Uses of Literacy: Aspects of Working Class Life*. London, 1957.

———. *A Local Habitation: Life and Times, 1918–1940*. London, 1988.

INSEE. *Les immigrés en France*. Paris, 2005.

INSEE. *Immigrés et descendants d'immigrés en France*. Paris, 2012.

Jaillet, Marie-Christine. *Les pavillonneurs*. Paris, 1984.

Laacher, Smaïn. *L'institution scolaire et ses miracles*. Paris, 2005.

Laé, Jean-François, and Numa Murard. *L'argent des pauvres*. Paris, 1985.

Lagrange, Hugues, and Marco Oberti, eds. *Émeutes urbaines et protestations. Une singularité française*. Paris, 2006.

Lahire, Bernard. *La Culture des individus*. Paris, 2004.

———. "The Individual and the Mixing of Genres: Cultural Dissonance and Self-Distinction." *Poetics* 36 (2008): 166–88.

Lambert, Anne. *"Tous propriétaires!" L'envers du décor pavillonnaire*. Paris, 2015.

Lapeyronnie, Didier. *Ghetto urbain. Ségrégation, violence, pauvreté en France aujourd'hui*. Paris, 2008.

Légé, Bernard. "Les castors de la Monnaie." *Terrain* 9 (1987): 34–39.

Lehingue, Patrick. "L'objectivation statistique des électorats: que savons-nous des électeurs du Front National?" In *La politisation*, edited by Jacques Lagroye, 247–78. Paris, 2003.

Low, Setha. *Behind the Gates: Life, Security and the Pursuit of Happiness in Fortress America*. New York, 2003.

Magri, Susanna. "L'intérieur domestique. Pour une analyse du changement dans les manières d'habiter." *Genèses* 28 (1997): 146–64.

———. "Le pavillon stigmatisé. Grands ensembles et maisons individuelles dans la sociologie des années 1950 à 1970." *L'Année sociologique* 58, no. 1 (2008): 171–202.

Maison, Dominique. "Pionniers de l'accession." *Les Annales de la Recherche Urbaine* 65 (1993): 46–53.

Marangé, James, and André Lebon. *L'insertion professionnelle des enfants d'immigrés*. Paris, 1982.

Marichalar, Pascal. "Vers le bon voisinage: Enquête ethnographique sur les entrepreneurs de la morale résidentielle." Master's thesis, ENS-EHESS, 2006.

Maruani, Margaret. *Travail et emploi des femmes*. Paris, 2000.

Masclet, Olivier. "Mission Impossible. Ethnographie d'un club de jeunes." *Actes de la recherche en sciences sociales* 136–37 (2001): 62–70.

———. *La gauche et les cités. Enquête sur un rendez-vous manqué*. Paris, 2006.

Merle, Pierre. *La ségrégation scolaire*. Paris, 2012.

Michelat, Guy, and Michel Simon. *Les ouvriers et la politique. Permanence, ruptures, réalignements. 1962–2002*. Paris, 2004.

Ministère de l'éducation nationale. *Repères et références statistiques*. Paris, 2014.

Newman, Katherine. *Falling from Grace: Downward Mobility in the Age of Affluence*. New York, 1988.

Noiriel, Gérard. *Les ouvriers dans la société française XIXe–XXe*. Paris, 1986.

———. *The French Melting Pot: Immigration, Citizenship, and National Identity*. Translated by Geoffroy De Laforcade. Minneapolis, 1996.

Oberti, Michel. *Ségrégation urbaine et scolaire dans l'Ouest parisien*. Paris, 2004.

———. *L'école dans la ville. Ségrégation-mixité-carte scolaire*. Paris, 2007.

Oberti, Michel, and Edmond Préteceille. "Les classes moyennes et la ségrégation urbaine." *Éducation et Sociétés* 14 (2004):135–53.

ONZUS. *Rapport de l'Observatoire des zones urbaines sensibles*. Paris, 2005.

Pan Ké Shon, Jean-Louis. "Ségrégation ethnique et ségrégation sociale en quartiers sensibles. L'apport des mobilités résidentielles." *Revue française de sociologie* 50, no. 3 (2009): 451–87.

Park, Robert. *Race and Culture.* Glencoe, IL, 1950.

Pattillo-McCoy, Mary. *Black Picket Fences: Privilege and Peril among the Black Middle Class.* Chicago, 1999.

Peretz, Henri. *Les méthodes en sociologie: L'observation.* Paris, 1998.

Pétonnet, Colette. *On est tous dans le brouillard. Ethnologie des banlieues.* Paris, 1979.

Peugny, Camille. *Le déclassement.* Paris, 2009.

Piketty, Thomas. *Capital in the Twenty-First Century.* Translated by Arthur Goldhammer. Cambridge, MA, 2014.

Pinson, Daniel, and Sandra Thomann. *La maison en ses territoires. De la villa à la ville diffuse.* Paris, 2001.

PISA. "France. PISA 2012: Faits Marquants." Paris, 2013, http://www.oecd.org/france/PISA-2012-results-france.pdf.

Préteceille, Edmond. *La division sociale de l'espace francilien. Typologie socio-professionnelle 1999 et transformation de l'espace résidentiel 1990–1999.* Paris, 2003.

Pudal, Bernard. "Politisations ouvrières et communisme." In *Le siècle des communismes,* edited by M Dreyfus, B Groppo, CS Ingerflom, R Lew, C Pennetier, B Pudal, and S Wolikow, 513–21. Paris, 2001.

Raymond, Henri, Nicole Haumont, Marie-Geneviève Dezès, and Antoine Haumont. *L'habitat pavillonnaire.* Paris, 2001.

Reed-Danahay, Deborah. *Education and Identity in Rural France.* Cambridge, U.K., 1996.

———. "From the 'Imagined Community' to 'Communities of Practice': Immigrant Belonging among Vietnamese Americans." In *Citizenship, Political Engagement and Belonging,* edited by Deborah Reed-Danahay and Carolyn Brettell, 78–97. New Brunswick, NJ, 2008.

Reed-Danahay, Deborah, and Carolyn Brettell, eds. *Citizenship, Political Engagement, and Belonging: Immigrants in Europe and the United States.* New Brunswick, NJ, 2008.

Retière, Jean-Noël. *Identités ouvrières. Histoire sociale d'un fief ouvrier en Bretagne 1909– 1990.* Paris, 1994.

Rivière, Jean. "Le vote pavillonnaire existe-t-il? Comportements électoraux et positions sociales locales dans une commune rurale en cours de périurbanisation." *Politix* 21, no. 83 (2008): 23–48.

Saint-Julien, Thérèse, Jean-Christophe François, Hélène Mathian, and Antonine Ribardière. *Les disparités des revenus des ménages franciliens en 1999. Approches intercommunales et infracommunales et évolution des différenciations intercommunales (1990–1999).* Paris, 2003.

Santelli, Emmanuelle. *La mobilité sociale dans l'immigration, itinéraires de réussite des enfants d'origine algérienne.* Toulouse, 2001.

Savage, Mike, Gaynor Bagnall, and Brian Longhurst. *Rethinking Class: Culture, Identities and Lifestyle.* New York, 2008.

Sayad, Abdelmalek. "A Displaced Family." In *The Weight of the World,* edited by P Bourdieu et al. Translated by Priscilla P Ferguson, S Emanuel, J Johnson, and S Waryn, 23–36. Stanford, CA, 1999.

Schwartz, Olivier. *Le monde privé des ouvriers. Hommes et femmes du Nord.* Paris, 1990.

———. "Sur le rapport des ouvriers du Nord à la politique. Matériaux lacunaires." *Politix* 11 (1991): 79–86.

———. *"La notion de 'classes populaires.'"* HDR thesis, Université de Versailles-Saint-Quentin-en Yvelines, 1998.

———. "Does France Still Have a Class Society? Three Observations about Contemporary French Society." *La Vie des idées* 2014 (2009), http://www.booksandideas.net/Does-France-Still-Have-a-Class.html.

———. "La pénétration de la 'culture psychologique de masse' dans un groupe populaire: paroles de conducteurs de bus." *Sociologie* 2, no. 4 (2011): 345–61.

Selby, Jennifer. *Questioning French Secularism: Gender Politics and Islam in a Parisian Suburb*. New York, 2012.

Siblot, Yasmine. "'Je suis la secrétaire de la famille!' La prise en charge féminine des tâches administratives en milieu populaire. Entre subordination et resource." *Genèses* 69 (2006): 46–66.

Simon, Patrick, and Martin Clément. "Comment décrire la diversité des origines en France?" *Population et sociétés* 425 (2006): 1–4.

Terrio, Susan. "Who Are the Rioters in France?" *Anthropology News* 27, no. 1 (2006): 4–5.

Townsend, Nicolas. *The Package Deal*. Philadelphia, PA, 2002.

Traïni, Christophe. "L'épicentre d'un 'séisme électoral.' Le vote Front national en région PACA." In *Vote en PACA. Les élections 2002 en Provence-Alpes-Côte d'Azur*, edited by C Traïni, 21–44. Paris, 2004.

Van Zanten, Agnès. *L'école de la périphérie. Scolarité et ségrégation en banlieue*. Paris, 2001.

———. "Les classes moyennes et la mixité scolaire: Collèges et parents dans deux communes des Hauts de Seine." *Annales de la Recherche Urbaine* 93 (2003): 130–40.

———. *Choisir son école. Stratégies familiales et médiations locales*. Paris, 2009.

Verret, Michel. *L'espace ouvrier*. Paris, 1979.

Villeneuve-Gokalp, Catherine. "Les jeunes partent toujours au même âge de chez leurs parents." *Économie et Statistique* 337–38 (2000): 61–80.

Weber, Florence. *Le Travail à côté*. Paris, 1989.

Whyte, William. *Street Corner Society*. Chicago, 1943.

Wilson, William. *The Truly Disadvantaged: The Inner City, the Underclass, and Public Policy*. Chicago, 1987.

Wilson, William. *When Work Disappears: The World of the New Urban Poor*. New York, 1997.

Wirth, Louis. *The Ghetto*. Chicago, 1928.

Young, Michael, and Peter Willmott. *Family and Kinship in East London*. London, 1957.

———. *Family and Class in a London Suburb*. London, 1960.

INDEX